W9-BWE-148

DISTANT DOMINION

University of British Columbia Press Pacific Maritime Studies

Distant Dominion is the second in a continuing series dealing with naval history and related maritime subjects published by the University of British Columbia Press.
This series has been established as a result in part of the success of the following University of British Columbia Press books:

The Wind Commands: Sailors and Sailing Ships in the Pacific, by Harry Morton
The Royal Navy and the Northwest Coast of North America, 1810-1914, by Barry M. Gough
Ocean of Destiny: A Concise History of the North Pacific, 1500-1978, by J. Arthur Lower

Other volumes in this series are:
1. *Russia in Pacific Waters, 1715-1825: A Survey of the Origins of Russia's Naval Presence in the North and South Pacific,* by Glynn Barratt

DISTANT DOMINION

*Britain and the Northwest Coast
of North America,
1579-1809*

Barry M. Gough

UNIVERSITY OF BRITISH COLUMBIA PRESS
VANCOUVER AND LONDON

DISTANT DOMINION

Britain and the Northwest Coast of
North America, 1579-1809

Canadian Cataloguing in Publication Data

Gough, Barry M., 1938-
Distant Dominion
(University of British Columbia Press Pacific Maritime Studies; 2)

Companion volume to the author's The Royal Navy and the northwest
coast of North America, 1810-1914.
Bibliography: p.
Includes index.
ISBN 0-7748-0113-1

1. Northwest coast of North America—History. 2. British Columbia—History—To 1849.* 3. Great Britain—History, Naval.
I. Title
II. Series: University of British Columbia Press. University of British Columbia Press Pacific Maritime Studies: 2

F858.G59   971.1'01   C80-091136-9

International Standard Book Number 0-7748-0113-1

Printed in Canada

To my parents,
John and Dorothy Gough

This book has been published with the help of a gift to scholarly publishing made in honour of Dr. Harold S. Foley for his distinguished services to The University of British Columbia,

a grant from The Leon and Thea Koerner Foundation,

and a grant from the Social Sciences Federation of Canada, using funds provided by the Social Sciences and Humanities Research Council of Canada.

Contents

Photographic Credits

Illustrations

Maps

Plates   *following page 96*

Preface

Why was the Northwest Coast of North America the last portion of the world's temperate zones to be brought within the orbit of emerging European-based empires? I attempt to answer this question in this volume. Separated from eastern North America by the immense Rocky Mountain cordillera and from the Atlantic Ocean by long, tenuous sea lanes, the Northwest Coast stood apart from the civilized world until late in the eighteenth century. From time immemorial the Northwest Coast Indians, secure and unmolested, had inhabited these shores. By the 1770's, however, forces were at work that ended forever the comparative isolation of the Pacific littoral that now includes Alaska, British Columbia, Washington State, Oregon, and northern California. In the last thirty years of the eighteenth century and the first ten years of the next, several nations vied for control of this distant dominion. Britain, Russia, Spain, France, and the United States extended national interests in an attempt to secure trade, sovereignty, or both. Britain's involvement in this rivalry, which forms the substance of this book, was by sea and land and laid the foundations for territorial claims to the Northwest Coast between Russian-held Alaska and American-held Oregon—in other words, the present Canadian province of British Columbia.

This book is a predecessor in terms of the period covered, 1579-1809 (though not in terms of the order of publication) to my *Royal Navy and the Northwest Coast of North America, 1810-1914: A Study of British Maritime Ascendancy*. Taken together, these volumes complete a task begun over fifteen years ago: to explain the role of the sea, oceanic commerce, and sea power in the history of the Northwest Coast in general and British Columbia in particular. As a native of Canada's most western province I confess a strong personal involvement in this undertaking. I was born near the sea in Victoria, British Columbia, sailed inshore waters of the coast in my youth and, in recent years, have examined as many harbours from Drakes Bay, California, north to Cook Inlet, Alaska, as time and money would permit. In many ways the preparation of this volume and its predecessor has been a labour of love and I am grateful for some rather intangible environmental and human considerations that have sustained me during the course of research and writing.

I have incurred numerous debts in writing this book, and I cannot begin to name all the institutions and persons who have helped me. I must pay special thanks to the staffs of the Public Archives of Canada; the Provincial Archives of British Columbia; the Hudson's Bay Company Archives; the National Maritime Museum; the Maritime Museum of British Columbia; the Public Record Office; the British Library; the India Office Library; the Oregon Historical Society; the Wilfrid Laurier University Library; the Special Collections Library at the University of British Columbia; the Beineke Library, Yale University; and the Perkins

Library, Duke University. The James Cook and His Times Conference at Simon Fraser University, April 1978, allowed me to compare notes with many scholars and afforded me the opportunity to speak on "James Cook and Canada: A Chapter in the Importance of the Sea in Canadian History," some material from which appears in this volume. I thank for their help W. Kaye Lamb, Glyndwr Williams, Margaret Waddington, Christon Archer, Raymond Aker, Edward Von der Porten, John Gordon, Derek Lukin Johnston, Kenneth Pearson, Arthur G. Rose, Joyce Lorimer, James R. Gibson, James Ogilvy, Jean Gourlay, Margaret Meston, Marcella Roth, and Norman Wagner. Grants in aid of research were generously provided by the Leon and Thea Koerner Foundation and Wilfrid Laurier University; and I owe a special debt of gratitude to the Canada Council for a leave fellowship that enabled me to complete an early draft of the manuscript.

BMG

1

Tyranny of Distance

Through or over the deathless feud
of the cobra sea and the mongoose
wind you must fare to reach us.
Through hiss and throttle come,
by a limbo of motion humbled,
under cliffs of cloud
and over the shark's blue home.
Across the undulations of this slate
long pain and sweating courage chalked
such names as glimmer yet.

EARLE BIRNEY, *PACIFIC DOOR*

From Tudor times until late in the nineteenth century, the Northwest Coast of North America was for the British the ocean's farthest shore. Though girdled by mountains and approachable only by sea via Cape Horn or the Cape of Good Hope, that remote shore was of compelling interest to explorers, merchant traders, scientists, and governments. Its resources and lands spawned an international rivalry dating from the sixteenth century that had important consequences in establishing political boundaries on the Pacific coast of North America and in changing the lives of native inhabitants—Indians, Aleuts, and Eskimos.

The Northwest Coast was a dominion, a future sphere of empire, whose distance at once shaped its development and kept it secret from the wider world until the late eighteenth century. Fifteen hundred years before this the Chinese had known of "Fousang." They called it the country of the extreme east.[1] But they chose not to pursue their discoveries across the Pacific and instead contented themselves with an active maritime commerce in their own immediate seas.

Even if the Chinese had possessed the deep-water capability to cross the Pacific, they might not have had the will to establish long-lasting contact with the Northwest Coast. A few trans-Pacific voyages would be insufficient in themselves to establish permanent trade and, in turn, sovereignty on the ocean's opposite shore. However, by the late eighteenth century, European maritime technology was sufficiently developed to enable traders and rulers to undertake expeditions to trade half a world away or to explore any of the ocean's far frontiers.

Yet the sheer size of the Pacific, one-third of the world's surface, was often enough to deter regular commerce. At 165,000,000 square kilometres the Pacific is double the area of the Atlantic. From Bering Strait to Antarctica the Pacific extends 15,900 kilometres; from Panama to the Philippines, 17,200 kilometres. In the age of sail, this awesome vastness defied description. The Pacific was a desert of waters, a vast empty space that posed psychological as well as physical difficulties. Only by sailing over its blue, profoundly deep watery wastes for weeks together, Charles Darwin said of the South Pacific, could man comprehend its enormous immensity.[2] A voyage from London round Cape Horn to the Northwest Coast might consume nearly half a year and seldom under five months of a ship's life.[3]

Montreal or Boston were not much closer to Vancouver Island than London. The passage round the Cape of Good Hope was even longer in distance than round the Horn. Yet it afforded a safer and sometimes faster entry to the Pacific by avoiding the hateful seas at the southern tip of South America, seas made volatile by the shallow shelving seabed, strong currents, and cyclones off the Andes. Sometimes the easier entry to the Pacific offered no compensation given the longer course and the tricky track that pilots would have to plot through the island-infested straits of Southeast Asia. However, by rounding the Cape of Good Hope and using the "roaring forties" of the southerly latitudes to carry their vessels eastward, a ship could have a fast entry to the Pacific south of Australia and New Zealand. The prevailing westerlies and southern ocean current in those latitudes would take the vessel east until a course could be shaped north and east to Tahiti. There a ship would leave the "roaring forties" and sail virtually due north in order to pick up the northeast trade winds blowing from Baja California, make for Honolulu, and then take the final, three-week leg to Nootka Sound, the Queen Charlotte Islands, or the coast to the north.

However, by the late 1700's, captains were not only entering the Pacific in increased numbers but were sailing with prized cargoes of fur pelts from the Northwest Coast to Asia. Their vessels followed a relatively easy track across the Pacific from Nootka Sound on the west coast of Vancouver Island to Macao, then the principal entrepôt of Pacific commerce, a voyage of some 15,750 kilometres. They set out for the China market early in September, confident of reaching their destination by late November with the aid of the trade winds and the north equatorial current. The return passage from Macao sometimes took longer, for the prevailing winds and ocean currents along what is now called the Great Circle Route were less dependable. The track along the northern route, especially through the China Seas, posed potential problems for even the most careful pilot. Ships would leave port after the monsoon season. They would then make their way between the thousands of islands, islets, and reefs that flank the northeast coast of Asia. The dangerous shores of Japan and Korea were not charted with any degree of accuracy until the explorations of Captain William Broughton of the Royal Navy in the late 1790's, and even then accurate data available to mariners was scanty. Still farther north, the Kurile Islands, Kamchatka, and the Aleutians provided an intensely intricate shoreline across the roof of the North Pacific, the Aleutians strung out like beads on a chain and blocking easy access to Bering Strait and Arctic seas. Unalaska and Kodiak provided havens for ships in distress or in need of wood or water en route from Macao to Cook Inlet or Prince William Sound on the Gulf of Alaska. Otherwise, mariners gave these a wide berth. If, by contrast, ships were to sail easterly from China in more southerly latitudes, their track across the Pacific would be reasonably safe north of the Hawaiian Islands, though delays could be painfully long if currents and winds proved obstinate.

Before the age of steam navigation, passages to the Northwest Coast from California and Panama were the most difficult of all approaches. The northeast trades proved to be the arch-enemy of northward bound sailing vessels hugging the shore. From a northern California port a ship would have to sail far out from land before reaching winds suitable for a reasonably easy reverse track to Nootka. Curiously enough, in these circumstances the shortest sea route from Monterey, California, to Nootka Sound or Cook Inlet lay by the Hawaiian Islands.[4]

While the northeast trades defied sailing ships and crews bound north, they could be the ally of pilots on the way south. For instead of beating into the wind between storms as was customary, captains could make their leisurely way south along the shore, investigating river mouths, straits, and inlets or putting into native coves to trade or to repair their vessels. Thus almost all the great European maritime discoveries on the Northwest Coast occurred on southward-bound tracks. Bruno de Hezeta's discovery of the Columbia River in 1775, for instance, came after he had been to the Gulf of Alaska. On separate occasions Charles Barkley and John Meares discovered the Strait of Juan de Fuca on similar courses. George Dixon did the same with respect to the waters separating the Queen Charlotte Islands from the mainland. By contrast, Francis Drake's northward advance was blocked, firstly, by the hazardous weather conditions in the belt of the northeast trades and, secondly, by the continuously close proximity of the continental shore which he found, to his surprise, running northwesterly. James Cook missed the entrance to both the Columbia River and the Strait of Juan de Fuca under similar circumstances and conditions.

When European ships began visiting the coast in the 1770's their captains knew only the barest outline of this very intricate and fickle shore. That more ships in the maritime fur trade did not find themselves wrecked on the fog-bound coast of Vancouver Island or the rocky bluffs or sand spits of the Queen Charlotte Islands testifies to the healthy respect with which mariners of that age treated the unknown and the unrecorded. Navigation to and on the Northwest Coast remained troublesome and dangerous as long as the hydrographic chart was incomplete and the patterns of tide and wind had not been systematically recorded. By Cook's time conspicuous advances in the design and construction of instruments

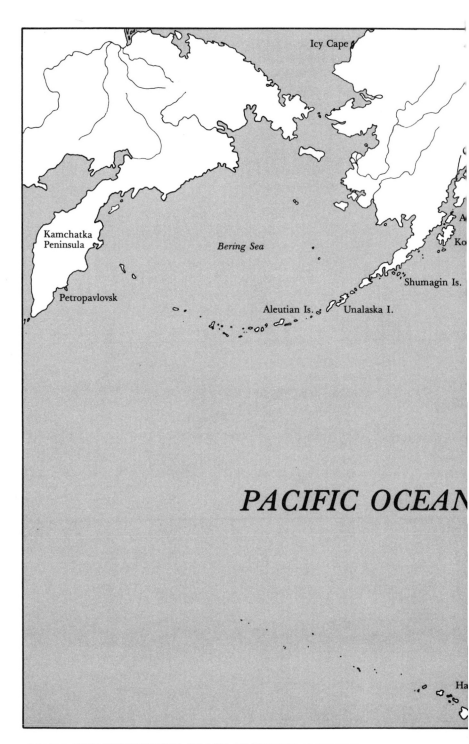

Icy Cape

Kamchatka Peninsula

Bering Sea

Petropavlovsk

Shumagin Is.

Aleutian Is. Unalaska I.

Ko

PACIFIC OCEAN

Ha

MAP 1: THE NORTHWEST COAST OF NORTH AMERICA
AND THE NORTH PACIFIC REGION

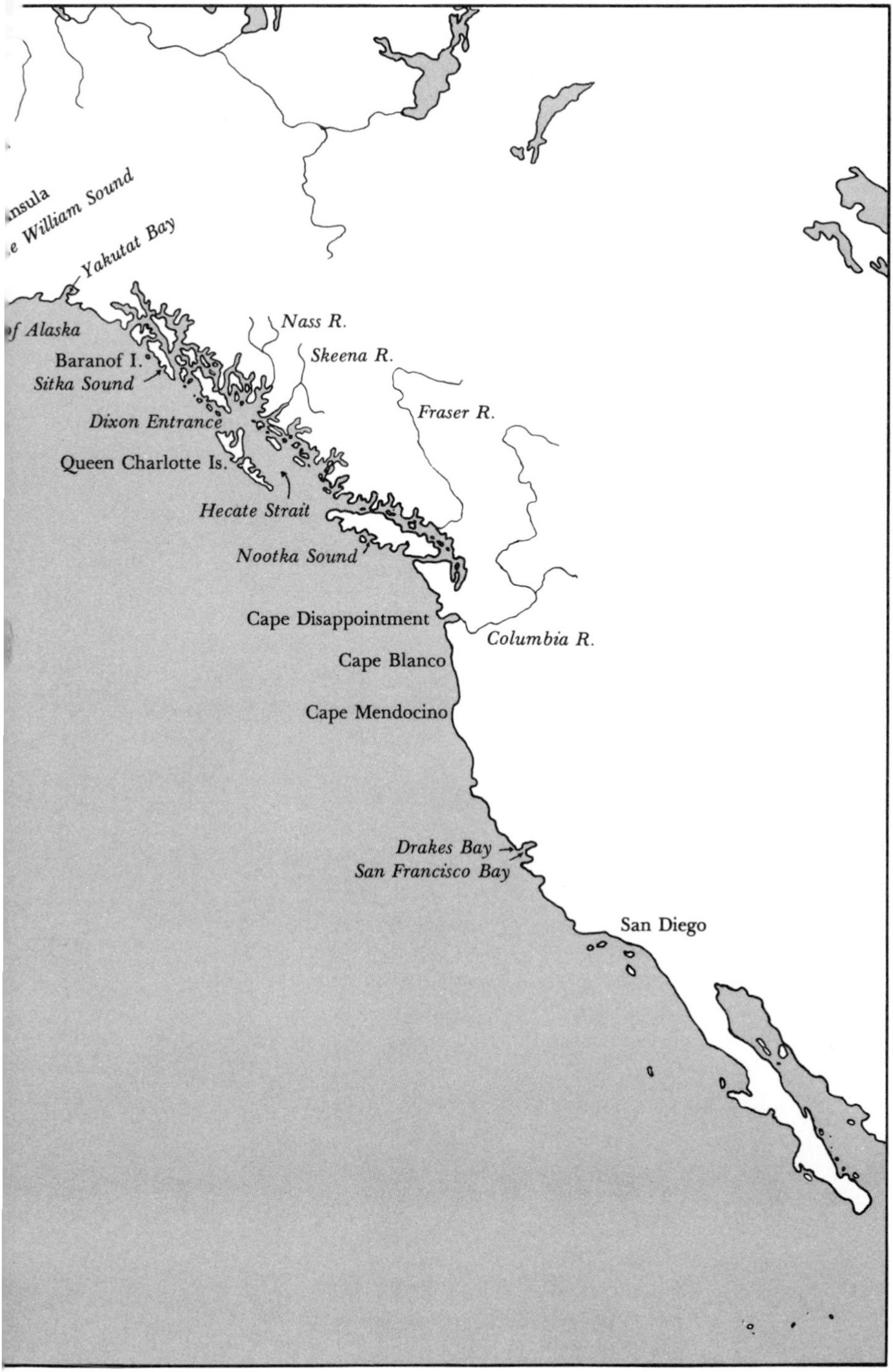

nsula
e William Sound
Yakutat Bay
f Alaska
Baranof I.
Sitka Sound
Nass R.
Skeena R.
Fraser R.
Dixon Entrance
Queen Charlotte Is.
Hecate Strait
Nootka Sound
Cape Disappointment
Columbia R.
Cape Blanco
Cape Mendocino
Drakes Bay
San Francisco Bay
San Diego

used for astronomical observation enabled mariners to determine their position at sea.[5] Harrison's timekeeper, for instance, gave Cook the means to carry his longitude accurately with him from place to place and to make charts such as had never been made before.

Captains wisely chose not to sail the inner reaches of inlets and passages in vessels larger than 300 tons. Craft of 150 to 300 tons, known as snows, were preferred in the late eighteenth century. These vessels, similar to brigs, had two square-rigged masts. They had convenient stowage, an economical complement, and a rig that made them more manoeuvrable in inshore waters than most other designs of their size. Other vessels could be used on the coast, of course. H.M.S. *Resolution,* Captain James Cook's command on the Northwest Coast in 1778, was a three-masted, square-rigged vessel known as a "ship." The Navy Board of the Admiralty classified her as a sloop-of-war, for she carried a mizzen topgallant mast that snows lacked. At 400 tons, Barkley's *Imperial Eagle* was among the largest "ships" in the maritime fur trade and the biggest to visit the coast until the nineteenth century. But whether the sailing vessels of the early explorers were snows or ships, their ultimate enemy was distance.

Voyages of this sort meant that provisions were always at a premium, and the few places where food could be obtained gradually became well marked on the charts. Salmon, cod, and halibut of the Northwest Coast provided a useful supplement to the biscuit and salt pork diet of men on the lower deck. Fruit was both expensive and difficult to keep. Fresh meats and vegetables could seldom be had anywhere within the Pacific during the eighteenth century. Sheep and cattle, goats and swine were seldom found on the shores of the Pacific rim; consequently, ships brought their own with them, leaving behind at Tahiti and Honolulu stock that it was hoped would multiply and could be slaughtered subsequently. In these circumstances only careful victualling could eliminate scurvy—the disease whose prevalence corresponded directly to the length of a voyage. Accordingly, captains and Boards of Admiralty tried various antiscorbutics. Sauerkraut, salted cabbage, and "portable soup," a dried beef to be dissolved in hot water, helped, but such measures as using malt extract and elixir proved unsuitable. In an age when no one had heard of vitamin C, dutiful naval surgeons successfully experimented with lemons, limes, and other citrus fruits, and in 1795 the Lords of the Admiralty ordered a daily issue of lemon juice to all hands. As a result, within five years scurvy virtually disappeared from His Majesty's ships.[6]

Sailors faced additional health hazards: lice and fleas, the latter prevalent among sea otter pelts; malaria, typhus, dysentery, and other disorders; sometimes filthy and always cramped quarters; and, not least, unhealthy new shipmates from England's diseased slums. Without dwelling on the horrors of a seaman's life between decks at this time, it can be noted that by 1800 life at sea had improved measurably over that of the previous century. This was the result of advancements in naval administration and medicine, better ships and aids to navigation, and more paternalistic attitudes of captains—all factors conducive to longer voyages.

The distinguished scientist Lord Kelvin once remarked that sailing round the world constituted in its day one of the great human accomplishments because it utilized natural elements to serve human ends.[7] Unquestionably this was so. Yet sailing into the Pacific for trading or scientific purposes was, in fact, more than a mere circumnavigation of the globe, for such voyages, lasting sometimes four or five years at a stretch, meant circling or criss-crossing the Pacific before returning to the North Atlantic. The strain was great, almost beyond description. As one historian put it so aptly, "Men and ships alike, whether bred or built on its shores or far away, had to measure up to the scale of the Pacific or disappear."[8] In difficult circumstances the healthiest and best of men were required to meet the ever-changing needs of the ship they were sailing.

Ships, like men, would give under the pressures imposed by distant voyaging. For weeks on end ships would have to keep at sea to reach their destination; and this meant wear and tear on hulls and rigging. Naval stores and supplies had to be of the best quality. Hulls, spars, and cordage had to withstand typhoons and gales. Problems of weather aside, wooden hulls proved particularly attractive to the shipworm, *Teredo navalis*. By the late eighteenth century, copper sheathing had become the customary means of protecting hulls against the ravages of this ubiquitous worm and against marine growths that hindered a ship's progress. Moreover, hulls could be damaged on uncharted shoals, shores, and rocks. Repairs had to be made en route or, preferably, in port. For these reasons places of refit and repair for a ship and for the crew's rest were needed at key points in the far-off oceans.

In short, distance presented tyrannical obstacles to the European approach to the Northwest Coast. Until North West Company fur traders penetrated the Rocky Mountain cordiliera in the first decade of the nineteenth century and established a commercial network that linked the land with the sea, European nations interested in this distant dominion came by long sea routes. Resourceful mariners, spurred by the lure of profit, the honour of science, the service of the nation, or some other reason, conquered the watery wastes leading to the Northwest Coast. Few, if any, made the voyage for adventure alone. Most were motivated by a desire to further the profit and the power of their nation. In turn the nation, as in the British case, often supplied necessary material, financial, and diplomatic support.

2

Pacific Probes

What English ships did heretofore ever anchor in the mighty river of Plate? Pass and repass the impassable (in former opinion) strait of Magellan, range along the coast of Peru and all the backside of Nova Hispania . . . traverse the mighty breadth of the South Sea, land upon the Lucones, in despite of the enemy, enter into alliance with the Princes of the Moluccas and the Isle of Java, double the famous Cape of Bona Speranza . . . and last of all return home most richly laden with the commodities of China, as the subjects of this now flourishing monarchy have done?

RICHARD HAKLUYT, *THE PRINCIPAL NAVIGATIONS, VOYAGES, TRAFFIQUES & DISCOVERIES OF THE ENGLISH NATION* (1589)

For four centuries beginning with the sixteenth, Europeans came to chart and exploit the vast waters and shores of the Pacific Ocean. They rounded the Cape of Good Hope or Cape Horn in their small, gun-carrying sailing ships whose home ports were in far-off Portugal, Spain, England, France, or Holland. Some, including Russians, Spanish, Americans, and Canadians, made their way to the Pacific overland. As these men entered into commercial and political enterprises, they found themselves at times dependent on support from their respective governments—support that could only reach them over long, tenuous, and vulnerable seaways. The fact that the British were able to establish a firm and lasting foothold on a large part of the Northwest Coast of North America was owing in no small measure to their commercial enterprises by sea and the presence, strength, and explorations of the Royal Navy. A correlated factor was the emergence of Britain as a strong international power after the middle of the eighteenth century as a result of an economic revolution in agriculture, industry and commerce and of successes on the battlefields of Europe, India, and North America.

The first fruits of the age of discovery went to Portugal and Spain; and to prevent disputes between these rival maritime powers, the 1493 papal bull *Inter caetera* arbitrarily divided the world for Portuguese and Spanish colonial exploitation. The Treaty of Tordesillas of the following year gave further advantages to Portugal, but Spain still possessed a religious sanction for the conquest of most of the New World and the conversion of its heathen inhabitants. Thus Spain claimed the western lands of the Americas and the expanses of the Pacific Ocean as part of her empire, whether settled by the Spanish or not.

Dutch and English promoters of exploration and expansion disregarded the bold claims of Spain to all empire in the eastern seas by right of the Treaty of Tordesillas. A mere claim to ownership was not enough. The English aggressively argued that "the use of the sea and air is common to all . . . as neither nature nor public use and custom permitteth any possession thereof."[1] And as far as the land was concerned, the English argument was similarly disrespectful of Spain's policy of exclusive territorial ownership. Territorial claims were not enough; ownership depended on occupation.

The Pacific, with its allure as an eldorado, constituted the last frontier of European exploitation and influence. Ever since the fifteenth century, European merchants, explorers, and kings were captivated by the idea of a Northwest Passage. Tudor geographers thought the legendary Strait of Anian to be the western mouth of the passage. English geographical theorists, commercial promoters, and artful strategists kept the legend alive. On their maps they changed the position of the strait as it suited their purposes and as they learned of new discoveries from French, Spanish, American, and Russian sources.

Englishmen of the sixteenth century were also captivated by rumours of a great unknown southern continent, Terra Australis Incognita. Several Tudor voyages to the Pacific had the purpose of finding this land mass. Strategists and geographers reasoned that an easy access to it might be found across the North American continent. They agreed that the benefits to England in finding such a passage might be astounding in terms of commerce, religion, politics, and security.

The various propagandists of the empire in the Elizabethan age knew well the advantages that might accrue to their nation by advances in geographical exploration. One contemporary, Richard Hakluyt, said that English success would lie in the "advancing of navigation, the very walls of our islands." But such distant sea travel required seaworthy ships, healthy crews, capable commanders, and scientific aids to navigation. Moreover, such enterprises required venture capital from private persons who had to make large sums available for lengthy periods of time. These individuals were ably classified by the seventeenth-century writer Gregory King as "greater merchants and traders by sea."[2]

Although the commercial motive behind English expansion overseas was strong, what might be called the pre-emptive impulse—to forestall the ambitions of a rival by prior control—was never far removed from English thoughts. The motives for England's expansion beyond her shores were nearly always political or strategic, as is amply documented in Tudor writings. Hakluyt advised Queen Elizabeth I in his *Discourse on Planting* (1584) that Virginia should be settled in order to check Spain's New World empire. John Hawkins's memorials recommended to government how Spain could be humbled if England's navy severed her sea communications with her empire. Michael Lok and John Dee's idea of the Strait of Anian connecting the Atlantic and Pacific oceans had political overtones. These strategists hoped to find weaknesses in the geographical integrity of Spain's Pacific Ocean. It is true that these Elizabethan promoters of empire were motivated by a lure of immediate profits, by the prospects of adventure, and by a hatred of popery. They sought to check their Spanish Catholic rival and to keep Protestant England secure at home. As a shrewd observer of British expansion has written: "At all periods the development of England's colonizing activity has been largely influenced by the course of her foreign relations, and this not less in the days of its beginning than in the great eras of expansion in the eighteenth and nineteenth centuries."[3]

In the late sixteenth century, Spain was the pre-eminent European power. Her overseas commerce, tightly regulated by a zealous Council of Trade anxious to increase Spain's profit at the expense of foreign rivals, ranked second to none. Aliens could not engage in Spanish-American trade except by treaty, a rule of exclusion which lingered in some areas of the Spanish Empire well into the nineteenth century. Spanish seapower dominated the Atlantic. The King of Spain's fleets were strong enough to undertake reprisals against pirates and privateers, to war against any European foe, or to mount an armada for the invasion of England or the protection of national interests in the Spanish Lowlands of Europe.

Such seaborne ascendancy did not give Spain freedom from assault. Her weaker opponents, France, England, and Holland, conducted an undeclared war at sea. In peacetime, privateers often carried the unofficial sanction of their governments and differed only in legal terms from pirates and buccaneers who operated against Spanish shipping. In wartime these same corsairs might sail under letters-of-marque, commissions authorizing them to seize enemy vessels and to operate in conjunction with naval vessels.

During the 1570's, Anglo-Spanish antagonisms frequently approached a state of war. Not least among the causes of tension between the two countries was the prevalence of English privateers in the Atlantic. Sailing out of London, Portsmouth, Bristol, and other south-of-England ports, privateers prowled between the Azores and the Iberian peninsula intending to capture Portuguese carracks and Spanish galleons. They attempted to cut the flow of bullion from America to Cadiz or from Lisbon to Asia. They sought to capture the prized commodities of America, Asia, and Africa. Sometimes they raided the great Spanish home port of Cadiz or sacked distant Spanish ports in the Caribbean. Sometimes they mounted inshore expeditions, even going stealthily overland to Panama to ravage that great and sleepy Pacific town where they were least expected. Usually, however, they lay in wait on the known sailing routes to the rich Spanish ports in the West Indies, harrying Spanish treasure ships when the margin of men and armament rested in their favour.

Yet these corsairing activities carried with them great risk of capture. Traders with the enemy, or *rescatadores* as the Spanish called them, ran the danger of capture and even of being tried by the Inquisition. The case of Sir John Hawkins treacherously attacked by a superior Spanish fleet in the Mexican port of San Juan de Ulua in 1568, after he had been admitted to the harbour on pledge of peace to refit his ships, served as a painful reminder of what might happen to Englishmen attempting to engage in peaceful if not quite legitimate trade with Spain. To the English traders, Spanish monopolies were the pest from Mexico to Cape Horn on both sides of America. Elizabethan seamen who sailed as privateers were filled with a hatred of everything Spanish. They waged their own wars for business reasons, with patriotism, adventure, and religious fervour usually thrown in to season the motivation or please their virgin queen.[4]

How effective it would be, Elizabethan strategists reasoned, if English mariners could strike where they were least expected—on the "backside" of the Americas? They would circumvent Spain's stronghold in the Caribbean by attacking her precisely where she was weakest, in the Pacific. For these reasons, in 1574, the Secretary of State, Francis Walsingham, and his political ally, the Earl of Leicester, supported a venture headed by Sir Richard Grenville and other west-of-England privateering interests. This grand anti-Spanish project aimed to send armed ships to trade and settle near the River Plate of South America. They would penetrate the Pacific by doubling Cape Horn. These ships would also be used to link English interests in the Strait of Anian with Terra Australis Incognita.[5] This project was halted because of an easing of Anglo-Spanish tensions. However, by 1577 Walsingham again considered war with Spain unavoidable.

In 1577, Francis Drake sailed from Plymouth with a squadron of four ships, the most famous being the *Golden Hind,* to harry Spain in the Pacific. The alleged connivance of the Queen and Walsingham in the secret voyage is well known. Indeed, Drake admitted to Spanish officials he met during the voyage that he possessed a licence from his queen to engage in warfare.[6] Elizabeth and her advisers had determined on a policy of secrecy for several reasons: firstly, in order to overpower the Spanish settlements in the New World with the help of surprise; secondly, in order that the Spanish court would not suspect a raid, the mission being tantamount to a declaration of war; and, thirdly, in order to be ahead of Drake's former companion and now rival, John Oxenham, thought to be leading an expedition across the Isthmus of Panama to the Pacific.[7]

Born probably in 1540 near Tavistock, Devon, Drake exhibited those daring qualities that marked the West-Country expansionists of the sixteenth century. In 1567 he had raided Veracruz, Spain's eastern port in Mexico, in the company of his kinsman John Hawkins. In 1571-73 he had been engaged in various voyages which on the surface appear merely piratical in nature but in fact were military operations aimed at strategic points of Spanish communication such as Lisbon, the Azores, San Domingo, Cartegena, and Panama. As the first Earl of Essex said late in Elizabeth's reign, "The hurt that our State should seek to do him

[Spain] is to intercept his treasures, whereby we shall cut his sinews and make war upon him with his money."[8] This was especially significant in view of the fact that twenty per cent of Spain's revenues came from bullion overseas.

Drake's "piracy" was actually a military operation of great strategic importance. In 1572 Drake had seen the Pacific from the Isthmus of Panama and desired to "make a perfect discovery of the same."[9] What better than to implement the old Elizabethan project of penetrating the South Seas? Drake had long cherished this dream. Probably he himself conceived and developed the plan which he eventually carried through: a mission of revenge, a circumnavigation of the globe such as had been attempted only once previously by Magellan sailing for Portugal, and an exploration of the Pacific Coast of America to take possession of the regions north beyond the limits of Spanish occupation.[10]

The draft plan for the voyage reveals in the background the workings of Master John Dee, the geographer and adviser on the long-distance voyages of the 1560's and 1570's. Dee knew that the Ortelius map of 1564, based largely on Jacques Cartier's discoveries in the Gulf of St. Lawrence, showed a sea route to Cathay by the north and west. He placed great importance on finding this Strait of Anian and also exploring the shores of Terra Australis Incognita, supposedly lying south and west from the Strait of Magellan. The plan provided that Drake would first examine the southern continent right across the Pacific to south of the Moluccas. Then, by using southwesterly winds, he would cross the Pacific to the Northwest Coast, arriving there in late summer when no ice would be met with, and make his way back to England via the Strait of Anian.[11] Also he would concern himself with harassing the Spanish, opening new trades, making new discoveries, and annexing new lands to the Crown of England.[12] We will probably never know what specific importance was placed on prosecuting trade in the Moluccas or, more importantly for our purposes, on finding the Strait of Anian and the Northwest Passage. But there can be little doubt that these were integral motives of the expedition.

The design to attack the Catholic King in the Indies worked admirably, but the voyage had difficulties. Four of Drake's five ships did not complete the Pacific portion of the voyage, and near Cape Horn there was a mutiny. Yet Drake had destroyed the Spanish contention that the only access to the South Sea lay by way of the Strait of Magellan. By sailing southward along the South American coast on the Atlantic side, he had entered the Pacific south of Cape Horn, thus disproving the idea that Tierra del Fuego was part of a great southern continent.

Drake's activities on the Pacific side of the Americas caused Spanish authorities great concern. On the Chilean coast he made surprise raids on the rich cities of Valparaiso and Callao and, to prevent retaliation, destroyed Spanish shipping. His small ship (the *Golden Hind* measured but 100 tons and carried only eighteen guns) became increasingly laden with gold and precious stones while his enemies were made increasingly furious by his audacious acts. By April 1579 he had reached Mexico's west coast. Drake's main concern now was to get home safely with his booty, reported to have been worth a million pounds. He needed supplies and water, and for this reason he seized the little Mexican port of Guatalco, where he took on fresh water. Now he planned his homeward voyage. He had two options. On the one hand, he could sail north and seek the Strait of Anian; or, on the other, he might return to England via a western route, and in the process visit the Moluccas, the rich spice islands discovered by Magellan, and perhaps even find the legendary southern continent. Either option if successfully completed would have brought him glory. However, the route via the Moluccas was more likely to yield wealth for England than the cold route via the Strait of Anian. Yet the prospect of the northern strait to the Atlantic must have appealed to Drake when he knew that he was likely to meet Portuguese opposition along the Moluccas route. Drake weighed the merits of both courses and decided to make a brief search for the passage.[13]

He seems to have met with little Spanish resistance in pursuing his voyage from Guatalco. Francis Fletcher, Drake's chaplain, wrote that on 16 April they quit the Mexican port, "setting our course directly into the sea, whereon we sayled 500 leagues in longtitude, to get a winde."[14] Such a course, to get what sailors called an "offing" by standing well out to sea, was necessary on any sailing voyage north and west along the Pacific coast of North America. For six weeks, between 16 April and 3 June, Fletcher tells us, they sailed 1,400 leagues, perhaps 6,750 kilometres in all, until they came into the coast, "where in the night following we found such alteration of heate, into extreame and nipping cold, that our men in generall did grievously complain thereof."[15]

We do not know the exact position of Drake's northernmost landfall. Some documents relating to the voyage state that the farthest northern latitude he reached was 48°. Captain R. P. Bishop, formerly in the Royal Navy and after 1907 a British Columbia land surveyor, made a study of various charts, sailing directions, journals, and hydrographic and atmospheric conditions and concluded that Drake took the "Spanish course" from Guatalco. Then he sailed west, where he met and followed "Fleurieu's Whirlpool," the clockwise movement of winds and currents named after the French naval officer Claret de Fleurieu. By Bishop's calculation Drake reached Vancouver Island on 10 June 1579.[16] Drake evidently anchored in what Fletcher called a "bad bay," where he sought shelter from contrary winds and heavy weather and "stinking fogges."[17] That this could have been Port San Juan or some such similar harbour on the southwest coast of Vancouver Island remains only a guess. If indeed Drake saw Vancouver Island, he was the first Englishman to see the west coast of Canada.

Another, less northerly landfall has been claimed by the Drake Navigators Guild in their exhaustive inquiries into all things connected with the famous circumnavigation. The guild's conclusion is that by 3 June Drake had reached only the 42nd parallel near Cape Mendocino, where the northwest passage could have been expected to turn eastward. Drake's course to this latitude had been invariably northwest, and on 5 June, when he had obtained the required northing, he approached land in the vicinity of where the western entry to Martin Frobisher's reported passage might be found. Here, to Drake's surprise, the land bore farther west than expected, and the ship's steady course apparently had taken him closer to land than he had been aware. The claim for 44°N as the landfall rests, firstly, on a deposition by John Drake that the *Golden Hind* had been sailing on a north-westerly course in search of a good wind to aid the ship's progress to the north-east and, secondly, on data supplied on winds and currents by the United States Navy Hydrographic Office Pilot Charts for the months of May and June. This track also corresponds closely to the report of a Spanish pilot who wrote at the time that Drake, having arrived at 43°N at Cape Mendocino, would have picked up the westerly winds by which Drake "would continue sailing with the wind astern towards the east to the land of Labrador which is in the neighbourhood of England."[18] In other words, Drake was in a latitude where he could expect to find the supposed Northwest Passage.

However, to undertake such a search was untimely. He had found the shoreline lying invariably north and west, and though "a very large sea" tended towards the north, no ebb or flow of the sea promised a strait to the east. Now dubious of the existence of the passage, Drake feared spending too long in seeking it. The season was too far advanced for Arctic travel. Already Drake's northern penetration had proved that cold weather and fogs brought complaints from his crew. Might they not mutiny if he persevered? Moreover, now he must make his final repairs before proceeding across the Pacific on the known track of the Manila galleon that made its annual voyage to the Philippines and reach the Asian shore after the monsoon season had safely passed.

The Oregon coast in the latitude of 44°N affords scant security from the open Pacific. Drake had been driven towards land by a sudden encounter with stormy weather. The *Golden Hind* found shelter in South Cove, Cape Arago, just south of Coos Bay.[19] The cove, the best roadstead available, provided only marginal security from the westerly winds. This was no place to linger for any length of time. On the other hand, to proceed farther north remained out of the question because of the cold, the complaints of the crew, and the contrary winds. Thus, the *Golden Hind* having got under way, the winds "commanded us to the Southward whether we would or no."[20] Had good weather prevailed, Drake might have continued his northerly progress, doubtless sailing within sight of land until reaching some strait, river, or sea that indicated a water entry to the Atlantic. Such would have been time-consuming, and of little value for Drake at this stage of his voyage, except of course for a shorter way home if the passage proved navigable. For these reasons, Drake did not sail north again. He was forced to be content with the belief that beyond his northerly penetration lay lands and waters largely unknown to the European world. For the time being a mariner's chart would continue to show vast blank spaces of land delimited only by crude lines suggesting the coastline of present-day Oregon, Washington, British Columbia, Alaska, and Siberia.

Now Drake followed the coast closely south and east in search of a port in which to refit before continuing his voyage across the Pacific. He passed Cape Blanco, Cape Mendocino, Point Arena, and ultimately Point Reyes. Drake was in latitude $38°N$ and here "it pleased God to send us into a faire and good Baye, with a good wind to enter the same." On 17 June he entered a "convenient and fit harborough" and anchored, in Drakes Bay, not San Francisco Bay, for its opening would not have been visible to him from that position.[21]

Drakes Bay provided wood and water, security from attack but, above all, an excellent place within the bay, in Drake's Estero, to careen his ship for repairs. The area's white sand cliffs, river estuaries, and moderate climate reminded Drake and his men of the south coast of England. Here they stayed from 17 June until 23 July to repair the ship and then to take on wood and water before setting off on the long voyage across to the Moluccas. Drake's relations with the California Miwok Indians were most cordial. They voluntarily gave him a sort of crown and then he proclaimed the territory part of his Queen's realm, naming it Nova Albion. This he did for two reasons: firstly, that the white cliffs of Drakes Bay resembled to an extraordinary degree those of the Seven Sisters of Sussex; and secondly, that California might be given some affinity to England, which in that era sometimes was affectionately referred to as "Albion."

Drake knew that the Spanish had never set foot in this portion of California but were farther to the south in the region of San Miguel Harbour (now San Diego), discovered by Cabrillo thirty-seven years earlier. Drake accordingly laid claim to the territory on the basis of prior discovery. Before leaving for the Moluccas, Drake set up on a large post his famous plate of brass, a version of which, until recently proven fraudulent, confounded many students of history. The text on the plate was suggested in *The World Encompassed by Sir Francis Drake* (1628) and is here reproduced in modernized spelling.

Be it known unto all Men by these Presents
June 17 1579
By the grace of God and in the name of her Majesty Queen Elizabeth of England and her successors forever I take possession of this kingdom whose king and people freely resign their right and title in the whole land unto Her Majesty's keeping now named by me and to be known unto all men as Nova Albion.[22]
Francis Drake

Drake's claim—so characteristically bold for the explorers of that age and so disrespectful of Spanish claims—constituted the first assertion of English sovereignty on North American soil bordering on the Pacific Ocean. Obviously, Drake classified "Nova Albion" as territories north and west of Spanish territory. But how far north?—at least as far as his landfall, possibly 48°N latitude. Needless to say, the western periphery would be the Pacific, while the extent of the area to the east Drake did not define. We do have some notion of the size of Nova Albion from a contemporary map by the Dutch cartographer Nicola van Sype, which Drake evidently saw and corrected before its publication.[23] The chart shows two lines of demarcation on the North American continent. The first begins in the Gulf of California and extends across to the Mississippi River mouth. The second, centred on the River St. Lawrence, defines New France. The remainder, that is, all of North America between New Spain and New France, was to be Nova Albion, a continental Anglo-Saxon area. Four centuries later, the linguistic but not necessarily national divisions of the continent reflect to a surprising degree van Sype's cartography and Drake's dream.

As for Drake, he sailed for the Moluccas on 23 July 1579, and by the end of September had reached some Polynesian islands, probably Magellan's "Islands of Thieves," now the Marianas. Several weeks later he put into the exotic port of Ternate in the Spiceries, and purchased six tons of cloves from Babin, the Sultan of Ternate, who controlled the bulk of the clove trade and who had ejected the Portuguese from his port city. Drake may have entered an alliance with the Sultan and then he made his way to England, where the court welcomed the news of his successful negotiations in the Moluccas as being of much future benefit to the kingdom.

Drake's voyage contributed to geographical understanding, heightened English interest in plunder and trade in the Pacific, and promised that an eastern trade might be developed with Ternate and the Spice Islands and thereby counter the Portuguese monopoly in China and Cathay. It also gave England's national outlook much stimulus in an era when Spain's overseas empire seemed awesome, and increased the importance of national maritime endeavour and strength at sea. In its other aspects, the circumnavigation elevated Drake to the position of a great pioneer of English expansion. And, particularly noteworthy here, it laid claim to English sovereignty over Nova Albion, including California and the Northwest Coast of North America. Herein lies the origin of British dominion over Old Oregon and, after 1846, British Columbia.[24]

In Drake's wake sailed an infrequent series of English sailors who went to the Pacific side of the Americas to repeat his exploits. Thomas Cavendish in 1587 captured the Manila galleon near Cape San Lucas, California's southernmost point. English sailors had a dual purpose—to enrich themselves by capturing "the prize of all the oceans," the Manila galleon, and by raiding wealthy, unsuspecting coastal towns. Sir John Narborough and Richard Hawkins also undertook privateering ventures. Drake's sudden appearance in the Pacific had concerned Spanish authorities, but not until 1594, after further marauding by

English pirates, did Spanish authorities send Mendaña and Quirós to colonize the Solomon Islands and, about the same time, they instructed Sebastián Vizcaíno and Martín de Aguilar to find the legendary city of Quivira and investigate harbours in and around 43°N latitude on the North American coast. Still, English depredations continued. Woodes Rogers sacked Panama with a transisthmian overland expedition. Expeditions undertaken in the early decades of the eighteenth century by William Dampier, Woodes Rogers, and George Shelvock maintained the Elizabethan pattern of attacking Spanish colonies, fostering revolution in Spanish America, seizing Spanish shipping, and opening Spanish ports to English trade.

At the same time the South Seas were gradually being brought within the understanding of the literate public. Dampier's *Voyage,* Daniel Defoe's *Robinson Crusoe,* and Jonathan Swift's *Gulliver's Travels* heightened British oceanic expectations. Strategists and map-makers continued to concentrate on the distant ocean. Even Parliament was prepared to underwrite the growing national debt by chartering, in 1711, the South Sea Company of famous "bubble" fame, which was given a monopoly of British commerce over the west coast of the Americas, from the mainland to three hundred leagues at sea. In other words, by the early eighteenth century the islands and seas of the Pacific had begun to bulk large in British plans, complementing existing interests in America, Africa, and Asia. The several oceanic probes by English adventurers into the Pacific beginning with Drake formed the essential preliminary to the government-directed activity that began in earnest in 1740.

Late in that year, in the course of the war with Spain that lasted from 1739 to 1748, H.M.S. *Centurion* and five other warships under command of Commodore George Anson sailed from England for the Pacific. Anson's instructions, reminiscent of Drake's, required him to attack Spanish shipping in the River Plate, "to annoy and distress" the Spanish along the Pacific seaboard of South America, to assist Indians in recovering their freedom from their Spanish masters, to capture enemy treasure ships, especially the Manila galleon, and to return home by way of the coast of China.[25] After three years, Anson was left with only his flagship and scarcely sufficient hands to man her as a result of the gales off Cape Horn and the ravages of scurvy. He lay in wait for the Spanish galleon from Acapulco and captured her off the Philippines, this being the most significant success of the Anson expedition. Anson had plundered several Spanish towns of Pacific America and seized Spanish shipping. Yet he had failed to open those ports to British traders or to kindle the revolutionary desires of the subject peoples in the Spanish colonies, as hoped for by the British ministry. It is now clear that Anson was sent on his mission because Britain was aware of the growing importance of the Pacific and the international rivalry that would inevitably follow.

The bearing Anson's voyage had on the development of the Northwest Coast of North America is not as obscure as might be thought. The voyage showed, firstly, that Britain could take the offensive without fear of Spanish invasion at home; secondly, that her naval strength made possible the conquest of Spain's possessions overseas; and, thirdly, that British political and commercial interests desired territory and trade in the Pacific. This new self-assuredness was to carry Britain through the eighteenth century, especially after 1763 when she emerged as a world power and entered the era of her world pre-eminence known as the Pax Britannica. While she might have trouble in controlling her American continental colonies, with her naval preponderance she could act from strength in her dealings with France and especially Spain. The growth of Britain's interest in the Pacific, "the swing to the East" as it is sometimes called, reflected her growing ascendancy in Europe. Anson's voyage thus foretold the conflict between English and Spanish claims on the Northwest Coast that erupted in the Nootka Sound dispute in 1790.

Far to the north of the route where Anson had patiently hunted the fabulous Manila galleon, the Russians began to make inroads into Spanish territory. In two voyages, 1727-29 and 1740-41, Vitus Bering, a Dane holding a commission in the Russian navy, put in motion Tsar Peter the Great's plan, though shrouded in secrecy to prevent Spain's retaliation, for dominion and trade in the northeastern Pacific. The objective of the first voyage was to find a route to America for the dual purpose of developing trade with New Spain and securing Russia's Pacific frontier; that of the second was to establish sovereignty in North America and offlying islands and to exploit resources. Pragmatic objectives supplanted the value of geographical discovery for its own sake. Thus, in the first, Bering, using ships constructed at Kamchatka, opened the North Pacific to Russian enterprise. And in the second, with Aleksei Chirikov, he pushed trade along the continental shore as far south as $56°N$, almost to the southernmost limit of the Alaska panhandle, and in so doing disclosed swarming breeding grounds of sea otter, the principal resource that eventually underscored international rivalry for the Northwest Coast. In the years that followed, the Russians gradually set up trading posts throughout the Aleutians, using Petropavlovsk as their Siberian and Unalaska as their American headquarters, and carried sea otter pelts to markets in China, Japan, and Kamchatka. This Russian penetration into America provoked a Spanish response. Missionaries and soldiers pushed northwestward by land to found their first colony on the North Pacific coast at San Francisco in 1769. Soon the Spanish had colonized California and established a naval base at San Blas, Mexico. France later demonstrated her interest in the Pacific by sending Bougainville in 1768 and La Pérouse in 1786 to expand the frontiers of French political activity, commercial enterprise, and scientific inquiry to Tahiti, New Zealand, and California.[26]

To secure her interests in the South Pacific and stop the French advance, Britain dispatched successive naval expeditions under Byron, Carteret, and Wallis.

Especially noteworthy is that undertaken in 1764-66 by Commodore the Honourable John Byron, commanding H.M.S. *Dolphin*. It aimed at gaining the Falkland Islands, whose strategic position as "the key to the Pacific" and a base for future operations in the Pacific had been recognized by Anson. Byron's second objective was to find a Northwest Passage, an easy sea lane from the North Atlantic to the rich trading areas of the Indies, one that would give Britain a commercial advantage over her European competitors. Byron's instructions detailed the advantages to the honour of the nation, including the advancement of commerce and navigation and the usefulness of discovery in the South Sea. They also made specific reference to the Northwest Passage in the following words:

> And moreover as the country of New Albion in North America, first discovered and taken possession of by Sir Francis Drake in the year 1579, has never been examined with that care which it deserves, notwithstanding frequent recommendations of that undertaking by the said Sir Francis Drake, Dampier, and many other mariners of great experience, who have thought it possible that a passage might be found between the Latitude of 38 and 54 [that is between, say, San Francisco Bay and the northern extremity of the Queen Charlotte Islands] from that coast into Hudson's Bay: His Majesty . . . conceiving no Conjunction so proper for an enterprise of this nature as a Time of profound Peace . . . has thought fit to make those attempts which are specified in the following Instructions.[27]

Byron was to proceed to Nova Albion via the Strait of Magellan, find a convenient harbour for refreshing his crew, and explore the Northwest Coast as far as was practicable. If a passage were found, he was to return to England by it. If no passage existed, he was to return by the coasts of Asia, China, or the East Indies. Byron occupied the windswept port of Egmont in the Falklands and was not deterred by French occupation at nearby Fort St. Louis. But he flagrantly ignored his instructions to search for a passage on the Northwest Coast, saying that his ships were not fit for the California voyage, a claim which seems contrary to fact.[28]

What motivated Byron to violate his instructions is not known. The Lords of the Admiralty took Byron at his word and contented themselves with his explanation that his vessels were unprepared for the California voyage. Nonetheless, their Lordships were, at this time, keenly aware of the importance of the Northwest Passage. Well into the 1770's they continued to express the opinions held since Elizabethan times that finding an easy route to Asia by way of North America would give the nation new commercial, political, and strategic advantages.

In retrospect, the voyages of Drake, Anson, and Byron were uncertain approaches to the Northwest Coast by the English. They were little more than probes into the Pacific. Drake, for instance, never fully examined the coast. His voyage is especially noteworthy in that it laid the basis for English dominion on the west coast of North America, although its exact extent had yet to be defined. Anson's voyage showed that British commercial intentions for the Pacific were strong indeed and that the Spanish claim to *mare clausum* in the Pacific had no strength if it could not be defended by force. Anson's probe also foretold the conflict of international interests such as the Anglo-Spanish rivalry for the Falkland Islands in the late 1760's and Nootka Sound in 1790. Byron's voyage was less satisfactory than Drake's or Anson's, yet his instructions had indicated clearly that the British were in the 1760's keenly alive to the importance of finding the Northwest Passage. Nonetheless, the earlier expeditions to the Pacific, commanded by captains of some seniority, had yielded comparatively meagre geographical results. For all the British knew, the Northwest Coast was still what Jonathan Swift had described in *Gulliver's Travels* in 1726—a strange land of strange men, Brobdingnag. The search for the mythical strait would have to wait for a better, more faithful naval officer in the person of Captain James Cook to delineate the general outline of the Northwest Coast.

3

Cook's Reconnaissance

Whereas the Earl of Sandwich has signified to us His Majesty's pleasure that an attempt should be made to find out a Northern Passage by sea from the Pacific to the Atlantic Ocean, and whereas we have in pursuance thereof caused His Majesty's sloops *Resolution* and *Discovery* to be fitted in all respects to proceed upon a voyage for the purpose above mentioned, and from the experience we have had of your abilities and good conduct in your late voyages, have thought fit to entrust you with the conduct of the present intended voyage . . . .

FROM COOK'S INSTRUCTIONS, 6 JULY 1776

In the 1770's the vexing problem of the Northwest Passage remained unsolved. The munificent reward of £20,000, offered by the British parliament after 1745 for merchant ships finding a sea route through Hudson Strait and the rumoured great "sea of the west" to the Pacific, was still unclaimed. As a further inducement, the British government, on pressure from the Royal Society, decided to extend the reward to include ships of the Royal Navy; and in 1775, the government authorized payment of a £20,000 reward for discovering a passage north of 52° and £5,000 to the crew of the first ship sailing within one degree of the North Pole, as "such approaches may greatly tend to the discovery of a communication between the Atlantic and Pacific oceans." The government reasoned that such a discovery would have "many advantages to commerce and science."[1]

The shift to include science as a motive for Arctic discovery reflects the influence of the Royal Society on government.[2] Already instrumental in sending Captain James Cook, R.N., on his first voyage to the Pacific and involved in various endeavours related to exploration, the Society, through its leaders, was close to the seats of power in Whitehall. Daines Barrington, a member of the Society's council and a jurist, naturalist, antiquarian, and geographer, influenced by his Swiss scientific correspondent Samuel Engel, declared that the north polar sea was ice-free and in 1775 and 1776 wrote several pamphlets expounding this peculiar belief. At the same time he appealed to his friend the Earl of Sandwich, First Lord of the Admiralty, to send British warships to find a passage to the East Indies via the North Pole. These pressures were successful, for in 1773 the Admiralty dispatched the *Racehorse* and *Carcass* to investigate, under command of Captain Constantine Phipps, F.R.S. Assisted by ice pilots from the Greenland whaling fleet, Phipps found the ice barrier north of Spitzbergen impassable, and he returned to London full of pessimism. Strangely, Barrington remained full of optimism, and reasoning that Phipps had been sent in a "bad year" continued to lobby Sandwich on the subject of polar exploration. Now he revived the idea of a naval expedition seeking an approach to the Northwest Passage from the Pacific.[3] This was to be a renewal of the Byron project of 1764.

Barrington's new plan, which gave birth to Cook's third voyage, was adopted by the council of Royal Society in February 1774.[4] Subsequently, on 17 February, the Secretary of the Society wrote to the Admiralty as follows:

> The Council of the Royal Society having last year submitted a proposal to your Lordships, for making discoveries towards the North Pole (which was honoured with your approbation), are now emboldened to lay another plan before the Board of Admiralty, for the protection of Science in general, & more particularly that of Geography.
>
> They conceive that a Ship, or Ships, fitted out either in Europe or the East Indies may be victualled at the Port of Canton in China; from whence the run to the Northern parts of New Albion will not be, probably, longer than from England to Jamaica: such vessels therefore (even if no refreshment could be procured on the Coast of N America) might proceed up the North western side of that continent, so as to discover whether there is a passage into the European Seas.[5]

For financial reasons the Admiralty never undertook this project, but the Royal Society at least had the Admiralty's assurance that an expedition would be fitted out when James Cook returned from the Pacific, probably in 1775.[6]

The British believed they knew where to find the western opening to the Northwest Passage. The 1775 act regulating the reward for discovering the passage specified that the search be conducted north of the fifty-second degree of latitude. This can be explained by the existing state of Russian geographical exploration and by the discoveries of Samuel Hearne, a fur trade explorer in the employ of the Hudson's Bay Company. In 1773 the findings of Jacob von Stählin, Secretary of the Russian Academy of Sciences, were published as *An Account of the New Northern Archipelago, Lately Discovered by the Russians in the Seas of Kamchatka and Anadir*.[7] Stählin's map of Russian discoveries, published in the volume, was a startling reworking of the geographical theories of Gerhard Friedrich Müller, who had been with Bering and Chirikov in their great discoveries of Bering Strait and Alaska. Müller's 1761 map, regarded in England as the best authority, had firmly delineated New Albion and Kamchatka but only vaguely defined the Northwest Coast of North America and Alaska. By contrast, Stählin's chart showed "Alascha" as a large island, part of the Northern or Aleutian Archipelago, and separate from the North American continent. The authority for this map rested in the supposedly accurate surveys of Lieutenant Ivan Synd of the Russian Admiralty Office made in 1764-66.

The British reaction to Stählin's map was generally condemnatory, but this did not remove the lingering suspicion that such a passage might reach north and east from Alaska to the Polar Sea, as Stählin had proposed. Might not such a waterway join with the partly frozen Arctic Sea discovered by Hearne, who in 1771 had made his way across forests and barrens to the mouth of the Coppermine River? Moreover, would not the findings of Hearne's expedition in the region of Great Slave Lake and Slave River, without crossing a large body of seawater, confirm that no Northwest Passage existed in low latitudes? On the evidence, Hearne's discoveries greatly influenced Cook's instructions. For some years the British government kept Hearne's outstanding discoveries secret.[8] At this time the Admiralty, Hudson's Bay Company, and Royal Society co-operated closely on the subject of finding a Northwest Passage. All wanted to solve the riddle and were anxious to counter the unjust aspersions of Arthur Dobbs, Joseph Robson, and others who condemned the Hudson's Bay Company for not exploring the northwest interior.

Cook at this time was forty-eight years of age, a tall, solid, and unpretentious Yorkshireman and a seasoned and humane sailor. He had already been round the world twice, once in each direction. "I have been almost constantly at Sea from my youth," he wrote in 1775, "and have dragged myself (with the assistance of a few good friends) through all the Stations, from a Prentice boy to a Commander." Indeed he had reached the quarter deck "through the hawse-hole." He owed his rank to his repute as a marine surveyor rather than to influence among persons of power. He was the son of a Scots farmhand settled in a remote Yorkshire village, scholar between the ages of eight and twelve, apprentice to a grocer and drygoods merchant at sixteen, and sailor in the Whitby coal trade at eighteen. As mate to a ship-master sailing coal ships to and from the Port of London, young Cook found the spirit of ships and the sea compelling. The tricky and dangerous navigation of the North Sea was his seaman's nursery. In the coal trade he learned navigation, and before he had been four years at sea he was able to "keep a ship's way." Perhaps the sight of great three-decker armed ships at Chatham dockyard on the Thames or news of the wider world caught his imagination; in any case, at age twenty-seven Cook volunteered as an able seaman in the Royal Navy.

Soon he became "Master, R.N.," a prestigious though uncommissioned service rank which pointed him out as a career professional in the handling of ships and in the surveying of waters. A varied service took him to Ireland, Halifax, Louisbourg, Quebec, and Newfoundland. In those years he distinguished himself by charting the River St. Lawrence as far as Quebec, a service which allowed the amphibious expedition under Major-General James Wolfe and Vice-Admiral Sir Charles Saunders to dislodge the French from dominant power in Canada. Then, for five years, he patiently made charts of Newfoundland that facilitated the continued safety of that other important nursery of seamen, the cod fishery, and, more, the security of traffic in and out of the St. Lawrence—whether through the Strait of Belle Isle on the north or Cabot Strait on the south. Surveying was the harbinger of commerce and settlement; and this imperial service that reveals Cook's importance in several Canadian locales allowed him to meet two men subsequently influential in his life, Sir Hugh Palliser, Governor of Newfoundland, and Joseph Banks, Esq., F.R.S., the naturalist and later influential "fixer" of British scientific surveys by sea.

Cook's talents were known to these men and a few others inside the Admiralty who controlled appointments. His reputation as a quiet, competent seaman who was a capable commander of men and his connections with superiors in the service and government marked him out for early advancement. At age forty he received his first commission as an officer. The Lords of the Admiralty found in Cook the necessary qualities of character and technical competence. They gave him command of the *Endeavour*, an ex-Whitby coal trade bark, bound for Tahiti on behalf of the Royal Society to observe the sun's transit across Venus. Cook's appointment was made against the wishes of the Royal Society and in particular one Alexander Dalrymple, F.R.S., an irascible, eccentric East India Company hydrographer who had published, among other things, *An Historical Collection of the Several Voyages and Discoveries in the South Pacific Ocean* (1770-71). Dalrymple believed himself competent to handle one of His Majesty's ships for the long Pacific voyage. Instead, the Admiralty selected a skilled sailor-diplomat capable of completing the voyage with low risk to men and material, unlikely to embroil the kingdom in a war with the Tahitians, and yet one who was, as his own well-received paper on the eclipse of the sun in 1766 to the same Royal Society had shown, an able astronomer.[9] This 1768-71 voyage and its successor, 1772-75, allowed Cook to map most of the Pacific world; to delineate its island continents—New Zealand and Australia—and many of its islands and island clusters, including the Society Islands, Fiji, New Hebrides, and others; and, not least, to determine that the great southern continent Terra Australis did not exist.

Thus, by the time Cook reached home on 30 July 1775 from his second voyage round the world, he had already won prominence, promotion, and the nation's gratitude. The Royal Society awarded him the Copley Medal, their highest honour in the field of current intellectual achievement, for his report on the means by which he had returned his crew to their homeland without loss during the second of the two longest recorded voyages.[10] The Lords of the Admiralty advanced him to post-captain. In a rare act of royal favour they provided him with full security by appointing him to the Board of Greenwich Hospital. Here he could live in peace, work on his observations, and prepare his journals and narratives for publication. And, not least, from here he could spend time with his wife, then living modestly with their three children at Mile End Road, near Greenwich. When Cook left on his third and last Pacific voyage in 1776 he had been married for seventeen years with little time on shore. The Greenwich sinecure offered relative comfort after years of travel and recent illness.

Yet the Pacific still beckoned, its northern reaches and islands still unknown to him and to the pre-eminent seaborne nation of that age. Cook confessed that he was one "whose ambition leads me not only farther than any man has been before me, but as far as I think it possible for man to go." Who could resist the offer to fill in the remaining blanks in the charts of the North Pacific and reduce in that Age of Reason the speculation about the ocean's secrets, in particular its legendary Northwest Passage? Who, too, could resist accepting an appointment which the Lords of the Admiralty insisted would contribute nobly to the advancement of discoveries by completing the last phase of oceanic surface exploration and, at the same time, add to England's commercial prospects, power, and prestige? Who, again, could resist leaving behind what must have seemed a prosaic London life for the excitement of a veritable anthropological and botanical museum that passed almost daily before a sailor-scientist's very eyes? Or, who could resist, with perhaps a baronetcy in the offing, Their Lordships' request once again to command another "voyage to remote parts"? Cook's letter to John Walker, a Whitby shipowner and his former employer, tells as much as we know of his feelings about his decision to venture again to the South Sea instead of staying in the comfortable confines of Greenwich Hospital. "It is certain I have quitted an easy retirement, for an Active, and perhaps Dangerous Voyage," he told Walker. "My present disposition is more favourable to the latter than the former and I imbark on as fair a prospect as I can wish. If I am fortunate enough to get safe home, there's no doubt but it will be greatly to my advantage."[11]

Cook had every confidence in his ship, H.M.S. *Resolution*. She had, he wrote of the second voyage, been "found to answer, on all occasions beyond any expectation." Formerly the *Marquis of Granby*, she had, like her commander, been employed in the coastal navigation of the North Sea. Ships of this sort, Cook said, were "of a construction of the safest kind, in which the officers may, with the least hazard, venture on a strange coast."[12] When the Admiralty purchased the *Resolution* in 1771 she carried three masts but with no square sails on the mizzen-mast. However, extensive alterations included rerigging her with a square mizzen-topsail, fitting her with a horse figurehead, adding a "coach" or "round house" for the captain and additional accommodation for scientists and artists, raising her upper works for more interior space, and giving her a new armament of light carriage and swivel guns. This earned her the classification as a twelve-gun sloop of war. She measured 110 feet in length and 461 tons by the then current method and drew seventeen feet. By modern standards she seems a small vessel for distant voyaging, but we can admire the great space provided by her bluff bow and deep wide waist, her broad bottom that with her small size permitted easy beaching for repairs and provided stability if she were to ground, and, lastly, her additional armour, an extra skin of thin planking fitted to the hull over tarred felt and secured with thousands of closely spaced flatheaded nails—a precaution against shipworm. Normally she would have carried 110 men, but on Cook's third voyage she had twenty-two officers, seventy-one seamen, and twenty marines for a total of 113.[13] For a brief time after her purchase she bore the name *Drake*, apparently in recognition of ancient Tudor ambitions and achievements in Pacific oceanic expansion. However, the Admiralty were sensitive to the fact that this name would offend their Spanish rivals. They recommissioned her the *Resolution*, a name with which few persons, British or otherwise, could quarrel. Her consort, another collier, also bore an appropriate name, *Discovery*. Not to be confused with George Vancouver's ship, of later date, she was not much smaller than the *Resolution*. She measured ninety-two feet in length and 299 tons. She carried eighty-one officers and men, including her captain, Charles Clerke who, like Cook, would die in the distant Pacific.

The ships, however, had got a poor refit. They were victims of shoddy materials and nefarious navy contracts at a time when the Royal Dockyards were hard pressed to meet the demands on them owing to the dangers of war with the rebellious American colonies. Yet the vessels were given the best outfit and stores available. They were also given the best men, most of them still in their youth and some capable as Cook's successors to make their own mark in oceanic expansion. One of them, William Bligh, twenty-one-year old master of the *Resolution*, was a skilled mariner who learned much from his eminent captain. It was he who later, in an error on the side of generosity, allowed his ship's company some six months' leave at Tahiti and suffered a mutiny, after which a court-martial acquitted him for the loss of his vessel, the famous *Bounty*. The *Resolution*'s lieutenants included, by seniority, John Gore, a veteran of Cook's two circumnavigations, James King, sometime student of astronomy, and John Williamson, the only quarrelsome and woefully autocratic officer in either ship, who, as a fighting officer during the French Wars, earned Nelson's charge that he should have been shot for his undistinguished conduct. Listed among the midshipmen was James Trevenen, whose fabulously tattooed arms later delighted women of the English social set, himself subsequently a potential North Pacific discoverer for Russia and a distinguished commander against Sweden at the Battle of Vibourg. Another noteworthy midshipman was Richard Hergest, appointed in 1792 commander of the storeship *Daedalus* to succour George Vancouver's expedition. Also in the *Resolution* were David Samwell, surgeon's mate and Welsh poet; John Ledyard, Connecticut-born marine corporal who wrote a famous journal about Siberia; John Webber, draftsman and artist; and Omai, a Society Islander brought to London by the second voyage and who, having been painted by Sir Joshua Reynolds and poked fun at by English satirists, was being returned to his Polynesian home.

In the *Discovery*, in addition to Clerke, were Lieutenants James Burney, veteran of the second voyage and subsequently a post-captain, a fellow of the Royal Society, and distinguished historian of *The Chronological History of North-Eastern Voyages of Discovery* (1819), and John Rickman, another writer, who wrote the unauthorized and dubious account of Cook's last voyage and mysterious death at the hands of the Hawaiians. Among other notable figures on board were George Vancouver, an eighteen-year-old midshipman bound for the Pacific with Cook for the second time; Nathaniel Portlock, master's mate and later leader of the King George's Sound Company expedition to Nootka Sound which opened up the maritime fur trade; George Dixon, armourer's mate and afterwards involved with the Portlock project and British discoverer of the Queen Charlotte Islands; Joseph Billings, later another North Pacific explorer, though in Russian employ; and William Bayley, an astronomer working for the Board of Longitude on this his second Pacific voyage.[14]

In all, the officers and men of the two ships were a singular collection of capable seamen, talented artists, and scientists all bound for a new and not yet fully discovered Pacific world. Here was seasoned experience and learned expertise. Here, too, were personalities (all except Williamson) capable of living harmoniously with shipmates during the lengthy voyage. They were men willing to learn the sea's secrets, to tolerate its moods, and to train themselves as mariners and, not infrequently, as explorers who later would follow in the wake of their great leader. In the closing years of the eighteenth century they completed the pioneering tasks undertaken by Drake, Anson, Byron, and even Cook himself.

Cook's objective, according to his instructions of 6 July 1776, was to find a Northwest Passage from the Pacific. The Admiralty had directed him to enter the Pacific by way of the Cape of Good Hope, touch at islands in 48°S in the Indian Ocean near Mauritius, and go to New Zealand and then to the Society Islands. After refreshing his crews and taking on wood and water at Tahiti, Cook was to "proceed in as direct a course as you can to the coast of New Albion, endeavouring to fall in with it in the latitude of 45° 0′ North; and taking care in your way thither not to lose any time in search of new lands, or to stop at any time you may fall in with unless you find it necessary to recruit your wood and water."[15] Cook was instructed not to land on any portion of Spanish lands on the western portions of the Americas unless by accident or absolute necessity; and if he should meet any inhabitants, or any subjects of Spain or another European nation, he was not to disturb or offend them.

In reference to actual discovery of the Northwest Passage, Cook's instructions specified that upon his arrival on the coast of New Albion he should put in to the first convenient harbour for wood, water, and refreshment. This presumably was Drake's old landfall northwest of San Francisco Bay. Then he was to "proceed northward along the coast as far as the latitude of 65°, or farther, if you are not obstructed by lands or ice, taking care not to lose any time in exploring rivers and inlets, or upon any other account, until you get into the before-mentioned latitude of 65°, where we could wish you to arrive in the month of June next. When you get that length you are very carefully to search for and to explore such rivers or inlets as may appear to be of a considerably extent and pointing towards Hudson's Bay or Baffin's Bay.'' If, from his observations or on the basis of information received from native inhabitants, Cook learned of the certainty or probability of a passage, he was to proceed as he thought necessary and attempt to discover it. If certain that no such passage existed, he was to make his way to Petropavlovsk in Kamchatka for the winter. In the spring of the following year, at his discretion, Cook could search further for a passage, either to the northeast or northwest, and proceed to England, as earlier directed, ''by such route as you may think best for the improvement of geography and navigation, repairing to Spithead with both sloops, where they are to remain till further orders.''

The British government ordered Cook not to interfere with Spanish claims to the Northwest Coast. Nonetheless, with the consent of the inhabitants, he was to take possession in the name of George III of ''convenient situations in such countries as you may discover, that have not already been discovered or visited by any other European power, and to distribute among the inhabitants such things as will remain as traces and testimonies of your having been there. But if you find the countries so discovered are uninhabited you are to take possession of them for His Majesty by setting up proper marks and inscriptions as first discoverers and possessors.''[16] Cook was to extend British claims whenever and wherever possible, but not at the risk of conflicting with the claims of other European nations or with native tribes not agreeable to such an act of possession.

While Cook was to explore the Pacific coast for a sea lane to the Arctic, the Admiralty planned an attempt to reach the Northwest Coast from Baffin Bay. In 1776, Lieutenant Richard Pickersgill was sent in the armed brig *Lion* to protect British whalers in Davis Strait from American privateers, to capture any vessels belonging to the rebellious American colonies, and to explore the coasts of Baffin Bay preparatory to sending guides to help Cook find his way eastward.[17] By the time Pickersgill reached the whaling grounds, the British whalers had already left for home. Pickersgill faced difficult climatic conditions owing to the lateness of the navigable season. He despaired, became ill, drank heavily, and returned to England in the *Lion*. Early the following year, this ship was recommissioned under command of Lieutenant Walter Young, who was given detailed instructions that indicated that his voyage was also to be in conjunction with that of Cook. Young was to find if Hearne's Polar Sea could be reached from Baffin Bay and also if the natives of that bay used copper.[18]

Young's voyage was as disappointing as that of Pickersgill, and for no known reason he ignored his instructions and abandoned the project. Neither man was of Cook's quality, neither had the strength nor the determination to discover and chart the icy eastern access to the passage at the time when Cook himself was in the Pacific completing an equally difficult part of the project.

While these tentative penetrations of the dark and icy waters of the Bay were being made, Cook had left from Plymouth on 12 July 1776 in H.M.S. *Resolution* nearly three weeks in advance of the *Discovery*. The details of the voyage from the Cape of Good Hope across the South Atlantic and into the Indian and Pacific oceans by way of the Cape of Good Hope need not be recounted here. En route to the Northwest Coast, Cook called at New Zealand, the Friendly Islands, Tahiti, and the Sandwich (later Hawaiian) Islands.

Cook believed that the central geographical position of the Hawaiian Islands between the Americas and Asia made them extremely attractive as an imperial prize. He warned that prior discovery of those islands by Spain would give her commercial advantages over other European nations since ships sailing from Acapulco to the Philippines could use the islands as a place of refreshment.[19] He rightly understood that the chief utility of the islands at this stage of the opening of the Pacific lay in their strategic mid-ocean location, a fact which maritime fur traders later exploited to good effect.

Leaving behind this Polynesian paradise with its swaying palms, crashing surf, and salubrious climate for discovery in colder, northern latitudes must not have appealed to Cook and his men. Nonetheless, the summer months were approaching, a favourable time to complete an ambitious round of work that would take the *Resolution* and *Discovery* to Nootka Sound, Alaska, and Bering Sea before a return to the islands in November. It was an adventuresome prospect and the focal point and climax of the expedition's activities. Quitting the islands on 2 February under "gentle gale" conditions, the two ships stood towards the northward, steering northeast and east as the prevailing winds would allow. Soon the welcome signs of land began to appear—kelp from the coast of Lower California, pieces of driftwood, a few birds, seals, and whales, and finally, at dawn on Saturday, 7 March, "the long-looked for Coast of New Albion." At noon their landfall was determined as 44° 33′N and 235° 21′E. Cook's journal reflects no excitement: it was another day of duty for the laconic Yorkshireman, who thought the wood-covered land of moderate height rather undistinguished in appearance. Lieutenant James King, however, was more enthusiastic about what he saw. This was land hitherto unexplored as far as he knew: there was no certainty that Drake or Vizcaino had been higher than 44°N; and he knew nothing of Juan Pérez's voyage two years before. The passage from Hawaii had been exceptional, with fair winds and uncommonly mild weather. This was a surprising fact, King wrote, when "approaching so great a continent." The landscape was aesthetically agreeable, for the wooded land of moderate height possessed a pleasant, fertile, and diversified appearance.[20]

Soon the weather turned poor. For nearly a month the ships patiently tacked off the coast, inching their way north, all the while awaiting better weather. The high and craggy land mostly covered with snow, the frequent fog, rain, and snow, and the heavy winds and gales were an uninviting combination. Cook took out his feelings on the landscape by naming one rocky headland Cape Foulweather (in 44° 55′N). Other capes in the region—Perpetua and Gregory—received saintly names for the days of the English calendar which commemorated them. On the 12th, Cook reported seeing Cape Blanco where the Spaniard Martin de Aguilar had been during Vizcaíno's voyage in 1603 and supposedly had located the southern entry to de Fuca's Strait. In fact, as Vancouver later discovered in 1792, Cook was too far north to observe Cape Blanco. What is important about this claimed sighting is that Cook wrote that it was in this latitude that cartographers had placed the entrance to Aguilar's Strait to the interior, to Cook's way of thinking a most improbable geographical fact.

From time to time fair weather allowed the ships to approach the rugged shore, and on 22 March in 48° 15′N, while seeking a safe harbour, Cook saw an opening in the shore between an island or rock and the mainland. This place, if Cook's calculation is to be relied on, was not Cape Flattery at the entrance to the Strait of Juan de Fuca but instead Point of the Arches, the next most southerly headland and one marked by an offshore island that offered an opening. This disappointed Cook. "It is in this very latitude we were now in," he wrote in obvious disgust, "where geographers have placed the pretended *Strait of Juan de Fuca,* but we saw nothing like it, nor is there the least probability that ever such thing existed."[21] It may be observed that had he been in the latitude of Cape Flattery ten minutes of a degree to the north he might well have seen the famous pinnacle rock reported by de Fuca, a high, conspicuous feature that Cook would have seen clearly from the south.

Cook was then some fifteen to thirty kilometres from the Strait of Juan de Fuca and about thirty kilometres from the shore, a goodly distance to see the Strait. From his angle of view the shoreline apparently did not reveal any particular indentation. The cape he reported as Flattery did not seem out of the ordinary; indeed, it did not shield from view any great sea entry into the continent. Perhaps, Cook was, as his recent biographer hints, "a little too contemptuous" of the possibility of "any such thing" as a passage.[22] Cook himself once had written that the world could hardly excuse a man from leaving unexplored a coast that he had discovered.[23] Could it be that on this occasion Cook was quick to cast aspersions on the enthusiastic discoveries of his predecessors? After all, he had given Aguilar's entry to an island sea at Cape Blanco short shrift. He was unlikely to give any more credence to a Spanish explorer whose discoveries were far less apocryphal than de Fuca's.

But again, weather conditions determined his ships' courses. Here his exploration was a compromise between his standards and his opportunities. With approaching nightfall Cook had to abandon further investigations, and a storm that blew up overnight did not allow him to return to the coast to trace the shoreline north of Cape Flattery. The very day he was to look for a harbour, a storm forced him away from the coast for a week. Thus in the night Cook missed the strait, a body of water only twenty-one kilometres wide at its entrance. Under the circumstances his miss is understandable, for the pioneers of the sea did not have their successors' haven-finding aids at their disposal.[24] Still, it would remain for others on a different, southerly track or in better weather to find Fuca's Pillar and Fuca's Strait and place them accurately on the mariner's chart.[25] And others would determine the insularity of Vancouver Island.

For Cook, the weather was too heavy, the shore too hazardous to allow the ships to approach "this unknown Coast where we knew of no shelter," Surgeon Samwell recorded.[26] For days on end the ships cruised under reefed topsails and reduced courses, inching their way north by the evening "southerly blasts," as Cook wryly called them, those daily intermissions that came as a break in the great storms and allowed the ships to carry more sail but at the same time warned of the storm that predictably would follow the next morning. These storms were frequent and violent. "Our ships complained," the marine Ledyard dryly wrote.[27] Not until the 29th did the weather allow them to approach the shore and search for a place to get water, then in short supply.

Here Cook thought the landscape seemed different from the Oregon coast, for high mountain peaks covered with snow dominated the skyline, providing a dramatic backdrop to the valleys and seacoast that were "cloathed with wood." Breakers dotted the shore, indicating treacherous reefs. Rugged points stretched from the beach. Between two such promontories he spied what appeared to be a large bay. This he called Hope Bay, for there he hoped to find a good harbour. As the ships drew nearer the shore, Cook saw two inlets, one in the northwest corner of the bay, the other in the northeast corner. Winds did not permit him to sail on a course towards the former and probably closer inlet, which may either have been Kyuquot or Esperanza. Thus he made for the latter, cautious of breaking or shoaling water, searching for a safe channel leading to a hoped-for-haven.

At this stage Cook was not certain that his ships were in anything more than a deep bay. However, about four in the afternoon a crewman at the masthead called out the welcome news that he had sighted water over a low rocky peninsula on the southern extremity of what later came to be called Nootka Island. This was the famous point shielding within its welcome arms Friendly Cove. Just as they approached the entrance, which by Cook's estimate was three or four miles wide, the wind died. The ships' boats were hoisted out to tow the vessels into what Cook now saw to be a deep and extensive sound, divided in two by a large island or peninsula (Bligh Island) with two channels (Cook to the north and Zuciarte to the northeast) providing welcome security from the misnamed Pacific.[28]

When Cook's ships came into the harbour, the local Indians, known as the Moachat, did not understand what the strange vessels were. The chief sent his warriors in canoes to investigate. Oral tradition among the Moachat holds that they spied one sailor with a hooked nose and another who was a hunchback and identified them in turn with the dog salmon and the humpback salmon, an indication of their fish-like origins. They thought Cook's ship to be "a fish come alive into people" and consequently grew cautious. But the chief "told them to go out there again . . . and try to understand what those people wanted and what they were after." They did so and Cook's crew gave them biscuits. The Moachat decided that the whites must be friendly and that they, in turn, should welcome the white strangers, so they gestured, all the while telling Captain Cook "Nootka, Itchme Nootka, Itchme"—meaning, "you go around the harbour."[29]

Cook had reached Nootka Sound by chance rather than by design. His entry into this sheltered confine on Vancouver Island's west coast had been dictated by the elements and his need for water. He might have reached Kyuquot, Esperanza, Barkley, or some other sound, or indeed Juan de Fuca Strait itself, had wind and weather proved different. As it was, this place afforded more than Cook had expected, and a brief stop for water became a month-long stay for rest, repair, and trade. Here was a snug harbour on a stormy and uncharted coast, "luckily"[30] discovered and affectionately prized by the ships' crews, who came to mingle freely with the inhabitants in sexual activity and to sense the features of a bountiful and artistic coast culture never before known to the British, one quite different from the Polynesian varieties of Hawaii or Tahiti but one also dictated by the features of the great ocean and in this case by the flora, fauna, and climate of its northeastern littoral.

Now observers on the decks of the *Resolution* and the *Discovery,* the latter still lying at anchor outside the harbour awaiting wind, had a chance to observe the Northwest Coast environment. Cook noticed that the land bordering the sea was usually level and not high. Around the sound it was high and generally inaccessible, with deep valleys, and farther inland, large mountains seemingly naked except for their snowcaps.

The compelling feature of the landscape there, however, is not the mountains but the brooding forest, heavily treed and made less inviting by thick underbrush and fallen timber. To the explorers everything seemed green and tree-covered. In every direction could be seen the great species of the western forest—spruce, Douglas fir, yellow cypress, and cedar[31] among others—the larger evergreens standing stately, the biggest trees yet seen by Cook and his men. Deciduous maple, ash, and small crab-apple trees provided a less majestic contrast. Storms had taken their toll on the forest, and the devastating effects of the southeasterly gales could be seen at several places on Bligh Island. Many trees were blown down and others "confoundedly mutilated," Captain Clerke said, by the rough gales that had attacked them. However, the prize of all the trees, mistakenly called pine, was the great Douglas fir, admired by most of the officers. Cook himself went on shore with the carpenters to "choose a proper stick" which would serve as a new mizzen mast to replace one rotted in the *Resolution.* They found an appropriate spar close to the ship. As Clerke put it admirably, such a variety of sizes existed "that in going a very inconsiderable distance, you may cut sticks of every gradation, from a Main Mast for your ship, to one for your Jolly Boat; and these I suppose as good as are to be procur'd in any part of the world."[32] Other parts of the masts—bibbs or hounds, cheeks, and tressle trees— had to be replaced. This labour required the ships to stay longer at Nootka Sound than Cook had intended. Conveniently, however, fallen timber or driftwood on the shore, both seasoned and dry, provided the carpenter with stock. Again the mariners' material needs were there for the taking. As Cook said, "the principal thing wanting was to be had."[33] When Cook's *Voyages* were published in 1784, due notice was given of the timber resources of the Northwest Coast. This advertised another feature of the area's economic wealth that would be exploited by the British traders, Meares among them. They came in Cook's wake to trade for sea otter skins but often went away from the coast with a cargo of spars, boards, and square timbers.[34] In the end the forests provided the more lasting resource, while the sea otter population dwindled in the over-exploitation that attended the maritime fur trade.

The forests supplied other important needs of the *Resolution* and *Discovery* and other ships that subsequently called. Tops of trees were cut to make spruce beer in the brewery set up on shore, and within two weeks the local liquor had replaced brandy in the daily ration. The beer, an excellent anti-scorbutic, had other medicinal benefits such as providing a cure for gonorrhoea and serving as a diuretic for the same complaint or simply as a laxative.[35] In that season, only local wild garlic and nettles provided edible produce. Grass, available in quantity, was acquired for the ships' cattle. However, the early approach of spring, noted by Lieutenant King with enthusiasm as being far in advance over the east side of North America, foretold a rich bounty for a variety of plants—strawberry, gooseberry, and currant among others—growing in heavy rich soil.

The sea also provided some food for the sailors. Salmon was not plentiful at that time of year. Herring, anchovy, cod, and other species augmented the diet, but the British were "grievously disappointed" at not getting an ample supply of fish which would have partly corrected their salt meat diet and spared their dwindling food reserves. They saw the ingenious fish weir and herring rake used by the Indians to take the fish with little apparent work. They felt disappointed, indeed cheated, that all their own labours with hook or net went unrewarded in seas seemingly abounding in fish if the number of seals, sea elephants, and sea otter seen were reliable indication. The ease of native self-sufficiency grew increasingly apparent to them as they came to realize that fish and sea mammals were the Indians' staple food. The British could see no indication of soil cultivation. "All seemed to remain in a state of nature," Ledyard said.[36]

In other places where the ships had called, the Europeans' attention had invariably been drawn to the natives. At Nootka Sound, cross-cultural contact began even before the ships entered the sound. Several canoes had come from

Yuquot to the ships. The inhabitants seemed self-assured, supremely confident in the strength of their own civilization, and rightly so because their predecessors had inhabited Yuquot for four thousand years. They welcomed their guests rather than shying away from them, and were inquisitive about these strangers who had sailed into their midst in their great winged vessels. To them the "white men" were those who lived on the ocean.

According to native traditions, one of the greeters was Maquinna,[37] Chief Tsaxawasip of the Moachat tribe of the Nootka. He was in the first canoe to come alongside the ships. He stood up, gave a long speech unintelligible to the English, but he pointed to the sound, indicating that the ships should proceed farther inshore. He wore a cedar bark hat in the shape of a buck's head and offered it and other objects for sale. He had announced the natives' commercial motivation from the outset of the ships' visit and, as a midshipman recorded, the British were immediately convinced that the Indians were no novices at that business. The chief went away content with a large axe.[38]

The Moachat were forward people who showed no fear or distrust. As many as thirty-two canoes filled with Indians had surrounded the ships immediately; and ten or twelve stayed with the *Resolution* most of the night. Cook's first impression of the Moachat, one that lasted for only two days, was that they were mild and inoffensive, quick to trade, and strictly honest. Soon, however, the Indians trespassed on English manners and customs: they laid aside all restraint, mingled freely with the whites on the ship's decks, and began helping themselves to the ship's iron articles. Sometimes they did so for sport. They stole a twenty or thirty-pound fish-hook used for fishing the anchor; on another occasion, though being closely guarded, they stole Cook's gold watch from his cabin. Many items, including the valued timepiece, were returned, not voluntarily but by force. Cook learned that the Indians were willing to impeach one another, and thus it became easy to identify the thieves. The British learned, as Master Thomas Edgar expressed it, that the Nootka "had a very great genius and passion for stealing." Consequently, Cook and his men, perhaps too trusting in the first place, now took appropriate precautions to stop the "thievish tricks" of people who considered property not personal but communal in nature.[39]

However, the English could go about their duties without fear of molestation. The Indians, though sometimes armed with bows, arrows, clubs, and spears, did not threaten. Any brandishing of a weapon (as when a chief in a canoe paddling round the ship stood up with his spear) seemed merely a ceremonial courtesy. Only when some neighbouring Indians, perhaps some Muchalat who were not then in the confederacy and who wanted to approach the ship, reached the vessels' anchorage at Ship's Cove did matters become troublesome. Even then, when Cook had armed and mustered the workmen on shore near the observatory, their native hosts gestured that they were not preparing to fight against the whites but against some of their own race.[40] The Moachat, jealous of their new allies, made a show of arms sufficient to ward off the intruders. The ancient internecine rivalries, the constant intertribal enmities, and the new economic divisions had surfaced quickly. The Moachat had a recent and newly acquired ascendancy that they were anxious to defend at all costs, a superiority that would make them for the time being lords of the coast. They claimed the English as their "exclusive property."

Doubtless the Moachat must have wondered at the Europeans' strange weapons. They did not understand their use until Lieutenant Williamson demonstrated a musket by firing a ball through a native's skin robe mounted twenty yards away on a tree. The Indians "gazed at one another for some time with fright & silent astonishment," Williamson wrote of himself, "and he felt obliged to bribe the robe's owner with copper and iron pieces before he could be persuaded to retrieve his hitherto impenetrable armour."[41] A hint had been given of the explosive, destructive qualities of the musket; the European had demonstrated his technological superiority. However, few could have predicted what firearms in native hands would do to diminish native populations by making internecine violence more intensive and deadly.

Nonetheless, at this stage, cross-cultural contact remained peaceful on both sides. Cook, King, Clerke, and Samwell were among those who looked on the natives with sympathy and understanding. The Indian thieves exasperated them, of course, and Cook was struck by the high notion they held of the resources of their country. "This is an American indeed!" he remarked in smiling admiration of an Indian who refused to be bullied by the captain's demands but who instead took him by the arm, thrust him away, and pointed the way for him to go about his business.[42] Cook took no offence, and the episode led to a meal in the Indian's house, where Ledyard claims a roasted human arm was produced as part of the fare, a course which the whites did not accept. There were other signs of cannibalism at Nootka, too many to discount the existence of the practice.

The strange appearance of the Indians also gave offence, not to the officers, who seemed tolerant, but rather to a young midshipman, Edward Riou, who thought them "the dirtiest beings ever beheld," their faces and hands marked with red and black, their bodies covered with animal skins.[43] Such condemnations do not appear in Cook's writings and seldom in those of his officers. Instead we are given observations, scientific in intent, that provide some of the best ethnological data in English about Northwest Coast life at that time.[44] Their accounts tell in splendid detail of the inhabitants, their villages, animals, produce, manufactures, foods, artistry, equipment, religion, political structure, and even language.

In short, what emerges from this ethnological report is a clear picture of an active, energetic, migratory society, spending the summer at the confederacy site at Yuquot and dispersing for the winter to some fifteen villages on the more sheltered waters of the sound. It was a populous society. Perhaps fifteen hundred lived at Yuquot alone, estimates varying from five hundred to two thousand, in any case a number sufficiently large to cause Cook to shy away from anchoring at Friendly Cove but to choose instead an unpopulated spot at Bligh Island for his ships' berth. This was also a maritime society of whalers and sea hunters, dependent on the ocean's bounties for their food, readily supplementing the sea's resources with the land's. These were Pacific peoples too, though different from the Maori, Tahitians, or Hawaiians, but people who came from some sort of common and as yet mythical well of mankind, their weapons resembling those of the Maori, their art forms curiously mirroring Polynesian norms.

They lived in large cedar-planked houses whose interiors were much more interesting than their ramshackle exteriors. The houses' inside corner posts, as the expedition's artist John Webber portrayed, were carved with figures. The Moachat called these columns *Klumma*. Their carvings were strange to the Europeans but full of meaning for the inhabitants, for they spoke of their ancestors and of their distant origins. Inside the houses were vast drying racks for herring and salmon, a long raised sleeping platform, cedar boxes for cooking, large baskets, and various utensils. Webber's illustration is among the important visual sources for the study of the Northwest Coast life in that time and place.[45] Above all, it reveals that here was a society living communally and in harmony with its maritime environment, its beliefs infused in part into great carved posts, its patterns of life and art built up through the millenia.

Yet for all the stability of this ancient order of things the Indians were quick to acquire what their own splendid society lacked most—iron—and to give in return what seemed most prolific—skins of mammals. None could imagine the rapid train of events that would follow. None could conceive that the era of primal innocence would quickly give way before firearms, disease, alcohol, a wage economy, and Christianity. The British arrival at Nootka forecast changes that could not then have been foreseen or appreciated.

Nonetheless, on the European side, a glimpse, ever so casual, existed as to the new order of things to come, of new place names and of new classifications. "Captain Cook has honour'd this place with the Name of King Georges Sound," a lieutenant scratched in his journal, "but it is call'd by the Natives Nook'ka."[46] Nootka seems an appropriate name indeed, for according to one source it meant in the native tongue "to go around" or "to make a circuit."[47] It meant to circumnavigate Nootka Island, the large island which the British in Cook's time thought part of the mainland. Eventually Cook also came to call it Nootka Sound and recorded it as such on his charts along with King George's Sound. During Juan Pérez's voyage in 1774 the Spanish had called it San Lorenzo after the saints' calendar date of their landfall; and their Iberian successors termed it San Lorenzo de Nuka. For half a century the simple appellation Nootka became the mariner's key place name on the whole coast between San Francisco Bay and

Bering Strait. It was known in the courts of Europe and the halls of commerce as a focal point of European rivalry.

Cook also helped to establish in the minds of Europeans the name Nootka for this particular tribal grouping. Whereas the Nootka used specific tribal designations rather than broad inclusive classifications, Cook called them Wak'ashians on account of the commonly used word *Wak'ash,* meaning an expression of applause, approbation, or friendship.[48] Thus in another way, the place name Friendly Cove took on a more subtle meaning, though natives now less anxious to receive outsiders prefer ''Yuquot'' [*Yukwzt*]—''where winds blow''—its name before Cook's call.[49] Even today ''Wakashan'' denotes the languages of the natives living on the northwestern coasts of Vancouver Island, including Nootka Sound and of the Kwakiutl, who inhabited the island's north and northeastern coasts and the mid-coastal region of the mainland. Thus in time these terms of place and of language became points of identification for the natives themselves. At the time of Cook's call, however, the Nootka did not designate themselves by any particular appellation except in the use of such phrases as ''people we can understand.''

Cook knew little of the region's geography. He did not know, for example, that Yuquot lay on an island. Nor did he know that the whole region constituted an integral part of the much larger Vancouver Island. Obviously Nootka Sound provided no access to the great ''Sea of the West'' and to no Strait of Anian or Juan de Fuca Strait. Thus three weeks elapsed before Cook decided to investigate the labyrinthine channels and islands of Nootka Sound. The heavy work of cutting spars, trimming masts, and loading water was now finished. On the morning of 20 April he set out in the *Resolution*'s pinnace and barge cutter to view the sound. This voyage took Cook first to Yuquot, Friendly Cove. Here the natives showed him every mark of civility. They asked him to visit their houses, which he did. From Friendly Cove, ''a very snug harbour,'' the boats proceeded up the west side of the Sound via Kendrick Inlet, Tahsis Inlet, and Tlupana Inlet. Soon he came to realize that Ship's Cove, where his ships were anchored, formed part of an island—Bligh. During this voyage, which became as the day advanced a forty-eight-kilometre circumnavigation of Bligh Island, they found several other Indian villages. At one of them, on Hanna Channel, Cook received a surly reception from a chief who objected to the British intrusion. Presents from Cook could not change the chief's demands that they be gone. A plaintive song sung by young Indian women seeking the affection of the sailors provided a pleasant contrast to the chief's welcome.

For the young midshipmen at the oars of the boats it was an interesting but laborious day. For Cook, tired and in poor health, it was a day to relax and, almost out of character, to ''condescend now and then, to converse familiarily with us,'' as one midshipman so wryly put it.[50] In verse he recalled the contrast of their day in the "jolly-boat" with the usual midshipman's work and the humdrum of ship's routine.

Oh Nootka, thy shores can our labour attest
(For 30 long miles in a day are no jest)
When with Sol's earliest beams we launchd forth in thy sound,
Nor till he was setting had we compass'd it round.
Oh Day of hard labour! Oh Day of good living!
When Toote* was seized with the humour of giving!
When he cloathd in good nature his looks of authority,
And shook from his eye brows their stern superiority.[51]

The boats' return to the ships in the evening marked the end of the first European reconnaissance of Nootka Sound, and the rudimentary charts produced revealed an intricate maze of islands and passages. Now the British had a precise position for the Sound's entrance, which would allow mariners after Cook to locate it with certainty. From his *Voyage* they would know that life could be sustained here, that ships could find a good place for refreshment and repair, and, not least, that the inhabitants were generally friendly and anxious to trade. They might well become important commercial allies if their customs were not violated by the intruders.

Now the voyage must continue in pursuit of its objectives in northern latitudes. On the 23rd, 24th, and 25th preparations were made to sail: sailors took down the observatory on shore, readied the sails, and then stowed the last spars and timbers on board. The outward passage was not easy owing to unfavourable winds and tides. However, even a dramatic drop of the barometer did not prevent Cook from determining to put to sea at all events, leaving behind his new friends.

"Our Friends the Indians," he wrote in his journal of his last contact with the Nootka,

attended upon us till we were almost out of the Sound, some on board the Ships and others in Canoes a Chief named [name not given] who had some time before attached himself to me was one of the last who left us, before he went I made him up a small present and in return he present[ed] me with a Beaver skin of greater value, this occasioned me to make some addition to my present, on which he gave me the Beaver skin Cloak he had on, that I

---

*The Polynesian pronunciation of Cook.

knew he set a value upon. And as I was desireous he should be no suffer-[er] by his friendship and generosity to me, I made him a present of a New Broad Sword with a brass hilt which made him as happy as a prince. He as also many others importuned us much to return to them again and by way of incouragement promised to lay in a good stock of skins for us, and I have not the least doubt but they will.[52]

Cook's voyage north to the Alaskan coast was not easy: heavy weather drove him westward of the Queen Charlotte Islands, Prince of Wales Island, and even the Alexander Archipelago. Finally, in latitude 57° 3'N, near Cape Edgecumbe and present-day Sitka, he was able to find the coastline. This was adjacent to the pretended strait of Admiral Bartholomew de Fonte or river Los Reyes, supposedly discovered by de Fonte for Spain in 1640 in order to forestall Boston navigators trying to attempt a passage from Hudson Bay to the Strait of Anian.[53] Cook wanted nothing to do with de Fonte's fabrications: "For my own part," he recorded, "I give no credit to such vague and improbable stories, that carry their own confutation along with them nevertheless I was very desirous of keeping the Coast aboard in order to clear up this point beyond dispute; but it would have been highly imprudent in me to have ingaged with the land in such exceeding tempestious weather, or to have lost the advantage of a fair wind by waiting for better weather."[54]

His subsequent explorations on the Alaskan coast, especially in Cook Inlet, proved similarly unrewarding for finding a Northwest Passage. However, Cook showed that Alaska was no island but rather a large promontory extending west and north and then northeast from Bering Strait. He had nothing but disgust for Stählin's map, and must have felt duped.[55] By 18 July, Cook had penetrated into the Bering Sea as far as Icy Cape, Alaska. By the 29th, he had crossed over to Siberia, where he landed briefly. Then he made his way southbound through Bering Strait to the Hawaiian Islands, which he thought, quite correctly, would be the best place in the North Pacific to winter. His ice-bound alternative, Petropavlovsk, on the Kamchatka Peninsula, was quite unsuitable.[56] In an unfortunate train of events in which Cook seems to have lost his temper, he was killed by the Hawaiians in a melee on 14 February 1779.[57] Charles Clerke, the *Discovery's* captain, assumed command of the expedition; and after his own death some months later from consumption, he was succeeded by John Gore.

The following summer, 1779, found the *Resolution* and *Discovery* once more attempting the passage north of Bering Strait. Again pack ice blocked their passage back to England. They subsequently shaped a course for home not touching the American coast but instead calling at Petropavlovsk, sailing past Japan, stopping at Macao, doubling the Cape of Good Hope and, at last, in early October 1780, dropping anchor in the Thames. Their journey, then the longest single voyage in oceanic exploration, had lasted four years, two months, and twenty-two days.

On reflection, how is Cook's last voyage to be viewed? It might be interpreted as a failure: Cook did not find a Northwest Passage, he did not penetrate far into the Bering Sea, and he died unnecessarily. But this would surely be wrong. Cook's voyage was an achievement in exploration of the first magnitude: a rough outline of the Northwest Coast had been laid down for the first time on charts soon made available to the public, several myths had been disproven, and new scientific data had been compiled. Perhaps the most important result, the subject of the next chapter, was the discovery that the beautiful pelts of the sea otter could be purchased for paltry amounts at Nootka Sound and elsewhere on the coast and then sold for fantastic prices in Asian markets. The subsequent rise of the maritime fur trade was to change forever the remoteness of the Northwest Coast as traders from various nations sought easy profits and intensified the international rivalry for the area.

4

Spanning the Pacific

In the half century of busy and enterprising exertion in every field of activity which has elapsed since his death, no newer name in the same department has yet eclipsed the lustre of his, and with reference to the peculiar character of his fame, as contrasted with that of our other renowned seamen, it has been well and justly remarked that, ''while numberless have been our naval heroes who have sought and gained reputation at the cannon's mouth, and amidst the din of war, it has been the lot of Cook to derive celebrity from less imposing, but not less important exploits, as they tended to promote the intercourse of distant nations, and increase the stock of useful science.''

THE PENNY MAGAZINE OF THE SOCIETY
FOR THE DIFFUSION OF USEFUL KNOWLEDGE,
20 October 1832

Cook's epoch-making navigation of the North Pacific rim including Oregon, Nootka Sound, Cook Inlet, Unalaska, Kamchatka, Japan and ultimately Macao opened the maritime fur trade. This commerce was probably the first America-to-Asia trade in the latitude of the British Columbia coast: it did not predate the Russian trade from Alaska nor the Spanish commerce via the Manila galleon. It did not precede any aboriginal seaborne traffic with the Orient, if ever such existed. But Cook's voyage did inaugurate an important sea link between North American ports and the markets of China, one which in time would be superseded by an Asiatic desire for other staples, particularly wheat and minerals. This trade grew from small beginnings, and what seems particularly unusual is that it did not begin due to the efforts of merchants in the City of London or even by some preliminary trade mission authorized by the government, but rather by accident, and its repercussions were greater than Cook's men could have imagined.

At Nootka Sound trade was virtually thrust upon the officers and crew of H.M.S. *Resolution* and *Discovery* by the Indians. Even before the ships entered the harbour's inner reaches, natives had approached the vessels crying ''Macook?''—''will you trade?'' Out of custom, officers, midshipmen, and sailors bound for the Pacific took nails, knives, and trinkets with them to buy sexual favour or friendship and to acquire food and clothing. In every crew there were always curio hunters wishing to purchase items as souvenirs of their personal penetration into new and far-off lands. In all, it constituted a petty trade the like of which may still be carried on by travellers in the depths of the Brazilian jungle or on the golden road to Samarkand. At Nootka Sound, however, the trade took on serious proportions. Sailors traded away their nails and knives, then their buckles and buttons, and even took to robbing their ships' own hardware. They did so to satisfy the insatiable Indian demand for iron, brass, lead, tin, copper, and pewter in a land untouched by the industrial revolution. Iron was desired most and any flaw in a piece diminished its value, indicating that the natives worked it cold.[1]

The British had come to the Northwest Coast prepared to trade in beads. However, the Moachat Nootka held spherical glass in little esteem. They were discerning traders. "Nothing would go down with them but metal and brass was now become their favourite, So that before we left the place, hardly a bit of brass was left in the Ship, except what was in the necessary instruments. Whole Suits of cloaths were striped of every button."[2] Hardware from furniture, copper kettles, tin canisters, and candle sticks "all went to wreck."[3] There are individual stories, too, which tell of the native passion for metal. Midshipman James Trevenen was by chance holding a broken brass buckle in his hand, for which an Indian wanted to trade a splendid sea otter skin. He tried it on his wrist, admired it, and bought it as a bracelet. That same pelt sold for as much as three hundred dollars in China, sufficient for Trevenen to buy his own necessities, as well as silk gowns, teas, and other oriental items that he took home to England for family and friends.[4] In this case Trevenen had quite accidentally established his own round-the-world trade of metals from Europe, furs from the Northwest Coast, and teas from the Orient—paying cargoes on each leg of the voyage and sufficiently in demand at each place to make a new global commerce profitable. For their part, the Nootka had in their midst a great economic resource. They offered other skins, including bear, wolf, fox, deer, raccoon, cougar, and marten. However, none was so precious, none so prevalent, and none so attractive as the sea otter pelt, delicate, thick, soft to touch, and mysteriously luminous in appearance.[5] Next to a woman, maritime fur traders said, the sea otter pelt offered the most beautiful sight in the world.[6] The hairs of the fur were an inch to an inch and a half in length, and in colder northern waters they were especially attractive, being dark brown to jet black in colour. An adult pelt measured five to six feet in length and twenty-five to thirty inches in width. A number of these would make dazzlingly handsome robes for wealthy mandarins; tail and other small pieces made caps or borders for robes. Indians valued the fur as well; two skins would purchase a slave and only chiefs had the wealth to wear sea otter robes.

At the time of Cook's visit, sea otter were, as Falstaff said of reasons, "as plenty as blackberries." Except for small gaps of distribution, this mammal inhabited the whole 9,600-kilometre crescent littoral of the North Pacific from Baja California to Japan, including therefore the Northwest Coast, the Aleutians, and Kamchatka. The animal prefers waters of the open coast and bays of the outer sea coasts, never occupying inland waters far from the ocean such as Puget

Sound or the inside passage of Alaska. The sea otter favours waters adjacent to rocky coasts where points of land, large bays, underwater reefs, and large rocks or islets provide feeding and resting places. In these locations the sea otter eats invertebrate bottom fauna—clams, abalones, sea urchins—in abundance within a kilometre of shore. In some areas the sea otter feeds on fish and king crabs. Sea otter are always gregarious, congregating in large groups known as "rafts," floating on their backs eating and playing. They provided an attractive and easy target for a sea hunter armed with a spear or musket. The female's solicitous care for her young means that she seldom leaves her pups during an encounter with a hunter, a fact which hastened the despoliation of the breed. Because the female bears only one pup at a time and does not do so every year, the slow rate of reproduction could not offset the steady extermination of the sea otter by human depredations. In Cook's time this factor counted little, but by the close of Maquinna's era in the early 1800's it largely accounted for the declining wealth of the Nootka and of the sea otter trade.

In 1778, the Indians took sea otter pelts with relative ease and little concern. According to Ledyard's estimate, with Cook's ships they traded fifteen hundred sea otter skins, an average of thirteen skins per sailor. The crew took only the best, Ledyard said, for they had no intention of using them except to keep warm.[7] However, it seems likely that some of the sailors would have learned from Russian accounts of Pacific exploration about the possibilities of a trade in furs. They bought other skins—weasel, mink, and wolverine—but only a fraction of what they might have done had they known of the possibility of marketing them at "such astonishing profits."[8] By the end of their visit to Nootka Sound the British knew that the Indians hoped they would return to trade; indeed, as already noted, as an encouragement the Indians promised to lay in a good stock of skins.

Farther north, on the Alaska coast, the British again traded for sea otter skins. Cook's search for the western entrance to the Northwest Passage took him to Cape Hinchinbrook near the northernmost reaches of the Gulf of Alaska. Here he found that the shore lay almost east and west, and not north and south as the Russian charts showed. Thus the inlet before them, Prince William Sound, promised the possibility of a passage to the north. In fact, this body of water stood in $61°N$ latitude, the very place where the Admiralty had ordered Cook to investigate the probable entrance to the fabled Northwest Passage. Along the shores lived Eskimos and Tlingits, quite different people from those seen by Cook's men at Nootka Sound in their dress and cosmetics, their kayaks and canoes, their stature and features, their language and customs.[9] But, like the Moachat, they came to trade the sea otter, which here was a lustrous black and plentiful. Cook thought these natives had never traded with the Russians. He reasoned that the Russians had never been among them, for if they had the natives would not be wearing such valuable skins as the sea otter; "the Russians," he wrote acidly, "would find some means or other to get them all from them.''[10] Unlike at Nootka Sound, coloured beads, especially sky blue beads, were a prized commodity. Lamentably, the British came armed only with the clear crystal kind. The blue beads, about the size of large peas, were apparently of Russian manufacture handed down in trade from other natives to the west. A mere five or six blue beads might purchase a lavish sea otter pelt worth 90 or 100 Spanish dollars at Canton. Farther west the English traded with natives at Unalaska in the Aleutian Islands. Unalaska was the principal commercial centre of Alaska and Russian influence had long been strong. Here Cook met the cunning Russian chief trader G. Ismaylov, who had once voyaged to the Kurile Islands, Japan, and China but whose geographical knowledge seemed unreliable to the suspicious English. Ismaylov said that his countrymen had made several unsuccessful attempts to get a foothold on the continent but always had been repulsed by treacherous natives.

Cook correctly suspected that the Russians had tried to open up a trade with Canton but had been unsuccessful. The Chinese had effectively barred Russian access to the fur markets of Peking by the Treaty of Kiakhta of 1727. Once every three years they permitted a single official caravan to pass southward through the Chinese buffer state of Manchuria on the way to the imperial capital. Because all foreign commerce was excluded from China, Kiakhta, which lay on the border between the two states, played a role analogous to that assigned to Canton in the maritime trade of European nations. Gradually the mandarins closed Russian access to Peking. Thus when Cook visited Unalaska, no Russian caravans could travel the arduous overland route to the imperial capital.[11]

In these circumstances it is understandable why Ismaylov falsely told Cook that the sea otter pelt was not prized at Canton. Cook, however, read the mind of his opposite and was suspicious of this and other information supplied by the Russian. He hinted that Ismaylov was trying to induce him to divert his trade to Kamchatka instead of China by offering him the present of a sea otter pelt worth eight rubles at the Russian port. Cook declined this offer, not wishing to remain in his debt on that point.[12] They parted as friends, however, Cook bearing a letter of introduction from Ismaylov to the Russian governor at Petropavlovsk. Ismaylov had given Cook the useful warning that when Cook's ships approached Petropavlovsk they were not to enter the port unannounced for they would surely be shot at. Rather they were to declare their arrival by sending a boat to shore with Ismaylov's letter.

Now Cook knew the Russians were entrenched on the doorstep of the American continent, operating an emporium of trade with the help of a schooner sailing out of Petropavlovsk, 2,400 kilometres distant. At Unalaska about thirty Russians and seventy Kamchatka natives were busily pursuing a branch of commerce developed by Bering and his Russian successors. Everywhere there was evidence that Bering's discoveries had been important if not accurate, facilitating Cook's own inquiries and depriving him, as Ledyard rightly put it, of being sole discoverer of this particular part of the Pacific, the northwesternmost part of America.[13]

Yet Cook's painstaking surveys on the Alaska Coast and his probes into the Bering Sea and Arctic Ocean as far as Icy Cape in 70°N latitude in the summer of 1778 had yielded much geographical data about Alaska. Cook determined that Alaska was not an island, as had been suspected. He also knew that the many sounds and rivers that his boats had investigated in that latitude did not lead to any northern ocean as reported by Hearne.[14] Cook had won a victory over speculation; he had disproved the existence of the Northwest Passage in that particular latitude. He had not, however, investigated the long coast from Nootka Sound north towards present-day Prince Rupert, Ketchikan, and Juneau. Because of bad weather and because his instructions had required him to investigate the coast farther north, he had missed a whole complex and mysterious quadrant of the Northwest Coast.

Paradoxically, though Cook's explorations disclosed no Northwest Passage that would enable the British to undertake a world revolution in trade by a shorter route to Asia, they did reveal the absolute requisite to carrying on any British trade in this region—profitability. Cook did not yet know of the possibilities of the China market when he wrote in his journal on 5 June 1778: "There is no doubt but a very beneficial fur trade might be carried on with the inhabitants of this vast coast, but unless the northern passage is found it seems rather too remote for Great Britain to receive any emolument for it."[15] He knew that the prized sea otter pelts were available in quantity. He also knew that the Indians would hunt the sea otter in order to obtain pelts to exchange for foreign products. If a high enough price could overcome the costs accrued by long-distance trading perhaps trade could become profitable. After all, were not the Russians already trading there?

Cook never lived to see the maritime fur trade thrive in English hands. However, at Petropavlovsk and again at Macao, Cook's men came to realize, unhappily all too late, that they had been on the doorstep of wealth without knowing it. At Petropavlovsk they disposed of two-thirds of their skins but not realizing their value naïvely traded them away freely to an exceedingly eager Russian merchant named Fedositsch. It was a surprisingly brisk traffic, carried on between decks, and eventually the price rose and good skins yielded thirty-five rubles or seven pounds sterling each. The most made by any of the officers or men was sixty pounds, a pleasant and unexpected return. Eventually they discovered (doubtless to their surprise and disappointment) that the Russians got more than double the price for their skins in China, and that Fedositsch was specializing in Russian trade with northern China.[16] Perhaps the British would have been wise to await their arrival in Macao. On the other hand, they did not know when they would reach Macao if at all, and indeed not until 1 December 1779 did the *Resolution* and *Discovery* sail into Macao Roads and then only on a brief call for supplies.

The river entrance to the Celestial Empire was much the same in that year as it was when the last of the maritime fur trading vessels called there in the 1830's. How very different it must have seemed from the forested, savage wastes of the Northwest Coast or from the salubrious Hawaiian Islands whence ships had come with sea otter and sandalwood cargoes. After a voyage of several weeks from Honolulu, a ship passed between Luzon and Taiwan, ran between piratical junks, passed on its port beam the Portuguese fort of Macao and summer residence of the "Taipans," the great traders, and anchored in the lower reaches of the Chu-Chiang (or Pearl) River, known as the Typa. Soon a Portuguese boat would come alongside and leave customs officers to tell the captain that he could not tarry there because the Portuguese claimed the Typa as their own under the Chinese emperor's grant of 1557 to them for their service to China. All foreign vessels would undergo the same inspection. Soon, however, the Chinese bureaucracy would appear in the form of the Hoppo, the superintendent of maritime customs, who would demand gifts for himself and family. Only when these were given would the merchantman be able to anchor and go about its business. All business had to be transacted through an organization known as the Hong or Cohong. The supercargoes could now make trading arrangements with one of the Hong merchants, numbering about a dozen, the sole Chinese traders licensed by the Viceroy of Canton to do business with the *fan-kwae*, or foreign devils. The Hong merchant in turn would make arrangements with the various foreign mercantile establishments such as the East India Company, Messrs Cox and Beale, or Perkins & Co. of Boston. "This strange oppressive, intermediate official merchant," was what the English fur trader John Meares termed the Hong's representative.[17] This "fixer" placed his own pecuniary interests high above those of the importer and exporter and exacted exorbitant duties for the Hoppo, at the same time skilfully keeping his own share of the extortions from the European traders.

Such a system controlled European access to Canton, the capital of Kwangtung province, China's major port of trade, which lay up the Pearl River some 130 kilometres above the Typa, depending on the channel taken. Foreigners were forbidden to enter Canton. Thus, for the purposes of wrangling with the Chinese mandarins, European agents set up factories for the winter's trade outside the city walls and outside the city gates at Whampoa the port of Canton, some twelve miles below. At every turn the Europeans were watched, imprisoned within their own commercial palaces by functionaries doing the Emperor's will.[18] Yet, because China was now assuming a central role in British trade in eastern seas, surpassing even India in the value of commercial transactions, British traders patiently suffered these indignities and exactions.[19] Resignedly they observed countless rules and regulations. The enormous profits in the tea and woollen trade pacified them. All the while they hoped that a British embassy to Peking might loosen the shackles on trade or, failing that, that British warships might be used to open the rich market of China to the western world. In the meantime, Canton remained to Europeans, as Charles Reade said, as difficult to enter as Heaven and as difficult to get out of as Chancery.

To Meares and others fresh from Nootka Sound or Cook Inlet, China presented an altogether different world. Its teaming populace, its active river traffic, its picky officialdom, its terraced warehouses along Whampoa's Strand, as the English called it, provided a bewildering contrast to the quiet of the northern forest coast. Flags of the trading nations hung on poles from the English, French, Dutch, Danish, and Swedish factories. Sampans by the thousands darted here and there in the river. Mandarin boats coursed upstream and down busily maintaining the imperial facade. Countless junks stood along the wharves or at anchor, carrying on the ancient business of the coasting trade. Five or six English merchantmen would be anchored below in the roads—on official sufferance, of course—loading tea from the interior provinces and unloading opium from India. Occasionally a foreign warship might grace the same harbour, but then only by special permission, for foreign warships could not linger and threaten the ancient empire. The Chinese remembered that in the 1740's Commodore George Anson, R.N., had twice used force to impress the Hoppo with the dignity of the English flag. They were always alive to the possibility that armed ships would take advantage of their defenceless shore establishments and open the trade by a prolonged bombardment.

When the *Resolution* and *Discovery* reached the Typa they were met with these same restrictions on trade, these same sticky matters of protocol. Chinese business procedures seemed painfully slow to Captain Gore, who was anxious to transact the trade in furs, complete his stores, and begin his long homeward track.

The ships had been away nearly three years from the Cape of Good Hope, where supplies and stores had been taken on board most recently. Crews desperately needed rest before proceeding home to England, but Captain Gore was anxious to quit port in two weeks whether he had the supplies or not. When Captain King was sent ashore to make necessary arrangements, East India Company agents told him that he could not pass the Chinese guards without a permit. Captain Gore thus pressed the Company to provide as many of the required stores as possible and asked it to expedite the purchase of two hundred pounds of beef a day and appropriate stocks of vegetables.[20] The East India Company's Committee of Supercargoes at Canton offered sympathy. They were, they said, "in a situation without power; and in a country where delay and form take place of activity and effectual Service." Another reason making trade difficult was that international relations were now at a flash point: the American war had not ended (much to Gore's surprise) and hostilities had spread to eastern seas. Britain and France were now in an undeclared state of war in the Indian Ocean.[21]

In these circumstances the Chinese objected to the presence of two British warships that had not come to trade but were armed and prepared to defend themselves against the French or their probable Spanish allies. Generally speaking, the Chinese proved unco-operative. Their actions in denying both captains access to Canton were motivated, the supercargoes said, by "a mixture of fear, jealousy and folly by which every official Mandareen is governed whenever Europeans are concerned." The company came to the Navy's aid in supplying ships' stores. From the Company vessels *Worcester, Royal Henry,* and *Alfred,* the *Resolution* and *Discovery* received various items, mainly flints, powder, twine, and pitch. The Company also advanced Captain King the necessary £1,519.1.3 to pay for the stores. Further, the Supercargoes gave to the officers of the *Resolution* and *Discovery* a "trifling supply of provisions." This was a compliment made in the Company's name "to Gentlemen who have been so long and so hazardously employed in their countries' service."[22]

Nonetheless, the British were able to dispose of their valuable cargo. A company boat going upriver to Canton gave Gore the opportunity for which he had been waiting. Midshipman Nathaniel Portlock and twenty men provided the crew for this passage. Because the permit of trade was not forthcoming to Gore or King, the company trader Ferguson provided a means of satisfying Chinese trading requirements. A box of sea otter skins was given the East India Company to be used as a favour to the mandarins. On 15 December Gore sent Captain James King accompanied by Lieutenant Lannion, R.N., and Lieutenant Phillips, R.M., from Macao to Canton in a small boat to expedite the tricky arrangements for cannon, ammunition, and stores. Canton seemed likely to be the best place to sell furs, so King took some twenty pelts with him, chiefly the property of the late captains Cook and Clerke. This commission gave King, he wrote sarcastically, the opportunity to become acquainted with "the genius of the Chinese for trade."[23]

King was first required to meet with a representative of the Hong, who blatantly told him that he could depend on his integrity. Then, when King produced his wares, the Chinese agent shrewdly studied the peltry, examined the skins repeatedly and with care, and eventually told King that he could offer only $300 for the lot. King knew he had to drive a bargain, for knowing the market prices at Petropavlovsk he realized the Chinese had not offered nearly half their valued worth. He demanded a thousand in return. His opposite cautiously advanced to $500, then offered a private present of tea and porcelain worth $100, then $100 more in cash, and then offered $700. King reduced his demand to $900. The Chinese produced a list of India goods King should take in exchange, but this King refused because he did not want merchandise. Now the Chinese gave the surprising ultimatum that they would divide the difference. King, now quite wearied by the whole business, settled for $800.[24]

There is more to this transaction than meets the eye. The Chinese specie supply was closely guarded by imperial regulation. For years the Emperor had demanded that if westerners were to trade with the Chinese they would have to receive in return processed commodities such as silks, teas, and porcelain. All too frequently, as in King's case, the Europeans were looking for cash settlements. Nonetheless, the Hong merchant had bought the sea otter skins for cash, for they were prized items of clothing in China among people of wealth and influence. Sea otter were the ermine of Asia and highly in demand at the Chinese court.

King was not alone in completing a transaction, for other sailors sold what they had brought to Macao. One seaman peddled his stock for $800. Some prime skins, clean and well preserved, yielded $120 each.[25] Trevenen's pelt, acquired for the broken brass buckle at Nootka Sound, brought the splendid sum of $300, perhaps the highest price of the lot.[26] Another index of capital gain is William Bligh's purchase of thirty large green Spanish beads from Tahitians for a shilling hatchet. At Prince William Sound he bought six sea otter skins with twelve of the beads, skins which sold in China for £15 each. As one of his shipmates put it, "Here we find a quick return of £90 for one shilling!"[27]

In all, King estimated that the value of furs in both ships, in specie and goods, counted at least £2,000, a large sum when it is recalled that many of the poorer quality had been given away or traded at Kamchatka. "When in addition to these facts," he wrote in summary,

it is remembered, that the furs were at first collected without our having any idea of their real value; that the greatest part had been worn by the Indians, from whom we purchased them; that they were afterward preserved with little care, and frequently used for bed-clothes, and other purposes, during our cruize to the North; and that, probably we had never got the full value of them in China; the advantages that might be derived from a voyage to that part of the American Coast, undertaken with commercial views, appear to me of a degree of importance sufficient to call for the attention of the Public.[28]

The seamen of the *Resolution* and *Discovery* knew they could make their fortune by going to the Northwest Coast, obtaining another cargo of the black, lustrous sea otter pelts, and returning to Macao or Canton. "The rage with which our seamen were possessed to return to Cook's River, and, buy another cargo of skins, to make their fortunes, at one time, was not far short of mutiny," King wrote.[29] Just before the *Resolution* and *Discovery* left the Typa two men—John Cave, a quartermaster, and Michael Spencer, a seaman—stole the *Resolution*'s great cutter under cover of a dark morning and made their way unopposed to sea, bound for the Northwest Coast. They were neither heard of nor seen again, the first casualties of the new trade. Now the officers and watch were on guard against such desertions and although a few did occur, the ships were soon at sea.

Here was the design of future voyages, some of them originating in Macao, others from Bengal and Calcutta, still others from Europe and the United States, but all of them certain to concentrate on Nootka Sound, and especially on Cook Inlet. Who knew what sea otters lay uncaught in the coastal waters between $50°$ and $60°N$ not investigated by Cook? If the peltry of Cook Inlet and Nootka Sound were any indication, who knew what regal fortunes might be acquired given strong ships, good crews, adequate supplies, and, not least, the nails, buttons, and beads held in such high esteem by the Northwest Coast Indians?

In short, Cook's last voyage had given promise of wealth for those who could overcome distance and who could serve the needs and answer the peculiarities of the consumers on both sides of the Pacific. The Europeans, with their advanced deep-water technology, could link Asia with America, provided of course accurate charts were available. Some of these scientific aids to sea travel Cook had supplied, and his reports (and those of his officers) on the prospects of the trade soon affected the course of British expansion in the Pacific. Cook's third voyage established a new trade with the native peoples of the Northwest Coast. Cook not only brought the west coast of Vancouver Island and the coasts of Alaska out of the shrouded mists of the map-makers into the realm of scientific understanding, but also linked them with the oceanic channels of world trade.

5

The Fortune Seekers

Commerce is universally known to be the chief source of the prosperity, and also the power, of the British empire.

DAVID MACPHERSON,
ANNALS OF COMMERCE (1805)

Cook's third and final voyage had hinted to the wider world the great commercial prospects for a maritime fur trade between the Northwest Coast and China. The Russians, of course, had been secretly involved in a similar trade since 1740, but the Russo-Chinese Treaty of 1648 restricted their access to Canton; the Muscovites were obliged to trade only on the Chinese-Siberian border.[1] They thus had to content themselves with a cross-border traffic of marginal value. The Spanish, too, knew of the sea otter but satisfied themselves with the bountiful trade in the immediate Alta California area, not needing to venture much farther northward than the Farallone Islands near San Francisco Bay to hunt seal and sea otter. They took no steps to exploit the China market directly because it was the understood preserve of the Portuguese, and Spanish ships were nominally barred by the Portuguese from returning to Europe via the Indian Ocean. Until the late 1780's the Spanish kept to a coasting trade on their Pacific seaboard of the Americas, never stretching across the vast ocean separating America from Asia except on the Manila galleon that yearly took treasure and other western commodities on the long and hazardous track from Acapulco to Manila and the Moluccas and then returned with oriental produce for Spanish America. Finally, in 1786, Spain exported to China the first sea otter cargo from California under the auspices of a Spanish version of the East India Company, the Royal Philippine Company, chartered the year before as a state monopoly.[2]

Neither Russia nor Spain had explored the Pacific and its littoral in any systematic way. Their discoveries had been occasioned by trading ventures or by accident. No judicious plan had been adopted by either nation to examine the ocean's shores except where their traders or mariners might go. Russian sea routes from Kamchatka to Unalaska were used by the seaborne *promyshlenniks* alone, and the dangers of Pacific navigation in these northern latitudes were not published in a reliable chart or sailing directions before Cook's time. Similarly, coasting voyages and the trans-Pacific galleon route appeared in no well-documented or accurate report. In fact, any announced discoveries caused debates about findings and provoked nagging doubts in British minds about the achievements of the Spanish and Russians.

Cook's discoveries, by contrast, were authoritatively documented. Charts, views, and official narratives published with government permission after completion of the voyage were not cloaked by the secrecy with which their Spanish and Russian rivals usually hid their findings. The voyage had been prosecuted with disinterested views, Nathaniel Portlock boasted, and the discoveries had been described without reserve; in his words, "every nation and every individual had thus an opportunity of forming new designs, either for the cultivation of science, or for the advantage of traffic."[3]

Indeed, the official account of Cook's voyage, published with Admiralty approval in 1784, contained a blueprint for commerce.[4] In it James King, who knew the trading arrangements at Canton from personal experience, described a scheme for a surveying and fur trading voyage, which was read with enthusiasm by several entrepreneurs. King reasoned that profits could be high and that the East India Company would necessarily be involved. He proposed that two of the Company's China ships, one of 200 and another of 150 tons, could be purchased in Canton, where victualling was no more expensive than in Europe, and fitted out for a cost of £6,000. Each ship would carry five tons of unwrought iron, a forge, and a skilled blacksmith who would forge whatever tools the various Indians wanted. Iron was the only sure commodity for the Northwest Coast market, he said, but knives, woollen cloth, glass, and copper trinkets could also be shipped from China.

King specified that two ships should undertake the expedition. This would provide greater security for the traders in regions where discoveries ought not to be undertaken by a single ship. Where risks were to be run and hazardous experiments tried, he said, a single ship should not venture far unless some security could be provided against an untoward accident.

The ships, King wrote, would sail with the southwesterly monsoon in early April. They would steer northward along the China coast, and would survey from the Nanking River into the Yellow Sea and the Japanese Islands as time and weather permitted. When they reached Sakhalin and the Kurile Islands they would take on wood and water before heading for Cook Inlet. Trading would occur all along the coast of North America trading as the ships sailed eastward and then southward. However, in latitude $56°-50°N$ the ships should trace the coast with great accuracy; this was the area from Prince of Wales Island south to Nootka Sound, where Cook's ships had been driven out of sight of land by contrary winds. After spending three months on the Northwest Coast the ships would set sail early in October on their return course to China. They should proceed by hitherto unrecorded tracks so that the Pacific would be further charted.

King's scheme took account of several elements which were necessary for the successful prosecution of the venture: the nature of winds in the Pacific; the consent or involvement of the East India Company; the demands of the Northwest

Coast Indians as consumers; the necessity for two suitable ships; and the obligation of traders to undertake further surveys. On the other hand, he did not mention the possible importance of the Hawaiian Islands as a wintering place for traders who might wish to repair their ships and refresh their crews between cruises on the Northwest Coast. King envisioned the voyage as taking no less than a year; but subsequent voyaging by vessels from Britain and the United States revealed the necessity of spending several years in the Pacific, making Hawaii an interim "home port" until ships could complete the last phase of their "golden round" back to the Atlantic. This consideration aside, King's plan was the basis for several expeditions, though not all fur traders were as active as Portlock, Dixon, Duncan, Barkley, and Meares in conducting surveys of hitherto unfrequented harbours and island clusters.

King's plan would have been on the stalls of London booksellers in late 1784. Unofficial versions—by Ellis, Rickman, and perhaps Ledyard—were already on the shelves. These reports aroused widespread public interest, and in late 1784 several traders contrived to be first in the lucrative trade. Meanwhile, an ambitious scheme was advanced in 1781 by the Dutch-born adventurer William Bolts, formerly an East India Company entrepreneur in Calcutta and Bengal. Bolts, whose dreams of wealth knew no bounds, proposed that the newly formed Imperial Company of Trieste for the Commerce of Asia, an Austrian company trading to Asia, should in late September 1782 send a ship, the 500- to 600-ton *Count Cobenzell,* and a tender of forty-five tons stowed in the *Count Cobenzell*'s hold, from Trieste to the Northwest Coast, Canton, and then back to Trieste. The ship would carry twenty-two guns and twenty Austrian soldiers as well as other crew. George Dixon, armourer's mate on Cook's last voyage and a man of considerable talent and experience in the trade, had entered the service of the Austrian company along with three other officers who had been to the Pacific with Cook. But intrigues among company directors in Vienna and Trieste and insufficient funds stopped the project. In April 1786 Bolts then proposed to the French ministry that it work with the Compagnie des Indes to send an expedition to the Northwest Coast to take part in the sea otter trade.[5]

Meanwhile, in London, the East India Company's Court of Directors anxiously watched these developments, fearing foreign rivalry in a trade which might otherwise be turned to their advantage, and fearing that Dixon's skills might be employed by rival traders.[6] They knew that British traders would enter into foreign employ in order to circumvent the Company monopoly and that of the South Sea Company for licensing all British ships in eastern seas. They also knew that British ships would sail under foreign flags of convenience, usually Portuguese or Austrian, in order to bypass these monopolistic regulations and gain unrestricted access to the Portuguese port of Macao. The Court of Directors early realized that they must either become adventurers in the lucrative trade or partners with other British traders.

The first independent voyage undertaken in the maritime fur trade seems to have been conducted with the consent or at least knowledge of the East India Company. The owner of the appropriately named *Sea Otter* (or *Harmon* as she was previously called) is unknown. She was outfitted by John Henry Cox, a British trader in Canton who doubtless knew of Cook's crew's success in selling sea otter skins on the China market. The *Sea Otter,* a sixty-ton brig manned by twenty men, departed from Macao on 15 April 1785 and arrived at Nootka on 18 August, only 115 days from China. To her captain, James Hanna, the Northwest Coast land appeared remarkably high. He could see several bays and rivers, a promising sign for a mariner in search of a safe anchorage after a distant crossing in uncertain, foggy weather.[7] Almost at nightfall some Indians had paddled out from the shore in three canoes. Hanna, fearful of an attack, ordered his crew to arms. But the peaceful intent of the natives was quickly disclosed by their shouting at a distance "Macook," their request to trade. This was a familiar greeting to one who had read Cook's account. Soon the canoes were alongside. In the next few days an energetic traffic was entered into on both sides. By the end of December Hanna was back in Macao with a cargo of 560 sea otter skins that realized 20,600 Spanish dollars on the China market.

The *Sea Otter*'s voyage had not been without the serious portent that in trade relations with the Nootka and other Northwest Coast Indians the Europeans would have to be on their guard against Indian attacks: the *Sea Otter*, small by contrast to Cook's ships, may have been a tempting prize for the Nootka. It afforded an easy conquest given the size of the ship and her crew, a piracy that could be carried out with impunity. After all, the Nootka were sovereign. Was this not their land and their sea? They undertook an attack on the *Sea Otter* during daylight and were repulsed with considerable loss of life. But every reason exists to suggest that the fault lay with the whites. The skirmish occurred, Hanna claimed, after he fired on the natives for their stealing of a chisel. However, Maquinna later said that when he was visiting the vessel he was invited to sit on a chair under which was sprinkled gunpowder which was ignited and not only sent him into the air but burned his rump and wounded his dignity.[8] The native attack on the ship was motivated by revenge to re-establish chiefly prestige.

From the outset violence existed in the maritime trade at Nootka Sound, a fact with which traders and Indians almost always had to deal. Traders soon increased their ship armament. They built boarding nets around their vessels to keep Indians from climbing over the gunwales except in certain well-guarded places. They carried numerous small arms and swords. They augmented the size of their crews. On the other side, the Indians suffered from mistreatments and debaucheries, bad liquors, and the importation of firearms. They grew increasingly suspicious of the whites, more anxious to defend themselves against depredation and more determined to conduct trade relations on their terms.[9] The *Sea Otter*'s voyage not only pioneered the trade; it began hostilities between races that characterized the maritime fur trade for a generation or more to come.

The commercial success that Hanna enjoyed whetted the appetite of his supporters to try their chances once again. In May 1786, he sailed from Macao in a 120-ton vessel also called the *Sea Otter*, arrived at Nootka Sound in August, and found to his utter surprise and disappointment that two rival ships, the *Captain Cook* and the *Experiment* (of which more later) had been there already and had taken every scrap of fur available. This forced him farther afield, first northward to Queen Charlotte Sound and then southward to Clayoquot Sound, where he became allied with the Ahousat chief Cleaskinah, exchanging names with him as a token of mutual respect. Despite these labours, he did not garner many pelts. When he returned to Macao in February 1787, his cargo realized only $8,000, a paltry sum compared with his first expedition's return.[10] Already traders were learning that the source of pelts was not endless and that hitherto unfrequented sea otter haunts on the outer northern coasts would have to be visited in order to make these voyages paying propositions. And already traders were learning how fiercely competitive that trade was becoming.

In the same year that Hanna made his first voyage, 1785, a syndicate had been formed in London to trade to Nootka Sound under the name of King George's Sound Company, frequently referred to as Richard Cadman Etches and Company. The eight members of this group were mainly merchants and the principal subscriber and prime mover was Etches, a London merchant interested in whaling, fur trading, and convict settlement, indeed all imperial schemes for eastern seas. Two other members of the company were Nathaniel Portlock and George Dixon, already mentioned as seamen in Cook's ships and soon to be captains of the group's first two trading vessels, the *King George* and the *Queen Charlotte*, of 320 and 200 tons respectively, sailing from London for King George's or Nootka Sound.

This syndicate, through some delicate arrangements apparently approved by the British government, obtained a trading licence from the South Sea Company, which had by statute a monopoly of trade in the Pacific, and similarly got special permission from the East India Company to bring back to London Chinese teas in return for Northwest Coast furs traded in Canton.[11]

The identical instructions received by Portlock and Dixon, dated 3 September 1785, specified that factories were to be built on the Northwest Coast for the safety of settlers and traders of the company. Nootka Sound was mentioned as the central place of establishment, although the captains were given discretionary powers in this regard. Of the projected permanence of British settlement there can be little doubt. A William Wilby was to establish the trading post in a secure site on land purchased on liberal terms from the natives. "You are then to appoint as many men as you shall deem necessary," the orders ran,

> and who shall turn out as volunteers, to be companions to Mr. Wilby; you are to give them every possible assistance to erect a log-house, or such other building as shall appear to be necessary for their residence, and for

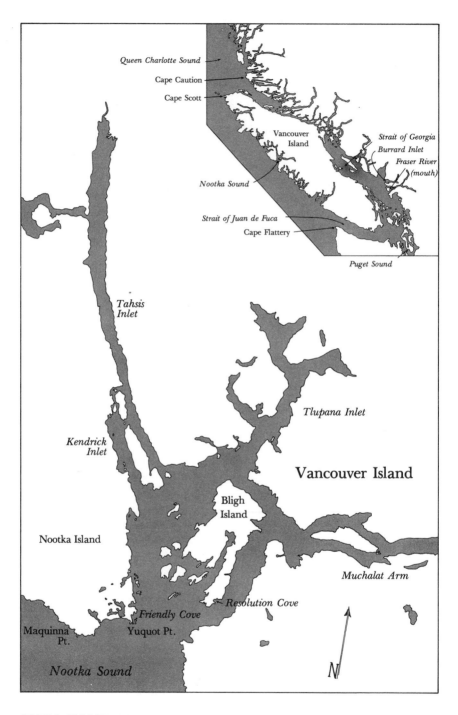

Inset labels: Queen Charlotte Sound, Cape Caution, Cape Scott, Vancouver Island, Strait of Georgia, Burrard Inlet, Fraser River (mouth), Nootka Sound, Strait of Juan de Fuca, Cape Flattery, Puget Sound

Main map labels: Tahsis Inlet, Tlupana Inlet, Kendrick Inlet, Vancouver Island, Bligh Island, Nootka Island, Muchalat Arm, Resolution Cove, Friendly Cove, Maquinna Pt., Yuquot Pt., Nootka Sound, N

MAP 2: NOOTKA SOUND

the carrying on traffic with the natives, &c. You are to give them every assistance to make such place tenable against the natives, and provide them with such arms, ammunition, &c. as you shall deem necessary for their defence and protection. You are to leave them such quantities of provisions and other articles for convenience, and the purpose of trade.[12]

The voyage was less successful than anticipated, although the two ships collected 2,552 sea otter skins. These were sold in Canton for $50,000, "well knowing," George Dixon wrote, "that the money would be more acceptable to our owners, than an account that we had left the furs on commission."[13] But the skins brought only twenty dollars each, well below the expected market price of eighty or ninety dollars.[14] In London, Etches blamed Portlock and Dixon for letting the furs go at such low prices; but the real culprit seems to have been the East India Company, which supervised the sale. Judge Howay, who studied these and other transactions between maritime fur traders and the Company, concluded rightly "that the real reason why the British lost the maritime fur trade was not the Napoleonic wars, nor the Keen Yankee opposition but the octopus hold and suction of the East India Company."[15] As for the South Sea Company's monopoly, he classified it as a nuisance, as the company, in Portlock's words, stood "in the mercantile way of more adventurous merchants."[16]

Portlock and Dixon were further angered when they dropped anchor in Nootka Sound, for here they discovered to their surprise that two English enterprises, one from Bombay and the other from Calcutta, had already been trading on the coast.

Curiously enough in 1785 almost identical projects had been launched simultaneously from London, Bombay, Calcutta, and Canton.[17] The fact is that after the American Revolution, merchant capital was available for distant ventures, young naval lieutenants were seeking employment in the merchant marine, ships in the carrying trade were waiting for purchase or hire, and government and traders were pursuing new branches of commerce.

One such fortune seeker was James Charles Stewart Strange, son of an engraver, brother of a jurist, godson of Bonnie Prince Charlie, and, later, the son-in-law of Henry Dundas. In London on leave from the East India Company establishment in Madras where he was a senior merchant, he was inspired by reading accounts of Cook's last voyage. Pondering the prospects of personal wealth and influence, he decided to discuss the matter on his return to India with prominent persons such as David Scott, a rising independent Bombay merchant and a famous publicist of projects such as this. With help from his two partners, Tate and Adamson, Scott obtained the approval of the President and Council of the East India Company at Bombay for an expedition to the Northwest Coast. Strange himself invested £10,000 in the project, borrowed from his patron,

Scott.[18] Two Bombay-built, coppered-hulled snows, the *Captain Cook* of 350 tons, commanded by Henry Laurie, and the *Experiment* of 100 tons, commanded by Henry Guise, were purchased. The Madras establishment provided all-European crews, stores for several years, provisions for fifteen months, guns and ammunition, instruments and charts. The Bombay government provided fifteen soldiers, to serve less as marines than as artificers "if our prospects succeeded, to form a settlement, and a military port on the coast of America."[19] Strange was more than a supercargo. He was in full charge, a Company servant embarking on a Company-sanctioned, private project that would, if successful, not only aid discovery and commerce but forestall rival attempts.

The ambitious outline plan was no less than a blueprint for the expansion of British trade and dominion in eastern seas. New discoveries, new trade with the Northwest Coast from India and China, and surveys of the Northwest Coast, Bering Strait, and the Asian shore were all set out in Strange's instructions of 7 December 1785. He was told to proceed to Goa on the Malabar Coast. There the resident Portuguese Captain-General would provide passes and letters to ensure his safe reception at Macao during a season when intercourse with English ships was not allowed at Canton. Scott and his associates took the added precaution of appointing an agent in Macao whose duty would be to service any request Strange might make, so as to avoid any difficulty with the Chinese or the East India Company. Strange was issued a considerable sum of money to purchase sandalwood and tinware on the Malabar Coast, a potentially profitable outward-bound cargo for the China market. His instructions also called for him to return via Bering Strait, the Arctic Ocean as far as the North Pole, then Kamchatka, and finally Canton, where it was left to his discretion whether a second voyage to the Northwest Coast should be undertaken.[20] Along the way he was obliged to serve two masters, discovery and trade, but in the end he served neither with distinction.

The first leg of the voyage was disappointing. Leaving Bombay 8 December 1785, Strange was unable to disburse a single rupee along the Malabar Coast, he wrote, and instead was forced to head directly for the Northwest Coast via Batavia, Borneo, and the Celebes, thereby missing the China market altogether. His expedition was now ill starred, for unless the profit on fur sales was exceedingly high the voyage's income would be reduced by not having a paying cargo on its first leg.

On the morning of 25 June 1786, seven long months out of Bombay, the *Captain Cook* and *Experiment* were off the coast of Vancouver Island. The next day they met forty canoes of Indians from Hope Bay. Strange asked repeatedly for directions to Nootka Sound. However, he could get no satisfaction from the natives who, anxious to trade with the visitors especially in iron (but not beads which they offered to the visitors in derision), pointed to nearby anchorages where the ships might safely stay in order to trade with them, and shouted "Wakosh! Wakosh! friend! friend!'' On the 28th the ships finally reached Nootka Sound, but Strange entered its tortuous northwestern passage by mistake, rather than its less dangerous southeastern one near Friendly Cove. He had intended to anchor at Ship's Cove, Bligh Island, as Cook had done eight years before. This error in navigation cost Strange dearly in time and labour. It necessitated a tedious and hazardous tow by the long boats through island-infested waters where he was unfamiliar with tides, currents, and winds. He was forced to find a shelter other than Ship's Cove. Boat crews sent to reconnoitre determined that Friendly Cove was the best site for his headquarters. Nine days after reaching the sound, the ships at last anchored at Friendly Cove.

Strange's immediate concern was to find a shore establishment for sick crew members, and from the Indians at Yuquot he purchased a house at the north end of the village in exchange for an adze and a saw. This was the first British purchase of property at Nootka Sound, predating John Meares's acquisition by a year. But the place, damp and frequently fog-bound, and "so near the noisome smell of the village," proved unsuitable. Strange thought it "more conducive to sickness than to health" owing to "the putrid state of the atmosphere" at Yuquot. He erected a tent some distance away from the village near the ships' watering place where the sick could be "more easily attended and protected."[21] Soon the men began to recover, aided by fresh berries and other antiscorbutics; and soon they were planting vegetables for use on a subsequent visit or voyage. Their garden may have been the first white man's attempted cultivation on the Pacific coast north of Spanish America but it is doubtful if the crop was ever harvested. Strange, meanwhile, traded with the Indians, getting possession, as he whimsically put it, "of every rag of fur within the Sound, and for a Degree to the Northward and Southward of it."[22]

Strange despised the Nootka Indians, whose filth, depravity, and uncivilized conduct, including cannibalism, he found deplorable.[23] He did not wish to quarrel with the more idealistic view of the Nootka as portrayed in Cook's *Voyage*. But his important account of the Nootka describes a native society whose personal cleanliness and public health differed from that of the European intruders. He had no delusions about the mythical noble savage, only the stern reality that he fortunately had not had to resort to violent measures. He had prevented Indians from numerous thefts by circumspect behaviour in all dealings with the natives. In Strange's narrative there is little of the lofty magnanimity of a mariner on national service but rather the hard-headed perspectives of a trader seeking to accord the great Cook his due yet at the same time providing his own personal and frank assessment of these Indians.

Unwilling to let the Nootka board his ships, except for the occasional chief, Strange's impressions of the natives are not as valuable as those of a thirty-two-year-old ensign of the Bombay Army, Alexander Walker, later a distinguished soldier, brigadier-general in the East India Company and Governor of St. Helena, who in 1785 did not seem to have any compelling military obligations, decided to visit "a Country little known," and shipped on board the *Experiment* with his friend, Captain Guise.[24] Walker's ethnological observations add greatly to the reports on the Nootka by James Cook and his officers and provide us with new data on the Nootka in the 1780's. Unlike Strange, who seldom visited shore, Walker mixed freely with the natives, particularly those at Friendly Cove. Unarmed, men from Strange's ships went on shore unmolested and lived there, Walker wrote, "with as much security, as if we had been on the banks of the Thames." Yet he did observe that the native civility "proceeded from fear" of the "power of our guns."[25] Having previously studied the language, based on Cook's vocabularies, Walker conversed with the Nootka and found them completely peacefully disposed and open to any questions asked. He found, to his astonishment, that James Hanna had been there twelve months before, though the Nootka concealed the items traded by Hanna from Strange's men.

The Nootka were astute traders, parting only with their furs, though they offered many things, when they had received and carefully examined the goods of exchange, mainly iron and brass items. Copper kettles they cut into bracelets and earrings, caring nothing for the utility of the kettle so designed. They zealously guarded their own property, demanding payment for everything and increasing their price as trade continued. As for prostitution, Walker reported that shortly after the ships entered the Sound's northern entrance, the visitors were offered women for iron. Later they met "two jolly wenches paddling in a canoe, who offered some significant gestures to be very kind, if we would favour them with some iron."[26] Yet at Friendly Cove, Strange's men encountered great difficulty in obtaining women for sexual intercourse, though on occasion, after determination and high bidding, a few "poor wretches," probably slaves, were produced though the discourse was undertaken "to raise a laugh against us."[27] The Nootka appeared healthy and uncontaminated by venereal disease though Walker, like Strange, deplored their filth, poor hygiene, garbage, and maggots and lice, the latter of which they ate along with salmon, their preferred food. Walker noted, at first hand, what he thought were cases of cannibalism among the Nootka and was offered hands and heads to eat. Later he changed his mind, believing that they only drank blood and used human pieces for memorials of achievement or charms against pain or sickness, and he concluded that displays of cannibalism may have been an Indian entertainment at the expense of the visitors.[28]

On the subject of chiefs and chieftainship, Walker noted the wealth, in property, and large families and houses of Maquinna (spelled by Walker, Makquilla) and Kurrighum. The latter chief was about fifty years of age, clean and undecorated, of stout, average stature, a marginally fraudulent trader, and a not-altogether friendly fellow. Maquinna, though dirty and slovenly in appearance, was "a stout handsome young man, with a fine manly countenance, and being fond of our company, soon became our favourite." He was honest and shrewd, though "vastly inferiour" to Kurrighum in activity, a fact owing to his domineering, handsome wife, Hestoquatto. "He was the most intelligent person we met with," Walker said.[29]

The son of the Maquinna who had greeted Cook, this Maquinna resented Strange's preference for Kurrighum on the basis of his older age, charging that he was wealthier and thus deserved preference. Giving more gifts to the younger chief, at the same time apologizing for their indiscretion, the British later observed the two chiefs laughing with one another, an indication that, perhaps again, the joke had been at the expense of the visitors. Not least among Walker's observations is his regret that Strange had used corporal punishment against a native thief, an event which nearly provoked a violent native response. "Our conduct on this occasion," he noted, "had neither justice nor policy to recommend it." In his view the restitution of property and the thief's imprisonment would have sufficed.[30] The stolen property was returned, but thereafter the visitors never regained the confidence of the Indians.

In keeping with his orders, Strange left behind at Nootka Sound a young Irishman, John Mackay,[31] surgeon of the *Experiment,* to live with Maquinna. Mackay, a former surgeon's mate in the Royal Navy, was a soldier of the Bombay establishment. He hoped to recover his former station in life and so volunteered to stay behind. With pen, ink, and paper provided (subsequently destroyed by the Indians), he had instructions to record the habits of the Nootka, to learn their language and customs, to compile a vocabulary, and cultivate the friendship of the natives before the vessels returned. Strange had Maquinna's assurance, sworn in the presence of one Enkitsun (The God of Snow), that Mackay should eat choice foods so that when the trader returned for the doctor he would be found as fat as a whale. Mackay had already won Maquinna's confidence, having cured his daughter of itchy, scabby hands and legs, a prevailing disease among Nootka children. Strange gave Mackay non-poisonous medicines, gifts to dispense to people who could protect him, a gun and ammunition, and, on Maquinna's recommendation, a red cap and a red coat to awe enemies. Strange also gave Maquinna lavish presents and the promise of more if he would take care of the surgeon until his return. Strange left Mackay goats and seeds. None of these things did Mackay much, if any, good.

Strange never came back, and yet the curious career of Surgeon Mackay has found its way into the history of the Northwest Coast. He lost Maquinna's protection when he stepped over the cradle of Maquinna's child, a native taboo, and was beaten by the chief and banished outdoors for weeks. The child died and Maquinna extended the exile. Mackay had the "bloody flux" in October, lived alone until the Indians returned in February to their seasonal village, and witnessed their brutal killing of more than a dozen captives. Though Mackay had been furnished with clothes and provisions, by the end of the winter he had been reduced "to the level of a savage."

When fourteen months later in the spring of the following year, white traders began to appear on the coast, he understandably attracted considerable interest. Portlock and Dixon knew he was at Nootka and intended to seize him as a poacher when they got there and take him in irons to Canton.[32] However Mackay suffered a less painful fate.[33] When Captain Charles William Barkley of the *Imperial Eagle* put into Nootka Sound in June 1787, he was absolutely dumbstruck when a ragged man, dressed and seeming like an Indian, meekly introduced himself as Dr. John Mackay. How surprised Barkley must have been to find an Irish surgeon among Nootka chiefs and shamans. He graciously offered to take Mackay aboard, and the latter seemed obviously pleased to leave the dreary surroundings. This first white to live among the Nootka became a trader for Barkley and aided in the latter's successful commerce and discoveries on the west coast of Vancouver Island.[34]

Had Strange returned for Mackay he might have profited from the knowledge the young Irishman had acquired about sea otter habitats and the nature of the insularity of Vancouver Island, knowledge which Barkley ably exploited. Barkley boasted to the rival trader William Etches, brother of Richard Cadman Etches of the King George's Sound Company, what an excellent cargo he had secured for the *Imperial Eagle*. We can imagine how this kind of jibe infuriated Etches. After all, he had told George Dixon that Mackay's theory that Nootka was one of a chain of islands rather than part of the continent could not be depended upon. In Etches' opinion, Mackay seemed "a very ignorant young fellow" given to contradicting himself frequently.[35]

As for Strange, the lateness of the season and the seductive prospects of trade at Cook Inlet led him to the conclusion that he should quit Friendly Cove. He failed to say that the poor trade at Nootka Sound, where he had gathered 540 sea otter pelts, also led him to this decision. More than this, he had to abandon the plan to build a fortified port. As Walker explains in a marginal note to his journal,

A more considerable establishment was originally intended and the Author of this Narrative was meant to have remained with the small Military party which is here mentioned. Motives of economical consideration however prevented the execution of this design & made it be abandoned, but not before a spot had been examined and fixed on for a Post which it was proposed to fortify. This was a small Island close to Friendly Village and appears to have been the same situation afterwards selected by the Spaniards. The great and excessive expectations which the projectors of the present Expedition had formed when it was first set on foot, were by this time much abated. The enthusiasm and ardour which are necessary to support such an enterprize, were likewise impaired & had been succeeded by contrary feeling of dispondency. Both extremes were equally dangerous but the last, which approached to despair, was much the most likely to produce failure & disappointment. It was this that now operated to prevent us leaving any establishment which might involve expense behind us, & probably unknown to ourselves paralized our exertions in other respects. It was this timidity probably that saved me from a Spanish prison, or a visit to the mines of Mexico.[36]

Strange left Nootka Sound on 28 July and four days later he found several islands off Vancouver Island's northwestern tip. Believing them to be a discovery, he called them the Scott Islands after his patron, a name still found on the charts. Landing at Cape Scott he took possession of it for the British Crown in the usual way by "hoisting the colours and turning a turf."[37] The place appeared desolate and deserted. Only fish weirs placed in sheltered inlets by the Newitty Indians indicated human activity. Although he conducted some trading with the local Indians, his attempts to find their village were fruitless and only increased his appreciation of the treacherous tide-rips, shoals, and reefs of that fickle coast.

Mistaking the region as part of the continental shore, Strange now discovered a large bay running east and southeastward from Cape Scott. It was several leagues wide and had extensive tides and currents, thereby indicating a flowing body of water that might well be a strait or river estuary. Strange speculated that this was Admiral de Fonte's famous Northwest Passage, the existence of which, admittedly, Cook had not disproven. Time did not permit Strange to probe the bay's extent. Such an inquiry, Strange wrote, would have to await a second voyage. For the moment he contented himself with the knowledge that this was a significant sound, and affixed the name "Queen Charlotte's Sound" to the chart.[38]

Strange understood that the wind and weather were important considerations in his attempts to delineate the shoreline. He took pains to draw sketch plans of the coast and make correct observations of longitude and latitude. Yet the tides and currents and "the rainy, dirty, foggy weather" dictated that it would require several voyages along the coast before a survey could be laid before the public with any assurance of being correct.[39] Strange knew that in this particular locale environmental factors made for uncommonly rough seas and tricky navigation.

The expedition's next objective was Cook Inlet. After a turbulent passage in thick weather, the ships came to welcome shelter on 20 August in a place aptly known as Snug Corner Bay. Here natives did not come to the ship in any numbers; instead the trading was tediously slow. Compared to the Nootka the Indians were almost destitute in furs. Strange concluded, rather painfully, that a second voyage to America could not be undertaken unless the expedition's costs could be vastly reduced: one small vessel such as the 100-ton *Experiment* might suffice, provided her establishment in men and supplies was restricted. Strange reasoned that his failure would deter others from the trade in that quarter. Ever optimistic, he wrote that his trading there would teach the natives to be prepared for subsequent traffic in furs "which this Coast would doubtless supply in no inconsiderable quantities."[40] For the moment at least, Strange believed that he could have the whole trade, marginal though it was, to himself.

On 5 September, however, a rival ship hove in sight. She was the British snow *Sea Otter* of 100 tons. Not to be confused with Hanna's ship, this one was owned by a syndicate calling themselves the Bengal Fur Society. From her captain, William Tipping, Strange learned that the *Sea Otter* had left India the previous March with her consort the *Nootka,* commanded by John Meares, the expedition's partner. The *Sea Otter's* captain carried instructions to survey the west coast of Japan before making the passage by the Aleutians to Prince William Sound; Meares meanwhile was to proceed directly to Nootka Sound.

In these circumstances, Strange and Tipping viewed each other with mutual suspicion, jealousy, and reserve. Here in a remote corner of the distant oceans they were at the outer limits of world trade serving different masters yet engaged in identical missions. The discussion at dinner hosted by Strange on board the *Captain Cook* seems like a chess match, with Strange and Tipping endeavouring to predict the other's next move. Tipping, the latecomer, took the more aggressive position. He knew Strange had been to Nootka Sound, but had he been to Cook Inlet? Strange told Tipping it was profitless for him to visit either Nootka Sound or any place in between. Predictably, Tipping reasoned that Strange had not yet called at Cook Inlet. Suddenly he made sail and sailed directly for that point. Strange had been dramatically and foolishly forestalled. Momentarily he entertained the idea of the *Experiment* wintering on the coast to await another trading season, but his provisions were low and he did not think the alternative possibility of the Hawaiian Islands a convenient place for refreshment between trading seasons. Thus he decided to proceed to China, sell his furs, and plan a further expedition. The *Captain Cook* reached Macao Roads on 15 November 1786 and the *Experiment,* having failed to reach Copper Island in the Aleutians to search for copper, arrived a month later.[41]

Strange had no delusions about his voyage. It had been a financial disaster. Tipping's arrival at Prince William Sound tolled the death knell of the expedition. As Strange admitted rather grandly, it was "the *coup de grace* to my future Prospect of Success in this Line of Life." To China Strange took only 604 fur pieces, and even they were of mixed quality. They were sold without any difficulty by the ship's agent for 24,000 Spanish dollars (about £5,600). This was a good price but hardly sufficient to defray the expedition's costly outlay.[42]

Nevertheless, Strange's expedition revealed several features important for future success in the trade. Nootka Sound was clearly the place to establish a base for coastal trade. Rivals from India were now in the trade, and competition could be expected to be fierce. Natives at various places were responding to the trade in their various ways: some, such as the Moachat Nootka, keenly entered into the new commercial pattern; others at Prince William Sound seemed uncertain about it. Above all, Strange learned that furs were not available with the ease and in the quantity that accounts of Cook's third voyage seemed to promise. This was a hard lesson, one that Strange was not the only trader to learn.

The *Captain Cook-Experiment* voyages also indicated that the East India Company would not derive great benefit from investment in a trade where risks were high and profits uncertain. In future, Bombay investors such as David Scott were unlikely to spend large sums of money and risk ships and men in marginally successful trade unless the East India Company became directly involved. This explains why Bombay now sought to interest the parent company in forming a settlement at Nootka Sound. Bombay's plan called for two small ships of 100 to 120 tons besides factors and a small garrison to be sent from Bombay to Nootka to build the depot. While one of the ships was to coast northwards as far as Cook Inlet, the other would sail regularly between China and the Northwest Coast.[43] This project was never undertaken. The group of company directors who comprised the powerful London-based "Shipping Interest" were unlikely to back Scott's expansive plans to use India-built vessels. This reflected the then prevalent if nascent contest for liberalization of Company seaborne trade, one in which Scott would later find Henry Dundas a willing parliamentary supporter. As for Strange, he does not seem to have enjoyed any pecuniary consideration from the Company for his Northwest Coast voyage. He re-entered the Madras service, returned to England in 1795, was elected a member of Parliament shortly thereafter, and returned to Madras in 1804, where he became Postmaster General and a senior member of the local board of trade.[44]

Meanwhile, Strange's rival at Prince William Sound, Tipping, had reached the Northwest Coast in 1786 in the Calcutta-based *Sea Otter*. Tipping was in the employ of the Bengal Fur Company, a syndicate of Calcutta agency house merchants of British nationality who traded with Canton and who were led by an enterprising scallawag named John Meares. This young former lieutenant in the Royal Navy, like so many others after the War of American Independence, had sought his fortune by entering the merchant service and sailing for India. He had no wealth, nor did he have political or commercial connections of note, but like Strange he knew about Cook's third voyage and the prospects for trade and fame. Like Strange also, in contrast to Portlock or Dixon, he had little experience in discovery and exploration. What he did have, however, was the unbridled character of the *agent provocateur,* which was sure to upset almost all rivals, whether British, American, or Spanish. He misappropriated place names, claimed priority of discovery to places already found by others, and was ungracious in not acknowledging the kindness of other mariners to him.[45] On the other hand, he was a propagandist for the protection of British interests and this placed him in good stead with the Cabinet. In the Nootka crisis he was prominent as the peaceful mercantile promoter who had been wronged by the highhanded Spanish dons. He assumed the role of the pioneering figure representing national interests that should be vindicated.

Much of this, of course, lay in the future, but it shows the ambitions of this fortune seeker and his manipulation of others. Unlike Strange he had sailed illegally from India under the Portuguese flag and in ships not licensed by the East India or South Sea companies. This meant that sooner or later his subterfuge likely would be disclosed or that he would have to enter into arrangements with the East India Company. Fortunately commercial success lay on his side, for the *Sea Otter* made a quick return to Macao, reached February 1787, where Tipping's furs yielded a handsome $8,000.[46]

At the same time that Meares was undertaking his first reconnaissance, Captain Charles William Barkley was scouring the coast of Vancouver Island for sea otter skins.[47] Barkley had taken up a seafaring life in the East India Company's service, commanding his own ships. In 1786, in his twenty-sixth year, he left the Company to command the former East-Indiaman *Loudoun,* a 400-ton, ship-rigged vessel mounting twenty guns, being outfitted in the Thames for a trading voyage to the Northwest Coast. At the time of her arrival at Nootka Sound she was the largest vessel to engage in the trade. She was owned by supercargoes in China in the East India Company's service and by several Company directors in London. However, she was outfitted by the Austrian East India Company, carried Austrian colours out of Ostend, and bore the appropriate Austrian name *Imperial Eagle*. This was really a poaching expedition, financed by East India Company servants intending to trade in ports and waters controlled by the East India and South Sea Company monopolies.

The *Imperial Eagle* reached Nootka Sound in June 1787, and here, as mentioned, Barkley found Dr. John Mackay. The young surgeon aided his rescuer's commercial transactions with various Indians by telling Barkley of the coastline's intricacies. Leaving Nootka, where he purchased a large number of sea otter skins from the Indians, Barkley entered Clayoquot Sound to the southward and then the large sound which now bears his name. Again he sailed southward, discovering to his surprise what he thought was the legendary Strait of Juan de Fuca, the entrance to which was about four leagues wide and stretched into the fading distance as far as the eye could see. Barkley was astonished that he had found the passage which in 1778 Cook had emphatically declared could not exist. He sailed southeastward into the strait as far as Destruction Island, where a boat's crew was killed by natives. From here he sailed for Canton, where his eight hundred pelts brought $30,000 on what had become an overstocked market. There Barkley suffered at the hands of agents of the *Imperial Eagle* and of John Meares, who confiscated Barkley's charts, journals, and private stores without remuneration.

Barkley never re-entered the trade, for the shadows of both private and East

India Company rivals and of French enemies lay across his path a number of times. In 1792 he sailed for Alaskan waters in the *Halcyon* as consort for the *Venus* which traded in the vicinity of Vancouver Island and the Queen Charlotte Islands, but the French subsequently seized his ship at Mauritius. His promising finds of Barkley Sound as a sea otter haven and of a great strait leading eastward from Cape Flattery were being pursued by other traders, including Charles Duncan and John Meares, who would profit by his pioneering efforts.

Meanwhile, Meares sailed along the Northwest Coast in the *Nootka* to trade at Nootka Sound and in Alaskan waters. He had intended to establish a permanent post at Cook Inlet, but there he was surprised to find forty or fifty Russians living snugly in a small and fortified settlement on the site of modern Anchorage. The Russians proved energetic trading rivals, preventing the natives from bartering with the English. In these circumstances Meares had no option but to withdraw. He did not do so until he had claimed Point Possession and thereby strengthened British claims previously made by Cook. Meares reached Prince William Sound on 25 September 1786, where no Russian opposed him. At Snug Corner Cove, he established an alliance with the Indian chief Shenawah and from him procured a considerable quantity of valuable furs. Under the terms of their treaty Meares promised presents in return for Shenawah's granting of exclusive trade with any ship under Meares's command.[48] Here, also, Meares constructed a rudimentary house for the ship's carpenter and his men, presumably the beginning of a shore establishment suitable for building a coasting schooner.

Meares was woefully ignorant of Alaskan winter conditions. In November his ship was iced in the creek mouth where he had foolishly chosen to anchor. There he and his men remained for seven months, prevented from retreating to warmer climates where food might be obtained. His stock of fresh vegetables eventually ran out and during the winter many officers and crew, twenty-three in all, died of scurvy and other diseases. Over the Christmas season Meares indiscriminately allowed unrestricted use of a spirituous liquor of a particularly pernicious kind, and there is reason to believe that its effects were no less fatal than scurvy. By the time Captain Dixon of the *Queen Charlotte* reached him in May 1787, only Meares and nine of his crew, still iced in, remained alive.

Dixon's superior, Portlock, took a harder line against Meares than Dixon had done. He treated his rival with disdain, although he was prepared to assist Meares for humanitarian reasons. According to Portlock, Meares did not have a trading licence granted by the South Sea Company. Nor did he have the approval of the British government. Consequently, Portlock believed that Meares was a poacher, an interloper. Portlock compelled him to sign a bond for £500 requiring that he would cease trading on the coast and immediately sail for Hawaii and China. Meares claimed that Portlock and Dixon were ungenerous and that they used his unfortunate position to compel him to quit the trade. On the other hand, he was in no condition to continue and was obliged to proceed to the closest port in any case, perhaps to re-enter the trade at some later time. He made his way to Macao and sold his 350 sea otter furs for 14,000 Spanish dollars, that is, about $40 per skin. By contrast, Portlock and Dixon arrived a few weeks later with the grand cargo of 2,552 skins, which sold for 50,000 Spanish dollars, that is, about $19 per skin.[49]

Meares was undeterred by Portlock and Dixon's attempts to gain exclusive trading rights on the Northwest Coast and by their bullying tactics. The China market had proved to his advantage, so he quickly enlisted the support of two Canton patrons, John Henry Cox and David Beale & Co., and formed a new trading alliance called the Merchant Proprietors, which likely included his old Bengal Fur Company associates. Two ships, the *Felice Adventurer*,[50] a British snow of 230 tons, and the *Iphigenia Nubiana*, of 200 tons, nominally owned by Juan Carvalho of Macao, were fitted out and sent from Macao Roads to the Northwest Coast under Portuguese flags.[51] Meares's objective was to reach Nootka Sound, stake a claim to trade there, build an alliance with Maquinna, acquire title to land, and forestall Portlock, Dixon, and their backers, the Etches concern. By destroying this competition Meares could gain exclusive control of fur sales at Canton and Macao, a rewarding prize indeed.

Meares's instructions, probably drawn up by himself in consultation with Cox and Beale, called for him to hasten to Nootka Sound. An early arrival on the Northwest Coast was important to check other traders, for Meares thought the Nootka Indians would have collected sea otter and other pelts. He would make Nootka Sound his headquarters. From there he would send his long-boat south to Wickaninnish, home of the hereditary chief of that name in the Clayoquot area, and subsequently to Barkley Sound where the rival trader Charles Barkley of the *Imperial Eagle* was known to have traded with great success. Then Meares would voyage south as far as the Spanish settlements that he thought existed on the shores of the Strait of Juan de Fuca.

Meares's main thrust was clearly to be southward of Nootka Sound, into Clayoquot and Barkley sounds and even into the famous strait itself. But he also intended, if time permitted, to examine the different bays north of Nootka, particularly the coasts of the Queen Charlotte Islands, where Dixon had done so well in 1787, and the shoreline as far as 55°N, in the latitude where Ketchikan now stands. Keeping in mind the lateness of the season, he intended to be back at Nootka by the first of September, where at his discretion plans were to be made for wintering on the Northwest Coast or in the Hawaiian Islands. In any event, the Nootka were to be told to expect Meares's return the following March. While Meares was concentrating on the southern area where sea otter could be had, his associate William Douglas, in command of the *Iphigenia Nubiana*, was to sail directly from China to Cook Inlet to begin trade and then trace the long coastal arc south—to Prince William Sound, Cross Sound, and ultimately to Nootka Sound—stopping along the way whenever Douglas thought it expedient but to rendezvous with Meares by 1 September.[52]

Pursuant to these instructions, Meares reached Nootka Sound in May 1788, traded with the Indians, bought land near Yuquot, and obtained from a willing Chief Maquinna a promise of exclusive trade, an important consideration at this mecca of the maritime fur trade. Meares consolidated his toe-hold by building his shore establishment and constructing a coastal schooner, the *North West America* of about forty tons, the first non-Indian vessel built on the west coast of what is now Canada. Meares wasted no time in returning to Macao to continue his commercial diplomacy to gain the monopoly of access to the China market. He left the *Iphigenia Nubiana* and *North West America* to scour the coast for furs and to winter in the Hawaiian Islands.

In effect, Meares had adopted James Strange's scheme of a permanent settlement served by coasting vessels in regular communication with the China market. His success in the trade as well as his priority of winning Maquinna's accord and settling near Yuquot placed him in a strong bargaining position compared with his main rival, Etches and Company. His opponents now would have to come to him. They would be obliged to treat with him for his right of trade on the Northwest Coast, for his alliance with Maquinna, and for his rights to have an establishment on shore.

On the other hand, Meares now faced challenges from other rivals, in particular the second wave of competition from Richard Cadman Etches and Company led by James Colnett. Colnett, an experienced mariner, was no less spirited than Meares himself. He had served with Cook in the Pacific and like his great teacher had attained the service rank of Master before being advanced to lieutenant. In September 1786 he obtained Admiralty permission to command the *Prince of Wales* and *Princess Royal* owned by Etches and Company. These ships were then fitting out in the Thames for Nootka Sound, where they were to follow the *King George* and *Queen Charlotte* in the maritime fur trade. Colnett traded on the Northwest Coast during the summers of 1787 and 1788, spending the first season in a search for furs from Cape Hinchinbrook, Alaska, to the Queen Charlottes, sketching charts, and learning that the best way to trade with the Indians was to beat off the coast, waiting for the natives to come from shore with their prized peltry. Colnett concentrated on the northern coast, leaving his associate Charles Duncan in the sloop *Princess Royal* to work the coast southward. They effected a rendezvous at Nootka Sound, wintered in the Hawaiian Islands, and in March 1788 returned to the Northwest Coast.

During their second summer on the coast Colnett and Duncan made several discoveries. Colnett, who continued to trade in northern latitudes, found that near Cape St. James in the Queen Charlotte Islands the Haida evidently were unfamiliar with trade and frightened at the appearance of the *Prince of Wales*. Colnett also discovered that the coast in the latitudes between $53°$ and $60°N$ was so complex, so studded with islands, that the western entrance to the Northwest Passage might well be concealed from view. "It's a doubt with me," he wrote in his journal, "if ever I have seen the Coast of America at all."[53] Such information, in the hands of the Secretary of the Admiralty, indicated the need to complete Cook's survey in those latitudes.

Meanwhile, Duncan in the *Princess Royal* was proving the insularity of the Queen Charlotte Islands (thus confirming the speculations of Dixon and La Pérouse) and exploiting the rich sea otter habitats on the continental shore between the Skeena River mouth and Cape Caution, a mainland promontory near Vancouver Island's northern extremity. This trade brought him in contact with Kwakiutl, Bella Coola, and Tsimshian tribes. Using George Dixon's advice that a good market could be found in these latitudes, he had done well in the trade, anchoring in the inner channels or securing hawsers to trees on the rocky shore when a secure anchorage was unavailable. On one such occasion, Indians attacked and he nearly lost a boat's crew, but he reached the security of Safety Cove, Calvert Island, before leaving for a rendezvous with Meares off Ahousat, Clayquot Sound, in early August 1788, where he traded with the tribe of Chief Wickaninnish.

Sailing south, as Barkley had done thirteen months previously, Duncan found the entrance to the Strait of Juan de Fuca. Here he put his skills as a surveyor and draftsman to good use. He drew an important sketch plan and views of the famous waterway, published by Parliament's authority in 1790. For some years this remained a valuable navigational aid to successors in the trade and to explorers such as Vancouver. Duncan's chart showed a pinnacle near the strait's entrance. This, Duncan assumed, was the famous pillar reported by the Greek pilot Juan de Fuca after his supposed voyage to the Northwest Coast in 1592. The chart also showed some useful data on the local Indians of Cape Claaset. The Indians had told Duncan that a "Great Sea" lay to the east which ran a great length northward and also southward, a speculation which like Colnett's conjecture of a Northwest Passage stimulated belief in England that the strait led to the polar sea. This "Great Sea" was doubtless the Strait of Georgia and Puget Sound. Duncan's discoveries made him a firm, even fanatical believer in the passage's existence. On his return to London from Canton in the *Prince of Wales* with a cargo of tea, he commanded a Hudson's Bay Company expedition to sail for the west coast of Hudson Bay, find the passage, proceed through it to the entrance of the Strait of Juan de Fuca, and either return home or go to China. Twice Duncan attempted this voyage and the last known reference to this pioneer in distant voyages to the Northwest Coast is that distressed by his disappointment he made several unsuccessful attempts to commit suicide on his last voyage home from Hudson Bay.[54]

Despite Duncan's emotional problems, the successful voyages of the *Prince of Wales* and *Princess Royal* increased the Etches Company's opposition to Meares and his merchant partners. Meares still did not have full access to the Canton market although Etches did by arrangement with the East India Company. Consequently it became apparent that a merger of India and China traders would benefit both, especially since each was operating at a loss. This would allow the partners to acquire government protection more easily and help British vessels compete with American ships such as the *Eleanora* of New York and the *Columbia* and *Washington* of Boston.[55]

In Macao in the autumn of 1788, Meares and his Canton associates Cox and Beale met with John Cadman Etches, brother to Richard. Etches had recently returned to China from the Northwest Coast with the intention of forming a new organization, a partnership rather than a merger, that would aid both parties in prosecuting the trade and in renewing licences from the East India and South Sea companies. The subsequent union of Meares's Associated Merchants and Etches's King George Sound Company under the new name the "Associated Merchants of London and India Trading to the Northwest Coast of America" was at once a marriage of convenience and a realization by the rivals that each could profit by the other's advantageous arrangements on either side of the Pacific. The agreement, dated 23 January 1789, required that all ships were to be on a joint account and the profits to be equally shared.

By 1789, therefore, British activity in the maritime fur trade was far advanced from its earlier uncertain developments of the late 1770's and early 1780's. Cook's voyage had revealed the trade to the English commercial community. Several independent expeditions had been undertaken by the British—from London, Bombay, Calcutta, Canton, and Macao. Since 1785, according to Meares's estimates, five British ships had entered the trade from Europe and nine others from eastern seas.[56] British sales in the maritime fur trade had reached a value of 288,000 Spanish dollars. By comparison, French, Spanish, and American rivals had engaged in trade worth only 142,000 Spanish dollars, or about half that of the British. Even then, according to Meares, foreign competition was closing in on the British. These figures indicated to the British ministry that the maritime fur trade was worthy of government attention, and that permanent steps should be taken to put the trade on a firm footing. More important, as we shall see later, the British now had a grand project in motion for the extension of British settlement and trade in eastern seas. Furs, settlers, convicts, naval stores, factories, and depots were to be well-placed pawns, so to speak, in the emerging international contest to win the trade and sovereignty of the Northwest Coast.

6

Beachhead of Empire

We made these chiefs sensible in how many moons we should return to them; and that we should then be accompanied by others of our countrymen, and build more houses, and endeavour to introduce our manners and mode of living to the practice of our Nootka friends. This information seemed to delight them beyond measure; and they not only promised us great plenty of furs on our return, but Maquilla thought proper, on the instant, to do obedience to us as his lords and sovereigns.

MEARES, *VOYAGES*

The first maritime fur traders on the Northwest Coast recognized the need for store establishments to enable them to pursue their business activities. Ships on distant voyaging needed places for repair; crews needed places for rest and refreshment; traders needed secure, fortified stations where commodities could be stored and traffic conducted with the natives. In short, such places, "factories" as they were commonly called in the eighteenth century, seemed essential to a profitable commerce on the Northwest Coast.

On the coast's far northern and southern extremities, the Russians at Unalaska and the Spanish at Monterey already had their respective bases of operation. Unalaska served the Russian coasting trade as far east as Prince William Sound; Monterey succoured the Spanish sea otter trade at the Farallones and other islands off the California coast. Between these Russian and Spanish areas of activity was a lengthy shoreline still unoccupied by European nations or the United States in the spring of 1788. Nootka Sound, lying midway between Russian and Spanish possessions, offered a tempting prize to the first nation that could gain control of it not only for use as a fur trading station but, more important in the long run, as a beachhead of empire.

Though his predecessors and rivals planned to build at Nootka Sound, John Meares was actually the first to plant an establishment there, and since his claims to having done so assumed major importance during subsequent Anglo-Spanish antagonisms, it is necessary to examine his shore activities in some detail. On 13 May 1788, Meares's two ships, *Felice Adventurer* and *Iphigenia Nubiana,* cast anchor off Yuquot, Friendly Cove, after a passage of three months and twenty-three days out of Macao. Both ships carried carpenters and smiths, almost all of whom were Chinese and who were intended to become settlers. "They have been generally esteemed a hardy, and industrious, as well as ingenious race of people," Meares wrote of the Chinese, "they live on fish and rice, and, requiring but low wages, it was a matter also of economical consideration to employ them; and during the whole of the voyage there was every reason to be satisfied with their services."[1] The labour and skills of the Orient were being employed to develop the potential of the occident. Though Meares's scheme was being conducted on an experimental basis its legacies would have subsequent importance in Chinese-North American relations. As Meares foresaw: "If hereafter trading posts should be established on the American coast, a colony of these men would be a very important acquisition."[2]

At Nootka Sound, Meares sought the consent of Chief Maquinna. The great chief, then "about thirty years, a middle size, but extremely well made, and possessing countenance that was formed to interest all who saw him." Maquinna and the Nootka welcomed Meares and his crew as "wacush, wacush," or friends, and an exchange of presents followed.[3] Meares now obtained Maquinna's assent to build a house on shore for the people intended to be left there; and Meares says that Maquinna "consented to grant us a spot of ground in his territory" on which the dwelling would be built. The chief not only offered his assistance in building the place but promised to protect the party who would remain behind during Meares's winter absence.

The Nootka Indians were cordial and generous: they brought timber from the forests and they gave whatever help was requested of them. They seemed anxious to do any tasks assigned. For their labour they received daily payments of beads and iron. Unfortunately, there was not enough work for all the Indians who wished it.

By 28 May, Nootka Sound's first European dwelling was ready for occupation. Meares describes it as sufficiently spacious to hold the men to be left at Nootka. On the ground floor ample room existed for sail-makers, coopers, and other artisans to work in bad weather. There was also a room for stores and provisions, while an armourer's shop was attached to one end of the building. The upper storey consisted of eating and sleeping quarters. "On the whole," Meares mused with characteristic pomposity and some mirth, "our house, though it was not built to satisfy a lover of architectural beauty, was admirably well calculated for the purpose to which it was destined, and appeared to be a structure of uncommon magnificence to the natives of King George's Sound."[4] Perhaps recalling Maquinna's attempts to overpower Captain Hanna's *Sea Otter* in 1785, Meares decided to take precautions. He built a strong breastwork enclosing a large area around the house to provide a modicum of security from intrusion though only one three-pounder cannon commanded the cove and villages. The Yankee Robert Haswell thought it "a tolerable strong garrison or place of defence."[5]

The factory, a curious counterpart to the long, low Nootka lodges nearby, stood north and east along the shore from Yuquot in a small, flat coastal indentation divided from the Indian village by a high rocky escarpment and dense bush.

The visitor to Nootka today sees that Meares had chosen a good site—conveniently near enough to Yuquot for communication with the Indians yet sufficiently distant so as not to interfere with the natives' activities. The place was relatively well sheltered from the weather. A small stream afforded a water supply. Timber was available on the beach and in the forest. Berries, fish, fowl, and deer were also readily available. A gently inclining pebble beach afforded an excellent place for beaching and careening small vessels and for conducting those numerous shore activities so essential to keeping a ship seaworthy.

As soon as Meares's establishment had been built and fortified, the Chinese artisans began to construct a coastal sloop. During the passage from Macao the shipwrights had tried to construct models and moulds for a forty- to fifty-ton sloop to be built immediately on their arrival at Nootka, one carefully designed for exploring and trading in coastal waters. A London carpenter superintended the project, aided by Chinese fellow craftsmen whose techniques of naval construction were quite different from the British. Language barriers added to complications. Thus when the *Felice Adventurer* reached Nootka Sound little had been done. The spirited Meares wrote, "our timber was standing in the forests of America, the iron work was, as yet, in rough bars on board, and the cordage which was to be formed into ropes, was yet a cable."[6]

Construction went ahead as planned, with a pressing completion date of October. In late August Meares deployed some of the *Felice Adventurer*'s crew to assist the shipwrights and soon "the business of our temporary dock promised a very speedy completion."[7] At high tide on 20 September, the vessel slid from her makeshift ways. It was an important moment in shipbuilding history, Meares realized. Never one to miss an opportunity, he adopted the ceremony of other dockyards by displaying the English ensign both at the house and on board the new vessel.[8] At the right moment, the sloop was named the *North West America* in honour of being the first European ship built and launched on the coast.

Meares's 1788 mission had now been completed: he had conducted a successful coasting trade in the Nootka area, particularly in the region of Clayoquot Sound, and his coasting vessel had been built. Yet the season was running late. He had to think of his crew's health and the long, damp winter ahead. He had not come prepared to winter at Nootka but rather had planned to sail for Canton in the *Felice Adventurer,* leaving the *Iphigenia Nubiana* and *North West America* to make for the Hawaiian Islands and be back early in the 1789 season to begin the coasting season in April.[9] Such a plan made eminent sense: already Maquinna's Yuquot Indians had begun to make their annual retreat to their inland settlement at the head of Tahsis Channel to gain protection from winter winds and severe weather during this part of the year. Besides, Indians did not ordinarily conduct trade during the cold months and no rival ship was likely to winter there when the Hawaiian Islands offered such a salutary, even festive alternative. In short, Meares must have expected no opposition during the time he would be away from Nootka Sound, no threats to his small coastal establishment, no rivalry to his pre-eminent position with Maquinna, Callicum, and other chiefs.

Nevertheless, at this juncture Meares had to face opposition from an unexpected quarter. In September 1778, the *Lady Washington* out of Boston, Captain Robert Gray commanding, anchored in Friendly Cove to find Meares's two ships there and a partially built schooner on the way. The Americans learned that the *Felice Adventurer* had coasted northward while the *Iphigenia Nubiana* had traded southward and collected a sizeable cargo of furs for the China market. The English officers tried to warn off the Bostonians in order that they might maintain their newly acquired ascendancy on the coast. "All the time these gentlemen were on board," young Robert Haswell of the *Lady Washington* astutely wrote in his log on 16 September, "they fully employed themselves fabricating and rehursing vague and improvable tales relative to the coast of the vast danger attending its navigation of the Monsterous Savage disposition of its inhabitants adding it would be maddness in us so week as we were to stay a winter among them."[10] Meares swore to the Americans that his ships had not collected fifty skins, a claim the wary Gray and Haswell regarded as a "notorious falsity."[11]

But Gray had good reason for wintering at Nootka Sound. The *Lady Washington*'s rudder and stern post had been badly damaged in a gale just north of the Columbia River. Moreover her mizzenmast head had sprung at sea and needed replacing. In addition the crew had been struck by scurvy and two men had actually died of it. Gray needed a place for rest and repair, and apparently, unlike Meares, he had sufficient provisions to last the winter. When Captain John Kendrick, in charge of the Boston expedition, arrived in the *Columbia* on 23 September he decided that both ships should winter on the coast. He believed that no useful trading with the natives could be conducted so long as the English ships lingered there, and so he cunningly sent his carpenters, caulkers, and blacksmiths to Meares's ships to help them prepare for a quick departure.[12] Indeed, on 26 October, when the *Iphigenia Nubiana* and *North West America* eventually put to sea, boats from the American ships courteously towed the *Iphigenia* out of Friendly Cove. No sooner had this vessel and her consort cleared the sound for the Hawaiian Islands than the natives approached the *Columbia* and *Lady Washington* in great numbers and a feverish commerce in provisions and furs was kept up for some days. The Nootka, however, pestered the Yankee traders, stealing water casks and five small cannon given Kendrick by Douglas.[13] Perhaps Meares was right after all in warning Kendrick and Gray against staying the winter. Nevertheless, the Yankee traders completed repairs to their ships, wintered in safety, and in mid-March 1789 began to range the coast in search of furs. They concentrated on Meares's favourite area, Clayoquot Sound. Like Meares before him, Captain Gray found trade in the great inner reaches of Clayoquot Sound agreeable and the natives friendly. The Americans secured new trade alliances with chiefs at Ahousat, Tofino, Echahchist, Opitsat, and elsewhere in the area.[14]

Not surprisingly, when the *Columbia* returned from her second voyage, Gray wintered here in 1790-91 and built the coasting sloop *Adventure*, brought out in frame from Boston.[15]

Meares meanwhile had promised Maquinna that he would return to trade, to build more houses, and to introduce European manners and modes of living to the Indians. Meares wrote with characteristic boastfulness that the Nootka were very pleased; they promised to have furs ready for Meares when he returned, and Maquinna accepted the English "as his lords and sovereigns." Maquinna, Meares claimed, now had conferred powers on the Englishman by an elaborate ceremony whereby Meares's superiority and sovereign power over Maquinna were recognized. Maquinna's act of allegiance was followed by all the Indians present.[16]

Meares clearly expected to return the following spring to start a permanent colony. He had already won Maquinna's friendship and promise of sovereignty at Friendly Cove. Provided some other rival ship or ships did not arrive in the meantime and Kendrick or Gray did not interfere with his plans by upsetting his newly forged alliance, all would be well. He believed he had acquired sufficient knowledge of the coast, its winds, and seasons to give him an advantage over all his competitors. Thus he was confident when he prepared to leave the Northwest Coast for Macao. "The years 1790 and 1791 bid fair to be the most productive that we may ever meet with," he wrote to Captain William Douglas of the *Iphigenia Nubiana*. And he continued: "Having these flattering prospects before us, our exertions must be redoubled, effectually to sweep the coast before any vessel can arrive from England."[17] Meares recommended that Douglas ought to be back on the coast from Hawaii as early in 1789 as possible and should trade in the Hecate Strait area as far north as 54° with the *Iphigenia Nubiana* and *North West America*. This would leave the coastal trade of Vancouver Island to Meares upon his return from China by the first of May.[18] Meares sailed from Friendly Cove on 24 September, leaving Douglas in charge of the shore establishment.

Meares's occupation at Friendly Cove in 1788 was only one of his acts of territorial possession on the coast. Farther south, he had obtained from Chief Wicanninish the promise of a free and exclusive trade in the Port Cox-Port Effingham area and permission to build whatever shore establishments he needed to conduct his business. Similarly, at the entrance to the Strait of Juan de Fuca, he had acquired from the Makah chief not only rights of trade but a tract of land. One of his officers took possession of it in the King's name and called it, in the chief's honour, Tatooche.[19] These pretensions to title provided the basis for subsequent English claims to Nootka Sound. Nonetheless, in 1792, Maquinna vehemently denied that he had sold permanent title to the Englishman he later blatantly referred to as Aita-Aita Meares, that is, "Liar Meares." Enough gift-giving or trading had taken place between the two that although Maquinna may not have thought it an actual sale, Meares had nonetheless gained the chief's required consent.[20] The Americans Robert Gray and Joseph Ingraham, perhaps harbouring anti-English prejudices after the American Revolution, sided with the Nootka chief—not out of friendship for the Indians but because they did not want to see exclusive British control at Nootka Sound. They thus supported rival Spanish claims to sovereignty and argued that only Captain Kendrick had acquired land from the Indians. The Englishmen William Graham and Robert Duffin, however, confirmed Meares's purchase.[21] Not least of the evidence in favour of Meares against the detractions of Gray and Ingraham is that Bodega offered Captain George Vancouver in 1792 the land on which Meares's small establishment had stood in 1788, an acknowledgement of Maquinna's sale of land and granting of title.[22]

On his return to Macao, Meares effected the partnership with Etches and Company. This allowed for the redeployment of ships for the following season and the rapid building of a Nootka shore establishment. James Colnett, in command of the *Prince of Wales,* owned by Etches and Company, now became commodore of all United Merchants' vessels in the Pacific—five ships in all—and had command of an expedition to start the colony at Nootka. He carried with him in the snow *Argonaut* from China the authority of a commercial pro-consul. However, he took with him no guarantee of support from London; he had no royal commission of authority. His duty was to execute his orders as given under Meares's master plan.

His responsibilities are revealed somewhat by the nature of the cargo on his outward-bound voyage. It included twenty-nine Chinese artificers—carpenters, blacksmiths, bricklayers, tailors, shoemakers, seamen, and a cook—who had been put on board to build a settlement at Friendly Cove and also carry on a large-scale trade with the Indians. Colnett had had some difficulty in getting the Chinese on board the *Argonaut,* and he had to smuggle them from the shore in order to prevent interference from the mandarins. Many more Chinese had wanted to undertake the expedition than could be carried, and Colnett would have shipped more if he could.

The object of having these artificers and seamen on board was to implement the plan that Strange, Meares, Etches, and others had had all along to establish a *permanent* factory for British trade on the Northwest Coast. "In placing a Factory on the Coast of America," Colnett's sailing orders of 3 April 1789 read, "we look to a solid establishment, and not one that is to be abandon'd at pleasure; we authorize you to fix it at a most Convenient Station only to place your colony in Peace and Security and fully protected from the fear of the smaller Sinister Accidents."[23] The port's object was to attract the Indians, to be a place to lay up the small coasting vessels during the winter, to be a place to build and repair ships, and to be a location for other commercial activities related to the fur trade. The establishment was to be the first of several and was to be named Fort Pitt, in honour of the Prime Minister, William Pitt, doubtless a ploy to gain government support. Once the post had been built other trading houses would be established at various coastal locations. For the time being, however, Colnett was to send traders to live with some of his Haida friends on the Queen Charlotte Islands in order to keep competitors away and, not least, to conciliate the Haida.

The Company's plans called for Fort Pitt to be the haven for a small but growing fleet of company ships. These coastal vessels, having cruised the north coast and sailed into various harbours, would rendezvous at Friendly Cove in August. The peltry, bundled and packed to ensure its preservation during the long, damp voyage, would be transshipped at a coastal rendezvous to the larger vessel, *Argonaut,* for passage to China. During the winter the small vessels would be laid up at the factory under the superintendence of Robert Duffin, the first officer of the *Argonaut.* Meanwhile some larger vessels would sail for the Hawaiian Islands, bringing back to the Northwest Coast in the spring not only the vital provisions for the summer's trade but Hawaiian men and women to settle on the Northwest Coast and be in the Company's employ. Kanakas, as Hawaiians on the Northwest Coast were called for many years, were to complement the multinational labour pool the British were bringing to Nootka Sound. As excellent sailors, the Kanakas would man company ships either in service or to be built.

The time came for Meares and the Company to embark on their well-considered venture at Fort Pitt. They had vessels, skilled artificers, prospective settlers, knowledge of weather conditions, and a friendly relationship with the native peoples. They hoped that all these resources would enable them to undertake the development of an efficient network of trading ships and, equally important, secure for the British a beachhead of empire.

7

Imperial Dreams and False Starts

And you will be careful to embark on board these ships such articles . . . for building etc. . . . in order to enable them to fulfil the object of forming such a settlement as may be able to resist any attacks from the natives, and lay the foundation
of an establishment for the assistance of his Majesty's subjects, in the possession
of the fur trade from the N.W. coast of America.

INSTRUCTIONS TO GOVERNOR PHILLIP, MARCH 1790

Nootka Sound symbolized newly won prosperity for British mercantile interests
in eastern seas, a fact that the government, ever conscious of traders' demands,
could ill afford to ignore.[1] By 1789 public and parliamentary interest in the prospects of the Pacific was so strong that the government decided that Meares, Colnett, Etches, Cox, and others needed official support. Persistent requests for official support had come from several quarters, and had been received by the
government almost simultaneously. These requests reflected various motives—
some commercial, others scientific, and still others humanitarian.

Yet at the root of these intentions lay the desire to promote the financial prosperity of the United Kingdom by generating new trade in eastern seas. To this
end David Scott, James Strange's ally, found parliamentary support from Henry
Dundas (later Viscount Melville) in pressing for a diversification of national interests by widening the East India Company's scope and adopting more flexible
methods of trade and regulation in eastern seas. Similarly, Samuel Enderby's
whaling interests lobbied Lord Hawkesbury at the Board of Trade to establish a
base in the South Pacific. Meanwhile, ex-maritime fur traders who had returned
to London and vested interests such as the East India Company and the Hudson's
Bay Company turned their attention to these changes in eastern affairs. Similarly, armchair geographers, scientists, and members of learned societies made
known their positions. The government came under pressure during the three
years before the celebrated seizure of British ships at Nootka Sound, and this
same pressure resulted in official decisions to send an armed expedition even before news of the outrage at Spanish hands reached London in 1789.

At this time the British were anxious to secure Pacific trade and direct or indirect dominion over lands in the component parts of that ocean. On opposite sides
of the Pacific, the Northwest Coast and the Antipodes lay unoccupied, though
not unclaimed, by European nations. Japan, China, and Korea largely remained
closed to foreign commerce. Hawaiian, Tahitian, and other island clusters at-

tracted beachcombers, mariners, and missionaries. Within two decades after the American Revolution, Britain had obtained some influence in many of these places and paramount sway in some others. Much British activity was spurred on by fear of rival activity by Holland, France, and Spain. In some instances, however, as in the cases of New South Wales and, to a lesser degree, Nootka Sound, British activity on these far-flung frontiers reflected the problems of the nation at home.

During the eighteenth century, the British practice of transporting felons as potential settlers rested on the expectation that they could become useful servants rather than a drain on the society they had sinned against.[2] Before the American Revolution, Britain gladly gave convicts to contractors who shipped them to Maryland, Georgia, and other southern colonies where they sold them to employers, mainly planters. It was a profitable trade for shipping interests and a means of reducing a growing national financial problem of maintaining criminals at home. Considering the dilapidated, unhealthy state of prisons or convict ships that lay along the Thames River, transportation afforded inmates a comparatively promising alternative.

However, convict export to the American seaboard ended with the Revolution, and for almost a decade after 1776 British jails and river hulks were overcrowded. The British shipped a few convicts overseas—to the Gold Coast to fight the Dutch or to British Honduras to serve as slaves—but by and large these experiments failed. Gradually, however, members of parliamentary inquiries into the growing problem became convinced that banishing prisoners to New Holland or Australia, whose eastern shores had been visited by James Cook and tempted rival Dutch and French expansionists, might provide the solution. Though the island continent was half-way round the world, which made transportation charges heavy on the outbound track, it might offer a new sea base for Britain in the east that would meet her commercial ambitions and might offer on the homeward voyage a paying cargo in Australian flax and New Zealand timber, then vital commodities for the maintenance of England's sea power, military strength, and national wealth.[3] Much evidence, as an Australian historian has written, suggests that Australia was colonized "with the twin hopes of giving England the naval supplies it needed and ridding England of the people it didn't need."[4]

Yet Britain's increasing influence in the Antipodes was also part of a growth of trade that profoundly affected British commerce and foreign policy in Asia. In 1784 Britain acquired by treaty from the Dutch the precious right of free navigation through waters of the Dutch East Indies. Coincidentally in that year, the China tea trade to Europe began to increase dramatically. In that year also, several projects were developed to exploit the maritime fur trade and to increase whaling in the Pacific. New South Wales remained central to this growth of British interests in eastern seas. However, the interrelationship of the component parts of the Pacific was becoming recognized by the British government as trade in tea, flax, timber, and sea otter pelts developed.

The government's decision to occupy Nootka Sound was part of this Pacific design and seems to have come about as follows. In early 1788, Richard Cadman Etches, a powerful proponent of the Northwest Coast fur trade, began a plan to establish a convict settlement at or near Nootka Sound. He found a willing ally in Sir Joseph Banks, President of the Royal Society. Banks had already given his blessing to the expedition of Etches's vessels *King George* and *Queen Charlotte*, the first London-based ships that had sailed for Nootka Sound. Previously in 1779 Banks had convinced a committee of the House of Commons of the expediency of establishing a colony of convicted felons at Botany Bay, New South Wales, although other sites had been considered, including Cape Breton, Bermuda, Nova Scotia, the Hawaiian Islands, the southwest coast of Africa, and the Gambia on the West African coast.[5]

Banks had been at Botany Bay with Cook and so had James Maria Matra, a midshipman in H.M.S. *Endeavour*. In 1783 Matra declared that a penal settlement at New South Wales would also "atone for the loss of our American colonies" by offering a colony for loyalists and a base to operate an extensive trade in the Pacific. The Northwest Coast was important in his thinking. Matra noted that an Australian colony would allow the British to expand their trade with China: the Russian trade in the Aleutians could be carried on by New South Wales ships. He astutely pointed out that just as Captain Cook's ships had brought a sea otter cargo to China from the North Pacific littoral so ships from New South Wales could easily carry on the trade and thus end the need to send immense quantities of silver to China in exchange for Oriental articles bought by the British.[6]

These two opinions—one favouring the promotion of penal settlement, the other for advancing settlement and Pacific trade—came to dominate cabinet members' minds. Other views were also promoted: that if national maritime power was to grow, Britain needed settlements in these seas; that New South Wales would give Britain a naval station in case of war with Spain; or that an Australian colony would benefit trade to the Philippines (in which the East India Company was interested) or to the western coast of America (where the Spanish proposed to have free ports). A plan for the settlement of New South Wales, by Captain (later Admiral) Sir George Young, R.N., envisaged not only the disposal of convicts but the establishment of "a very Extensive Commerce" and greatly increased shipping.[7] Such varied motivations led Alexander Dalrymple to write: "The project of settlement has appeared in many Proteus-like forms, sometimes as a half-way house to China, again as a check on the Spaniards . . . sometimes as a receptacle for transported convicts, then as a plan of asylum for American refugees, and sometimes as an emporium for supplying our marine yards with hemp and cordage or for carrying on the fur trade to the North West of America.''[8] Dalrymple did not oppose colonization, but he feared illicit trade.

The settlement at New South Wales would violate the chartered monopoly of the East India Company and upset its trade at Canton. Dalrymple could not stop the Botany Bay project. Nor did he bring about the merger of the East India and Hudson's Bay Companies. However, he did influence government thinking on the routes for armed expeditions that might be mounted to secure British interests on the Northwest Coast.

In the meantime, the government pressed on with its project to settle Botany Bay with convicts. In 1787 eleven ships under command of a naval officer, Captain Arthur Phillip, reached Sydney Cove and erected the first garrisoned shore establishment, Port Jackson. Though sixteen thousand kilometres across the Pacific from Nootka on Vancouver Island, this small beginning of sovereign authority affected the affairs of the distant Northwest Coast. The British thought of New South Wales as a springboard for the expansion of British trade and territory in eastern seas. From the far-off perspective of London, Port Jackson was considerably closer to the Northwest Coast than Portsmouth.

Once the government adopted penal settlement in New South Wales as its policy for relieving social distress at home and for reducing crime, various promoters advanced suggestions for the application of convict settlement to other places. In early 1788, for instance, Richard Cadman Etches wrote Sir Joseph Banks urging that the government consider the Northwest Coast as a colony for penal settlement. If a hundred felons and a few soldiers were sent out under the same conditions as the New South Wales scheme, Etches argued, this would not only "secure the complete discovery of that extensive and unexplor'd part of the World, but wou'd open, and secure a source of commerce of the most extensive magnitude to this Country."[9]

Etches saw both trade and convict settlement as conducive to national well-being. His plan suggested that a small armed government vessel, commanded by a lieutenant, should be sent to establish the settlement, survey the coast from Nootka Sound to Cook Inlet, develop the coastal timber and spar trade, build coasting trading vessels, and promote the trans-Pacific commerce in furs with Asia, especially Japan.

This project had the support of Patrick Wilson, an astronomy professor at Glasgow University, and Henry Robertson, a medical doctor, also of Glasgow. Their proposals indicate the widely held views of the advantages of this type of settlement. As Dr. Robertson put it, convict settlement would be the means whereby "the several Members of our Empire might link and connect together and form a solid and compact whole, comprehending every thing from St. James' and even to Botany Bay." "In such a station," he wrote with unmatched Scottish enthusiasm for northern latitudes, "we shall be possessed of a fixed Point, a *Fulcrum*, on which we may be able to poize and weigh up a World. By beginning in the South Pacific we are on the wrong side and must labour unsuccessfully, because we are working against Nature. Our Province is the North. It is the native and proper Seat of our Strength, whence it may spread far and wide, and be every where effectual."[10]

Despite these proddings, the idea of establishing a convict colony at Nootka Sound or elsewhere on the Northwest Coast does not seem to have been seriously considered by the British government until 1789. The reason is clear: the New South Wales experiment had been largely successful from the beginning, and the ready availability of arable land there for convict settlement meant that the government did not have to look elsewhere in the Empire for new sites. This did not preclude the possibility that the Northwest Coast might become a penal settlement in future. Even so, the links between Nootka Sound and Botany Bay were recognized in these nascent days of British enterprise in the Pacific; and it is not surprising that within a few years the government, ever optimistic and energetic, developed a project to extend the colony of New South Wales to include what is now British Columbia.

The project gathered impetus because of additional pressures. In July 1789, Captain George Dixon, commander of the *Queen Charlotte*, a fur trading vessel owned by Etches and the King George's Sound Company, urged Evan Nepean, Under-Secretary for Foreign Affairs, to send an expedition from England to the Northwest Coast by way of Cape Horn for purposes of trade and settlement. The government was bound to listen to this appeal. Dixon had long been known to Nepean, Banks, and others as a zealous officer, a successful maritime fur trader, and the one London resident who knew the Northwest Coast in any detail. He believed that sending an expedition by way of Quebec or Hudson Bay, as was planned, was "only losing time." Foreign competition from the Russians at Cook Inlet and Prince William Sound, the probable expansion of these two settlements southward, and the increased activities of Portuguese, American, Swedish, and Spanish vessels in the trade all augured badly for British commercial interests, Dixon argued. Unless the British government took active measures, "this valuable Branch of Commerce will be lost to this Country" and also to Canadian and Hudson's Bay Company fur interests.[11]

At the same time, support for government intervention on the Northwest Coast to bolster British interests was coming from yet another quarter. Dalrymple, then Examiner of Sea Journals for the East India Company, an associate of Duncan's, and a seasoned promoter of Pacific discovery and trade, had been keenly aware for some years of the need to find a Northwest Passage and promote the maritime fur trade. On 2 February 1780, in a memorandum to the government on the route for discoveries, he compared the access by Hudson Bay with that by Cape Horn. He maintained that a Northwest Passage existed, yet he tended to emphasize its possibilities rather than its difficulties. In his opinion, the old idea of a great inland or Hyperborean Sea in the northern wilds of Canada was still valid. Despite Cook's claim that it did not exist, Dalrymple meant no disrespect to the great explorer's memory or abilities when he said "I cannot admit of a *Pope* in Geography or Navigation.''[12] He clearly meant that the actual laborious work of surveying had to proceed on the Northwest Coast, even in minute detail, before the old idea could be laid to rest. He predicated his continual belief in the Northwest Passage on the seasoned argument that the Eskimos confined themselves to the sea coasts and vicinity and that because Eskimos lived in Labrador and the north coasts of America, it was reasonable to suppose that a sea existed between Labrador and the utmost extremity of North America. He noted that recent discoveries by Meares and Portlock indicated that sea communications lay eastward from the Northwest Coast and that Indians said there was a western sea beyond the mountains.

Thus, he argued, a ship should go from England to Hudson Bay and, if unsuccessful, return to replenish its stores and supplies and make its way by the Horn to the Northwest Coast.[13] Shortly thereafter, on 11 February, he was again advising government that his friend Samuel Wegg, chairman of the Hudson's Bay Company and his weekly dining companion at the Royal Society Club, had agreed to send a ninety-ton sloop at Company expense ''to examine if any outlet can be found from Hudson's Bay to facilitate the communication with the West Coast.'' Such an expedition, Dalrymple believed, would allow for further exploration of the interior of the Canadian northwest leading westward towards Cook's discoveries. Accordingly, Captain John Frederick de B. Holland, a British army officer in Quebec, submitted plans and estimates for expenses and instruments for a party of sixteen men ''for Discovering and Exploring the Interior Parts of the Northern and Western Quarter of America,'' lying between Lake Athabaska and the coastline discovered by Cook.[14]

Such advanced thinking was only a year ahead of its time. Dalrymple's scheme was surely the basis for what transpired in the voyages and explorations of Captain George Vancouver, R.N., and Alexander Mackenzie of the North West Company. It is noteworthy that although the Hudson's Bay Company became involved in this project, fur traders from Montreal first reached the Pacific overland.

It is similarly relevant that Dalrymple had another project in mind, this one to expand the maritime fur trade on the Northwest Coast. Arguing that British vessels would be forced out of the trade by Spanish, Russian, and American rivals, he declared that a government-supported merger of the Hudson's Bay and East India companies would allow British traders to dominate the North Pacific and its fur commerce. His plan included an East India Company ship with supplies meeting Hudson's Bay Company traders on the Northwest Coast, receiving furs from the coast and the interior of Canada, and then conveying them to China markets.[15]

The plan to occupy Nootka began to take shape. More and more it resembled the Richard Cadman Etches project, not as a convict settlement as such but rather as a commercial base for trade and navigation in the North Pacific. Such a plan involved the audacious act of forming an armed settlement manned by convicts on territory claimed by Spain, and was risky, reminiscent of the Falkland Islands episode of a few years before. It was a plan likely to invite Spanish reprisal. The government, however, was led to its decision by several pressures from an aggressive mercantile quarter, which in those days bulked particularly large in the affairs of the nation. Wegg of the Hudson's Bay Company, Etches representing the maritime fur traders, and others acting for shipping and whaling interests had spokesmen in the government.

The Cabinet came under pressure from one other quarter, for Samuel Enderby and his associates in the "southern" whale fishery were lobbying Charles Jenkinson, Lord Hawkesbury, the President of the Board of Trade, to establish a place of refreshment and repair for their ships in the south or even the north Pacific. After 1785 the government paid increasing heed to whalers who supplied significant commodities for the nation's energy requirements, to say nothing of its domestic, industrial, and ornamental needs. In 1786 the Board of Trade met with representatives of the whalers and adopted a new bounty scheme to encourage the southern whale fishery.[16] These premiums encouraged penetration of the Pacific via Cape Horn by ships owned by companies such as Samuel Enderby and Son, Alexander Champion, and John St. Barbe, who were profiting from the pioneering activities of the great Nantucket harpooners but sought barriers against foreign, mainly American, competition. The new regulations, which sharply circumscribed East India Company and South Sea Company monopolies of trade and navigation in the eastern seas and were adopted despite angry growls from these companies, allowed for the gradual opening of the western and northern Pacific to English whalers. In 1789 Enderby's *Amelia* became the first British bottom to enter the ocean. Subsequently, British ships came not only in search of the spermaceti whale but to hunt seals, sea elephants, and other sea mammals. The whalers did not wish to provoke Spanish resistance or to invite Spanish reprisal. Would it not be better, they asked government in 1788, to find an island base in the eastern Pacific close to the American coast that was not occupied by the Spanish?[17] Visions of Juan Fernandez Island off the Chilean coast, made legendary by Woodes Rogers and Daniel Defoe, came to their mind as a suitable islet. The matter grew more pressing when the Spanish arrested two British whalers, the *Sappho* and *Elizabeth and Margaret,* off the Patagonian coast in 1789 while they were refreshing and repairing. This incited the whaling lobby to petition the government once more, in October 1789, to bring British complaints before the Spanish government.[18]

Even so, the British government could not be persuaded to further penetrate the southern Pacific. London was not prepared to invite Spanish reprisals at Patagonia or conflict with the two chartered companies when islands in the South Atlantic remained possibly suitable sites for an adequate British whaling base. Thus, in October 1789 government revived a moribund project dating from

1784. The Navy Board was instructed to search for and purchase a ship of about 300 tons that could be outfitted for surveying three islands—Tristan da Cunha, Gough Island, and the mythical Isla Grande—as well as examining portions of the southwest African coast that were unoccupied by the Portuguese or Dutch. The expedition would have two objectives: to discover a base in the South Atlantic for whalers and to offset the advantage enjoyed by the Dutch at the Cape as the "Gibraltar of India."[19] This was the original service intended for H.M.S. *Discovery,* but that she did not sail on such a mission is important in showing how in the late 1780's the shifting course of events and sudden change in Anglo-Spanish relations could lure British interests away from the South Atlantic towards the emerging North Pacific world.

In fact, the 1789 proposal to send the *Discovery* to the South Atlantic proved to be the first of two false starts. Preparations for the ship's departure for the South Atlantic had gone ahead steadily as planned until January 1790 when the first news reached London that Spanish frigates had seized British merchantmen at Nootka Sound. British protests, described in the next chapter, did not bring any immediate assurance from the Spanish that British shipping could trade in those seas without molestation. Indeed, the Spanish ambassador in London boldly countered by asking the British government to restrain its "interlopers" in eastern seas.

The British response was not to yield to the Spanish request but instead to counter force by force by sending a powerful armed expedition under strictest secrecy to the Northwest Coast. Its object was to form a base—by armed force if necessary—to contest the vexing question of Spanish claims to sovereignty over distant, unsettled coasts on the basis of prescriptive right.[20] The British aimed to establish an effective occupation of Nootka Sound that would present their Iberian rivals with a *fait accompli.* By using a crowbar at Nootka Sound Britain hoped to pry open the sealed doors of Spanish American trade. Nootka was not an end in itself but a means to something much larger. Thus, in February 1790, Their Lordships issued instructions for H.M.S. *Gorgon,* a forty-four-gun frigate then preparing to sail for Port Jackson, New South Wales, with troops and supplies for the fledging penal colony at Botany Bay, to proceed from England to Nootka Sound via New South Wales. The *Discovery,* whose South Atlantic orders were now superseded by more pressing business, was to serve as her consort. As a surveying ship she would complete Cook's hydrographic work on the Northwest Coast. At the Hawaiian Islands, the *Gorgon* and *Discovery* were to join with a British frigate detached from the East Indies squadron, the *Sirius.* Then, in the spring of 1791, all three ships were to proceed to the Northwest Coast and form the armed settlement for prosecuting the fur trade.[21]

The establishment was imagined to be not more than thirty people (surprisingly close to the number Colnett had taken from China to Nootka the previous year), some of whom were to be drawn from the new New South Wales militia corps under the command of "a discreet subaltern officer" entrusted with temporary superintendence of the settlement. The rest of the establishment would consist of two or three Botany Bay overseers, a storekeeper, some volunteers, and a few of the most deserving convicts, who were to be promised parole as an inducement to go to this remote location. Governor Phillip was to provide the *Gorgon* and *Discovery* with stores, medicines, and tools sufficient to enable them to form a strong settlement that could resist attacks from the natives and lay the foundation of an establishment for the assistance of British subjects engaged in the Northwest Coast fur trade.[22]

This project was designed to strike where the Spanish were obviously weakest. A well-defended factory somewhere on the Northwest Coast on the east side of Queen Charlotte Sound, the main centre of the maritime fur trade some distance from Nootka, would place the British in the ascendant. Spain could not easily oust the British in view of the paltry naval forces available to the Spanish at San Blas, Guayaquil, or Valparaiso. Of course, the Spanish might send their own expedition from Europe, the Caribbean, or Manila to retake the British post. However, this was a risk the British evidently were prepared to take. Perhaps they knew that they were not contending with the Spanish navy as such but rather a provincial marine operating as an adjunct to the Viceroyalty of New Spain, whose commanders were not commissioned officers but poorly paid pilots commanding ships distinctly inferior to their British naval opponents. Even if the Spanish were to retake this distant Gibraltar, perhaps Britain would have had cause enough to war against Spain once more. War would not be desirable, of course, but previously it had come about for somewhat similar or even more trivial reasons; the severing of a British merchant's ear had sufficed to spark off the "War of Jenkins' Ear" with Spain in 1739. News of a similar outrage from the distant North Pacific might compel the British to declare war in defence of their sacred national honour and their new trade.

In terms of planning, the *Gorgon-Discovery-Sirius* project seems to have been wanting. London expected that after their arrival at Port Jackson, the *Gorgon* and *Discovery* would take in stores furnished by the new convict settlement and colonists supplied by Governor Phillip. Indeed the governor (who was to have jurisdiction over this domain many thousands of miles distant across the Pacific) was given discretionary powers as to "such articles of stores, provision, medicines and utensils for building, etc." as he thought necessary for a well-constructed settlement, one that would resist Indian attack and serve as a base for British maritime fur traders. Likely this would be a palisaded fort in an appropriate location near tidewater. Here seagoing vessels could be beached and repaired and here also wood and water would be readily accessible. London clearly misjudged the preparedness of the New South Wales colony for undertaking such a far-flung imperial venture. As an Australian historian has wryly written, "from the point of New South Wales it was no bad thing that the expedition never sailed."[23]

In the course of preparations, several modifications had to be made to the plan. At one time it was proposed that the *Discovery* would not go to Nootka as intended but instead pursue her original instructions to survey the South Atlantic and the southwest African coast for the encouragement of whaling. Then the frigate *Vestal* was detached from Indian service to proceed with the *Gorgon* from the Cape to the Northwest Coast. But because the *Vestal* was already bound home from the Cape, the Lords of the Admiralty decided that the *Discovery* would go with the *Gorgon* and, in addition, that one or two frigates from the East Indies squadron should be deployed by the senior naval officer, Commodore Sir William Cornwallis, to meet the *Gorgon* at Hawaii in December 1790. A subsequent modification called for the *Sirius,* the guardship at Port Jackson, if in fit condition, to sail for the Northwest Coast with the *Gorgon,* with some of the *Discovery*'s men and stores transferred to her. Later in the following spring or early summer a survey ship would be sent from England to the Northwest Coast.[24]

Ultimately, as the expedition's instructions became final in February 1790, it was evident that the government intended to send the force for the protection of British trade on the Northwest Coast and the establishment of an armed settlement near the north end of the Queen Charlotte Islands in 53°N latitude. The *Gorgon* and *Discovery* were to meet the *Sirius* from India at Hawaii. The *Sirius*'s captain would then assume command and sail for Nootka in the spring of 1791. On the coast he would establish the settlement near "a most favourable spot for communication" with the Canadian lakes and the suspected great sea of the west, survey the coast between 40° and 60°N to find the Northwest Passage, and ultimately rendezvous with a projected land operation crossing North America from the east. The expedition's commander was to ascertain if any British ships had been seized by the Spanish. If so, he was to demand satisfaction and restitution and, where necessary, capture the offending Spanish vessels. Then he would return to Botany Bay, where the *Discovery* was then to follow her previous orders for the South Atlantic.[25]

These instructions demonstrate the government's determination to underwrite the commercial enterprises of British merchants within the Pacific rim. The government had backed what Etches called in 1788 "our Intention . . . to adopt a Permanent system of Commerce direct from this country to the North West Coast and from thence to the Asian Coast, and Islands."[26] They had supported the demands of the Southern Whalers. They had co-operated with the Hudson's Bay Company in searching for the Northwest Passage from Hudson Bay. They had equipped an expensive expedition to establish a trading settlement under naval and military protection, not a private entrepôt but a government garrison to protect fur traders against any Spanish interference or native predators. All this had been done despite the fears of the East India Company and their supporters. England was embarking on a new phase of empire in eastern seas.

All was in readiness by 30 April 1790. The *Discovery* had been fitted and provisioned for sea; her complement had been filled. Lying at Deptford on the Thames, she was ready to proceed down the river to the open sea.[27] She might well have sailed had not John Meares arrived from Nootka Sound via Canton with startling information concerning Spanish interference with British trade and shipping on the Northwest Coast. This augmented what information the government had already received the previous January and forced it to reconsider the project of an armed settlement and, in fact, to employ a more drastic measure to convince Spain that they intended to open up the Pacific to British trade. For the moment, at least, the project was shelved. Stores and provisions from the *Discovery* were returned to their respective offices, officers and men were deployed in more active service, and Captain George Vancouver of the *Discovery* resumed employment under his old friend and patron Sir Alan Gardner, then in command of H.M.S. *Courageous,* awaiting further instructions from the Admiralty. The *Discovery* assumed the dreary task of receiving recently impressed seamen. She too was taking part, in a prosaic way, in preparing for war with Spain.

8

Conflicts of Ambition

The knowledge with which the foreign navigators are endowed and the superior quality of their ships at sea are two of the principal factors which make it impossible for me to affirm the solidity of the successes that one might have expected of the Russian fur-hunters . . . . there remains to us for a long time to come only the course of prudence and patience.

REPORT TO EMPRESS CATHERINE FROM THE
GOVERNOR GENERAL OF IRKUTSK, 13 FEBRUARY 1790

Britain had three rivals for the Northwest Coast—Russia, the United States, and Spain. Yet only Spain provided armed opposition to British designs. Spain's attempt to check British aggrandizement at Nootka Sound was only one act in a long series of such episodes between the two countries after the Seven Years' War ended in 1763. The Falkland Islands, Tahiti, and Nootka Sound are separated from each other by thousands of kilometres. Nevertheless, they formed focal points of Anglo-Spanish rivalry and integral parts of the contest for trade and dominion in the Pacific.

Spain claimed these and other realms within the Pacific as part of her imperial preserve. However, she was already overextended in Louisiana, Mexico, Central and South America, the Philippines, and west Africa. Given the resources at her disposal, Spain could not maintain her empire everywhere. The Northwest Coast lay on the fringe of her American dominions. She could not hope to check her rivals' ambitions here unless she had adequate naval and financial strength to meet any emergency that might threaten her interests in distant seas or, failing that, unless she had support from her ancient ally, France.

Spain's claims for the Pacific were unchallenged as long as Britain's interest in the southern ocean remained largely sporadic, as indeed it was before 1763. The long succession of English incursions into Spain's claimed oceanic preserve, including the voyages of Drake, Cavendish, Anson, and Byron, were fragile penetrations by armed enemy ships. Bold as they were, they hardly represented a grand design for English commercial and colonial hegemony in the southern ocean. In fact, they were little threat to Spanish claims.

After the Seven Years' War, the greatest chance for imperial aggrandizement lay with the paramount nation at sea. For the British, whose preponderant authority was now established, the way lay open to renew the old and largely unsatisfied Tudor ambitions. The nation had an expanding industrial base that needed new markets for manufacturers. Britain wanted to consolidate overseas trade and build trade alliances with native peoples. Not least, she fostered the scientific objective of delineating the most distant of oceans, the one least known to the European world.

In this great swing of British interests that laid the foundations of a new empire in eastern seas, the importance of bases, especially in time of war, seemed obvious to all imperial nations with overseas territories. In respect to both Nootka Sound on the Northwest Coast and Botany Bay in New South Wales, statesmen engaged in the same thinking as they did concerning the Cape of Good Hope and the Falkland Islands. These two imperial beachheads on opposite sides of the Pacific were important to the United Kingdom not simply because they might increase Britain's wealth but also because they would make foreign rivals—Spain or Russia in the case of the Northwest Coast and France or Holland in the case of New South Wales—more dependent on their existing holdings by excluding them from the advantages of trade that actual possession might provide. In other words, British strategists looked at these distant territories from two points of view: firstly, how they would suit national interests, and secondly, as a naval officer wrote, how they would "annoy us in other hands."[1] The British knew that the Cape of Good Hope, for instance, gave the Dutch a place of refreshment and repair for their shipping in the Indian Ocean and eastern seas as well as a place from which to extend their trade in South America. This "tavern of two oceans," as the Dutch affectionately called it, was coveted not only by Britain, but also by France, then smarting under the past humiliation of the loss of Canada. Britain could not afford to let France conquer and keep the Cape, for it was the key to India and eastern trade. During the wars of the late eighteenth century France captured the Cape once and Britain seized it twice, the second time in 1806, and kept it in order to forestall the French.

At the same time the British jealously watched rival ambitions with regard to the Falkland Islands. The importance of the Falklands to Britain had been pointed out by Lord Anson in the 1740's. In time of peace, he said, the islands could be of great consequence to the nation while in time of war they could make the British masters of the southern oceans.[2] Such a base would provide British whalers and other merchant ships with a convenient resting place en route to eastern seas. Subsequently, strategists believed a half-way house to the Pacific corresponding to the Cape should be established to stimulate trade in the Pacific and South America and to advance exploration of the Pacific. This base would counter Spain's head start in Chile, Peru, Mexico, and Manila. Perhaps also, they reasoned, it would check annexation of the Falklands by France or by Spain or, for that matter, by any other rival such as Holland.

In that mercantilist age the underlying national objective was to increase national security and military preparedness through trade. Thus, the Pacific assumed importance as a potential eldorado, a hitherto unknown world that might have riches that in some rival's hands would damage the nation's trade advantage or upset the delicate balance of power in Europe. Not only did the British want to go to the Pacific; they believed they were obliged to go there.

The rivalry for the Falkland Islands, these "few spots of earth, which in the deserts of the ocean had almost escaped human notice," as the satirist Samuel Johnson called them, were a prelude to the dispute over Nootka.[3] In 1764, after the loss of Canada, France had sent Bougainville to settle Fort Louis in the Falklands with Acadian refugees. Almost concurrently, the British Admiralty had sent Commodore John Byron to survey the islands and to establish a base there at Port Egmont. He found that the French had already established their rival base. The French withdrew, not because of Byron's demands, but because Spain claimed these lands on the basis of the moribund Treaty of Tordesillas. For the time being the British stubbornly maintained their fragile hold.

Meanwhile Spanish authorities in Madrid and Valparaiso watched this growth of British expansion with alarm and suspicion. Perhaps, they argued, Drake's anti-Catholic ambitions were being pursued once more. Perhaps the Falklands in British hands would give their ancient enemies a base from which to attack Peru's wealth or to settle Patagonia. Perhaps the annexation of Terra Australis Incognita, which had haunted French and British imaginations, would occur. Perhaps Tahiti, Hawaii, or even California would be seized. Thus, in 1767, the Viceroy of Peru sent ships to reconnoitre the Patagonian coast in search of British settlers. The Spanish also attempted to garrison the rocky and windswept barrens of Tierra del Fuego. Finally in 1770, a superior Spanish force captured the tiny and beleaguered British garrison at Port Egmont. War was avoided only by negotiations which restored the settlement to the British without prejudicing Spanish claims to prior right of discovery. The British, however, voluntarily abandoned the fort in 1774 and did so for financial reasons, leaving behind only a plaque and a British flag as a feeble register of British title.[4]

The Falkland Islands crisis showed that Britain could challenge Spain's imperial pretentions successfully. The Spanish had suffered, Dr. Johnson boasted, "a breach to be made in the outworks of their empire, and notwithstanding the reserve of prior right have suffered a dangerous exception to the prescriptious tenure of their American territories."[5] The "key to the Pacific," as the First Lord of the Admiralty glowingly described the Falklands in 1765, now became a frequent port of call.[6] Cape Horn grew as an entry to the Pacific. A varied collection of seafarers now doubled the Horn, including whalers, trepang hunters, pearl fishers, guano traders, and tallow and hide seekers. Missionaries from Spain, France, and the United States bound for Polynesia also passed the Horn. By the 1780's, the Falklands had become a frequent stopping place for some of these ships and for North Pacific whalers and maritime fur traders.

As in the Falklands, the Spanish attempted to check the rise of British activities in the South Pacific islands. Cook's voyages stimulated Spanish fears, for, as

Professor Harlow has written, "Generations of painful experience of English *corsarios* and smugglers did not make it easy for Spanish administration to accept the English in the unexpected garb of scientists."[7] The Spanish mistakenly regarded Cook's first Pacific voyage—to observe the Transit of Venus—as a mere pretext for further English raids and conquests. During his third voyage, Cook had possessed strict instructions to avoid Spanish-occupied dominions on the west side of the Americas and not to give offence to any Spanish subjects. The Spanish, however, aware of how much was at stake, made a feeble and unsuccessful attempt to secure their longstanding interest in Tahiti by sending two Franciscan priests there in 1775 to establish a protectorate and keep out the English.[8] As indicated by the potential costs of war with Britain and the insecurity provided by her unoccupied Pacific possessions' tenuous alliance with France, Spain could not hold these possessions. In these circumstances, British consolidation of claims to trade and dominion—at the Falklands in 1771, New South Wales in 1787, and Nootka Sound in 1789—could advance steadily, always with the real threat of war but with the margin of safety largely on the side of the British.

Spain's first concern for the fate of her claims to the far Northwest Coast began to mount in the early 1770's.[9] The Spanish ambassador at the Russian court at St. Petersburg warned Madrid that the Russians were advancing eastward across the top of the Pacific horseshoe. He reported that the explorer Alexei Chirikov had made investigations in 1769-71 and found that navigation along the Alaskan shore was less difficult than imagined. Alarmed, he reported that Tsarina Catherine II planned to send a fleet from the Baltic to Kamchatka via the Cape of Good Hope.

Such news brought an immediate response from Madrid. At the same time Spain learned that the British were mounting expeditions to find the Northwest Passage from Hudson Bay. Instructions were immediately issued to the Viceroy of Mexico, the closest authority, to learn if explorations were being pursued. Foreign incursions were to be halted by scouting the coasts for rivals and by developing appropriate plans for Spanish occupation. As the Viceroy put it, "any establishment by Russia, or any other foreign power, on the continent ought to be prevented, not because the king needs to enlarge his realms, as he has within his known dominions more than it will be possible to populate in centuries, but in order to avoid consequences brought by having any other neighbours [there] than the Indians."[10]

To check any foreign encroachment, in 1774 the Viceroy sent Juan José Pérez Hernández, then the most able and experienced pilot at San Blas, north on a secret voyage. Pérez made a landfall near the present Alaska-Canada boundary, where he met the Haidas of the most northern of the Queen Charlotte Islands and saw the southernmost point of the Alaska Panhandle, Dall Island. Pérez failed to push north, for the time that he could have used profitably in exploration had been foolishly wasted at San Diego and Monterey. All he learned of the Northwest Coast in that latitude was that it consisted of several offshore islands inhabited by vigorous natives. Timorous of proceeding north into heavy weather or of visiting shore to take on water and make a formal act of possession as instructed, Pérez sailed south to Nootka Sound, where he anchored in what he named "Roadstead of San Lorenzo." Pérez and the crew of his ship, the *Santiago,* became the first known whites to visit Nootka Sound. They traded with the Indians of Yuquot, who came to the ship in their canoes. Several warriors boarded the Spanish vessel, and one light-fingered Indian managed to steal several silver spoons. Four years later, James Cook bought these same spoons, recognized their provenance, and noted in his account that this was proof that the Spanish had been at or near Nootka Sound before him.

Pérez was much impressed with the strategic value of Nootka Sound, but did not send a party ashore to take formal possession. "This fateful omission," Warren Cook has written, "would have profound diplomatic consequences and be much lamented by Spanish officialdom."[11] Sailing south, Pérez missed the Strait of Juan de Fuca and reached his home port of San Blas with only a few charts and some rough notes of his voyage. Francisco Antonio Mourelle, who subsequently commanded a Spanish expedition over much the same track, complained of Pérez's voyage that despite considerable expense to the crown, "we are left almost in the same ignorance."[12] The Viceroy, obviously disappointed, told Madrid that Pérez's meagre accomplishments nonetheless would facilitate a follow-up voyage then in preparation. The following year, 1775, two explorers, Bruno de Hezeta and Juan Francisco de la Bodega y Quadra, were sent to reach 65° N latitude and then, on a southerly course, to take possession of convenient places on shore. They were also to trade with the Indians and demonstrate Spanish friendliness to the natives.

About this time the zealous Minister of the Indies, José de Gálvez, learned that Britain was sending James Cook to search for the western opening of the Northwest Passage. Now Gálvez recited a whole litany of fears: that the English by discovering the passage would outflank the Spanish on the north; that British traders would conduct illicit trade in these lands; that British settlers would settle the coast; that British agents would foment a revolution among Indians and colonial subjects in Spanish America. Might not "el famoso Capitan Kook" establish British claims to unoccupied territory and rights to trade and navigation and shatter dreams of a Spanish Pacific northwest?

On 20 May 1776, Gálvez directed the Viceroy of New Spain, Antonio Maria Bucareli, to take decisive measures to stop Cook's expedition: he was to withold supplies and all aid to the Englishman. If Cook's ships were encountered, they were to be apprehended and their papers seized so that a diplomatic presentation could be made to London protesting the encroachment. Two months later, after news reached Gálvez that Bodega had successfully explored the Alaska Coast and that Hezeta had discovered a great river on the Northwest Coast, later called the Columbia, he immediately ordered a third exploring expedition to be sent to the coast.

This development of Spanish policy by sea was related to a similar growth by land. At the same time, Gálvez reorganized the General Command for the Interior Provinces, a new jurisdiction in the American southwest separate from New Spain, one which would allow for the better administration of Texas, California and, in time, the Northwest Coast. Spain's power at Nootka depended on her power in the North American southwest. Eventually Indian raids in northwestern Mexico restricted the strength that Gálvez could draw on to extend his dreamed Pacific coastal dominion north and west and even to the Arctic.

For his part, Bucareli in Mexico City was anxious to oblige his superior and follow his instructions, but only if he had the necessary martial support to counter Captain Cook. The Spanish navy, he confessed to Gálvez, was too weak to oppose Cook by force, but he agreed to withhold supplies and aid from the British navigator.[13] Bucareli was plagued by a critical shortage of ships. He had few well-trained naval officers and men. His first concern was that Alta California be supplied regularly by sea. With some ships in dock, others in need of repair, and still others bound for the Alta California capital of Monterey with supplies, his slender marine resources were taxed to the limit. He believed that two frigates should be built at the naval yard at Guayaquil and sent north to further explore the Northwest Coast. Eventually the frigates *Princesa* and *Favorita* were readied. However, not until February 1779 did they head north from San Blas under command of Ignacio de Arteaga and Bodega to conduct an expedition ordered two years previously. This prolonged lapse augured poorly for Spanish interests.

In March 1779, one month after the *Princesa* and *Favorita* quit San Blas, Cook's ships left the Hawaiian Islands for the Arctic with no hint that two Spanish armed ships were in pursuit. In fact Arteaga was to be disappointed in his search: he never determined that Cook had visited the Northwest Coast though he explored north from Bucareli Sound (where the Spanish contemplated building a naval base) to Port Etches at Hinchinbrook Island, in Prince William Sound, the northernmost Spanish claim in America at 61°N.

Arteaga's investigations at Afognak Island near Kodiak revealed that the Russians, despite their energetic activities, were apparently confining themselves to the Aleutian Islands. These findings gave Spanish authorities a false sense of security. They allowed Carlos III and his ministerial advisers "to assume that Madrid could rest on its laurels and still retain dominion over that coastline, by virtue of previous discovery and symbolic acts of possession. No one foresaw that the decade to follow would bring traders of half a dozen nationalities swarming into the very area visited by Arteaga and Bodega."[14] In 1779, Madrid saw no reason to occupy the Northwest Coast with a garrison or settlement or even to claim Nootka. Indeed for nine years no Spanish navy ships ventured north from San Blas.

In 1788, however, Estéban José Martínez was given command of an expedition to Alaska. He had instructions to sail from San Blas in the frigate *Princesa* accompanied by the packet *San Carlos,* Gonzalo López de Haro commanding. He was to investigate vague reports that Russian ships were trading for sea otter skins on the Northwest Coast south of Mt. St. Elias in about 60°N. He was to determine if the Russians, as rumour stated, had erected establishments at various ports along the Alaska Coast.

Martínez, a central and controversial figure in the Nootka story, was a Sevillano, born in 1742. At the age of thirteen he began his naval career; and in 1773, at thirty-one, he was serving as second pilot at the Naval Department of San Blas. He had sailed north with Pérez to Nootka in 1774 and would have gone with Hezeta in the following year had not Pérez, no model himself, found him wanting in navigation and seamanship. For twelve years he patiently sailed supply ships between San Blas and Monterey, Alta California, a prosaic existence for such an ambitious man apparently destined to obscurity in the distant Pacific. Eventually his dedication brought him the approval of Bucareli as a competent and an able officer. Such an opinion ran counter to Pérez's assessment, and in view of Martínez's subsequent conduct during his Alaska voyage (which provoked the wrath of his fellow officers) and his high-handed actions at Nootka (which the British argued, precipitated the crisis) Pérez's report of incompetence seems the more reliable.

At bottom, Martínez was a patriot. In September 1786, he was in Monterey in command of two regular supply vessels from San Blas, the *Favorita* and *Princesa,* when the French explorer La Pérouse put into port for supplies.[15] La Pérouse had just called at Yakutat Bay, Alaska, and he gave Martínez first-hand information not only about the Russians' fort locations, but about their military strength and their future plans. Martínez, impatient for an important assignment, made the best of his information and warned both the Viceroy, Flores, and his superior, the Minister of the Indies, Gálvez.[16] Meanwhile, several British ships had come after Cook to exploit the sea otter trade. Martínez knew nothing of the details of Hanna's voyages, of Strange's two vessels, or of the Etches project. But he learned from La Pérouse the startling fact that the English were now conducting a highly profitable trade between Nootka and Canton. La Pérouse's news was sufficient to stir the Spanish from complacency. In the summer of 1787 preparations began at San Blas to assemble supplies and outfit ships for a northern voyage to regions hitherto unvisited by Spanish vessels.

At this time the Spanish had good reason to be frightened of Russian southward penetration from the Gulf of Alaska. As early as 1741 the Russian expedition of Bering and Chirikov had crossed the Pacific from the Kamchatka shore to Alaska—known to the Aleuts as the "great mainland"—where among the

Plate 1. Youthful portrait of
Sir Francis Drake from a locket miniature
said to have belonged to his first wife, Mary
Newman.

Plate 2. Drake's ship, the *Golden Hind,* rounding Point Reyes, 17 June 1579. Modern painting by Raymond
Aker.

Plate 3. Drakes Bay, California.

Plate 4. Plan of the Spanish port of San Blas, Mexico.

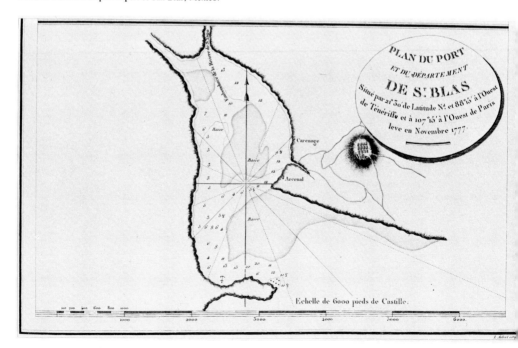

PLAN DU PORT
ET DU DÉPARTEMENT
DE St. BLAS
Situé par 21° 30' de Latitude N. et 88°15' à l'Ouest
de Teneriffe et à 107°35' à l'Ouest de Paris
levé en Novembre 1777

Echelle de 6000 pieds de Castille.

Plate 5. A young woman of
the Queen Charlotte Islands.

Plate 6. Maquinna, chief
of the Moachat tribe.

Plate 7. A view of the native habitations at Yuquot, Nootka Sound.

A CHART
of the
North West COAST of AMERICA and North East COAST of ASIA,
Explored in the Years 1778 & 1779.

N. The unshaded parts of the coast of Asia are taken from a M.S.
Chart received from the Russians.

PART OF AMERICA

Arctic Circle

PART OF ASIA

SEA OF OKOTSK

Plate 10. Cook's ships, the *Resolution* and *Discovery,* at Nootka Sound, 1778. Drawn on the spot by John Webber.

Plate 11. Interior of a native house at Nootka Sound, also by Webber.

John Meares, lieutenant in the Royal Navy
time fur trader. Engraving by C. Bestland
ainting by W. Beechey.

3. The long boat of the *Felice Adventurer*, Meares' ship, encountering native canoes in the Strait of Juan de Fuca.

Ship COLUMBIA of Boston off Point Ellice in the Columbia River
May 11th, 1792

Plate 17. Spanish exploring schooners *Sútil* and *Mexicana* off Point Roberts, Strait of Gerogia. The *Sútil* was commanded by Galiano and the *Mexicana* by Valdés.

Plate 18. The Spanish "insult" to the British flag at Nootka. This London engraving of 1791 shows the seizure of Captain James Colnett of the *Argonaut* by Don Estéban Martínez.

Clockwise from top left

Plate 19. Cayetano Valdés Florez.

Plate 20. Dionisio Alcalá Galiano.

Plate 21. Reputedly Captain George Vancouver, R.N.

Plate 22. Juan Francisco de la Bodega y Quadra, explorer of the northwest coast and Spanish emissary at Nootka in 1792.

Plate 23. Estéban José Martínez, commandant at San Lorenzo de Nuca.

Plate 24. Callicum and Maquinna, native chiefs from the west coast of Vancouver Island, 1790.

Plate 25. Vancouver's *Discovery* aground in Queen Charlotte Sound.

countless kelp beds they found immense quantities of two of the world's richest furs, Alaska seal and sea otter. The Russians soon erected advance posts for trade on the Okhotsk seaboard, the Kamchatka Peninsula, and the Aleutian Islands. Bering's second expedition, in 1741-42, yielded fifteen to eighteen hundred sea otter pelts. These were worth 80 to 100 rubles each at Kiatka, and defrayed a portion of the cost of the expedition.[17] Subsequently a large number of Russian fur traders were drawn to the Commander, Kurile, and Aleutian islands. They pushed eastward to the American coast and in 1784 had a fur station at Three Saints Bay on Kodiak Island. The closest European settlement was the Spanish presidio at San Francisco, founded fifteen years earlier.

By land and by sea the Russians pressed forward to establish their own distant dominion on the most northwesterly reaches of America. So extensive was Russian interest in the fur trade that between 1743 and 1800 some 101 ventures were undertaken by a total of forty-two companies, and nearly 187,000 pelts were taken (about ten per day)—worth in all about ten million rubles.[18] This was the most popular of all Russian merchant trades. What is surprising is that it took the Spanish and the English so long to discover that the Russians had established a prodigious new trade in Alaska.

In 1788 Martínez found that not only were the Russian traders building new settlements, as La Pérouse had reported, and sending ships from Kamchatka, but that Tsarina Catherine had outfitted an armed expedition commanded by an Englishman, Joseph Billings, a veteran of Cook's third voyage, to report on North Pacific prospects. Billings had elaborate instructions dated 1785 to explore the extreme northeastern parts of Asia, to visit the Aleutians, to make discoveries on the seas lying between Siberia and America, to report on the Alaskan fur trade, and to claim territory for Russia not previously discovered by any European power.[19]

Martínez's voyage to the Gulf of Alaska confirmed the worst fears of the Spanish court and the Mexican viceroy. From May to August 1788 he made a reconnaissance of the main islands and inlets of that remote coast. He found Russian traders solidly entrenched on many of the continent's island doorsteps east of the Aleutians. Martínez reported six Russian settlements in all, including those on Kodiak and Trinidad (Trinity) islands. Farther east, on the shores of Prince William Sound, he discovered a remnant of a European fort, an indication that Russians or perhaps Englishmen had been there already. The Russians had six small galleons, or "galliots," measuring fifty-three to fifty-eight feet, all armed—useful vessels for the then considerable trade with the natives. The Martinez expedition estimated the number of Russian occupants in the six posts at between 462 and 500, a considerable total in view of the obstacles of distance and environment.[20]

In itself, this information might have been sufficient warning to the Spanish that Russian occupation on the northeastern shores of the North Pacific was not only permanent but sizeable and increasing. As it was, Russian informants now told Martínez that the English were trading vigorously between Nootka Sound and Canton. And they warned him that the Russian sovereign had a better right to the Northwest Coast than any other nation because of the priorities of discovery. A further blow was that the Russian trader Potap Kaikov (or Cumsmich as Spanish accounts call him) candidly told Martínez that two Russian frigates and a schooner from Kamchatka soon would buttress Russian interests on the Northwest Coast by settling at the very focal point of what had now become every interested nation's concern, Nootka Sound. Specifically, the Russians aimed to block English commerce. According to Kaikov, his government intended to act in this way because a British maritime fur trader had boasted in Canton that Cook's priority of discovery gave the British the right to trade at Nootka and to possess land on the Northwest Coast.[21]

Martínez quickly decided to report these developments to his superiors. He recommended that his government forestall the Russians. The Spanish, he advised Flores, should send an expedition with as many forces as the Viceroy could spare for the object of occupying Nootka by May 1789. From his visit there with Pérez in 1774 and from Cook's account, he knew Friendly Cove would satisfy most requirements for a small naval base. By establishing such a garrison the Spanish would gain control of the whole coast from San Francisco to Nootka Sound and authority over all the native tribes.[22] The race to Nootka was on. Not only had Meares established his first, if only temporary, base there, he was also planning a substantial settlement. Yankee merchantmen were visiting the port and, more seriously, the Russians and Spanish intended to occupy the same place.

Spain also had a growing, though only recent, fear that the young United States might support their energetic Yankee fur traders by sending an expedition to cross the continent and establish a colony on the Pacific shore. "Obviously, this is a feat that would take many years," the Viceroy of Mexico warned Madrid, "but I truly believe that as of now we are threatened by the probes of Russia, and those that can be made by the English from Botany Bay, which they are populating."[23]

In fact by 1789, Spanish claims to the Northwest Coast had little chance of being upheld if Britain pressed her interests and if France did not support her Catholic ally.[24] Spain had no substantial interest in the fur trade between the Northwest Coast and Canton, although some pelts were arriving at Canton through Spanish hands.[25] However, in general, Spanish merchants had failed to prosecute a traffic that was giving American, Russian, and British rivals a bona fide claim to diplomatic support from their respective governments.

By contrast, Spain expected to maintain her claims by mere occupation of Nootka Sound and by rights of sovereignty under the Treaty of Tordesillas. She seems to have been outflanked on the coast between Alaska and Mexico by more aggressive commercial rivals, especially Britain, which was dominant in armed ships at sea. The cross and sword of Spain might be sufficient controls in Spanish America, but they would not answer on a maritime frontier where the economic wealth and the facts of oceanic geography dictated that a mere fort on the edge of the vast Pacific rim could not be held against all rivals, especially a great maritime power such as Britain, unless sufficient Spanish merchantmen and frigates could hold it through trade or by force. Thus all too late the Spanish came to realize, as Martínez had warned, that the Northwest Coast had a potential of its own and that true sovereignty over it could only be acquired by more than a small military garrison.

9

Dealing with the Dons

Superiority in naval power will henceforth consist in keeping up a proper naval establishment in discipline. The first naval nation to fall will be the one that is first caught napping. So that instead of resting upon our former naval renown it will be much more to the purpose to watch vigilantly that the renown is not made to suffer from the neglect of Governments to train fleets.

SIR CHARLES NAPIER, QUOTED IN
ADMIRAL SIR HERBERT RICHMOND,
STATESMEN AND SEA POWER

The immediate cause of the dispute between Britain and Spain for the distant dominion of the Northwest Coast was the thorny question of freedom of the seas. Spain, reactionary and defensive, wanted to exclude rivals. Britain, industrial and expansive, championed the rights of all nations to trade on the high seas. Nootka Sound saw these two principles in conflict. The same place subsequently witnessed the tide of the Spanish empire fall and that of the British empire rise. Ships of each empire, plying the distant seas of the Pacific, reflected the ambitions of their homelands. On the Northwest Coast, British merchant ships such as the *Iphigenia Nubiana,* commanded by William Douglas, posed no match for the armed might of Spanish naval vessels such as the corvette *Princesa.* By virtue of this local naval predominance Spain could exercise control at Friendly Cove. So far no British sloops-of-war loomed on the distant horizon of what still remained a backwater to English commerce.

Nonetheless, the merchant ships engaged in the maritime fur trade of the Northwest Coast in the five years beginning in 1785 were mainly English. Not counting Russian ships in Alaskan waters, of the thirty-three voyages of traders to the coast in this interval twenty-six were made by Englishmen; only seven were American.[1] When this profitable branch of seaborne trade became threatened by Spain in a manner they regarded as high-handed, the British government exercised its naval preponderance to force the Spanish to accept British commercial expansion in the Pacific. In the Nootka Sound crisis the British played a skilful game of diplomatic chess. Their sizeable fleet enabled them to make their moves from strength. No matter how exaggerated the claims of the intemperate trader John Meares, the cabinet of William Pitt the Younger believed that British merchants ought to be able to trade unmolested in what Spain regarded as her exclusive sphere of influence. In fact, these British statesmen intended to have their own way in dealing with the Spanish "dons"—by peace if possible, by war if necessary.

The *Iphigenia Nubiana*'s arrival at Nootka Sound on 19 April 1789 began a train of events that nearly brought Europe to war. In the spring of 1788 she sailed from China in company of Meares's *Felice Adventurer,* to spend the summer cruising the Alaskan coast in search of furs and to winter in the Hawaiian Islands with her consort, the *North West America.* Meares had taken particular pains to instruct her captain, William Douglas, to be on the Northwest Coast early the following spring in order to forestall any rivals. Douglas had faithfully arrived on time.[2] At Friendly Cove, he found that the rival *Lady Washington* of Boston, recently returned from a six weeks' cruise to the south of Nootka Sound with a good cargo of three hundred sea otter skins, would soon proceed to the rich north coast to trade.[3] To check his rival, Douglas, a spunky and highly competitive fellow, hastily readied the *North West America* for sea. His men beached her. Having no pitch or tar on hand, they nailed lead over gaping leaks in her hull. This done, they hauled her down the ways and quickly set to sea.

At this early stage the Spanish posed no threat to Douglas as his ship the *Iphigenia Nubiana* rode undisturbed at anchor. However, on 5 May, sixteen days after the *Iphigenia Nubiana*'s arrival, the *Princesa* anchored at Friendly Cove and immediately presented an overwhelming display of force to the British. Her commander, Commodore Estéban José Martínez, could now, if he so wished, exert the will of the King of Spain to exclude rival traders and claimants to sovereignty. However, the *Iphigenia Nubiana* bore Portuguese colours, to Martínez doubtless a curious national flag for an obviously British ship. First he cautiously inspected Douglas's papers. He found that one Juan Carvalho, a Portuguese merchant in Macao, apparently owned the vessel. He also discovered that the ship had not only Portuguese colours but, in fact, a Portuguese captain, Francisco José Viana. For these reasons he discreetly chose not to interfere with the *Iphigenia Nubiana.*

Nonetheless, Martínez did not want the foreign ship in the harbour. After all, his instructions bound him to fortify the port and exert his nation's influence to the exclusion of rivals. Could he not rid himself of the English threat by accepting Douglas's explanation, duly given, that the *Iphigenia* needed provisions and stores and was, in any case, waiting for Meares to arrive with these necessities before she could quit port? In this way Martínez could avoid an incident. Accepting this position, he quickly assisted the British to ready the *Iphigenia Nubiana* for sea. "At this time," the Americans Gray and Ingraham wrote, "there was not the least suspicion of any misunderstanding or disturbance among us, as Don Martinez was apparently satisfied with the answers each vessel had given to his request."[4]

On 12 May, however, the brig *San Carlos,* mounting sixteen guns, reached port from San Blas. Now Martínez had even more strength at his disposal. And on the same day the American trader Kendrick came from the inner reaches of the sound to Friendly Cove to welcome the Spanish. These new circumstances led Martínez to make his first arrest. His legal basis for doing this, he told Douglas, was that the *Iphigenia Nubiana*'s captain had orders to capture English, Spanish, or Russian subjects found on the Northwest Coast. They specified, to quote the document in question: "Supposing that in such a case you have superiority [in armament], then you should take possession of the vessel which attacks you, and of its cargo, bringing the ship and its officers to Macao, to be condemned as a legal prize, and officers and crews punished as pirates."[5] Martínez drew up an affidavit charging Viana and Douglas not only with trading illegally within the King of Spain's lawful domains but, even worse, with possessing instructions violating Spanish sovereignty. To these charges Douglas and Viana could not provide a suitable explanation, and on 14 May Martínez placed them under arrest. This was the first of several Spanish seizures of foreign ships, British and American, at Nootka Sound.[6]

Douglas clearly had not acted aggressively. Rather he had impressed upon Martínez that the *Iphigenia Nubiana* had been in a distressed state, that she lacked cables, thus making her less mobile in inshore waters, that she had no pitch to stop her leaks, and that she had no bread or other provisions except salt pork. Also Douglas made the telling point to Martínez that if the *Iphigenia Nubiana* had sailed for any port in Spanish America the Spanish would not have seized his vessel. Rather, as was customary, they would have supplied him with every material need. Heatedly he told Martínez that by making him a prisoner in a port where the King of Spain had never laid claim, he was doing "a piece of injustice that no nation had ever attempted before." However, Douglas sought to avoid a confrontation. He offered to leave Friendly Cove immediately rather than stay a prisoner, despite the fact that his ship was unseaworthy.[7]

Douglas's appeal to Martínez's good sense went unheeded. The Spaniard sent forty or fifty officers and men to board the *Iphigenia Nubiana*. They seized her as a prize and hoisted Spanish colours, disarmed her, and took her guns and ammunition on board their warships. They then demanded the keys to Douglas's sea chest. They took his charts, journals, and papers, indeed everything on the ship. In desperation, Douglas asked why Martínez had not captured the *Lady Washington* if he had orders to capture any foreign vessel on the Northwest Coast. To this Martínez could not answer satisfactorily. However, he repeated that Douglas's papers mentioned that the *Iphigenia Nubiana* was under instruction to take all English, Spanish, and Russian vessels of inferior force and to send the crews to Macao to be tried as pirates. In desperation Douglas countered by saying that although he did not understand Portuguese he had read English copies of the documents in Macao, and these specified that if he were attacked by any English, Spanish, or Russian ships he was to defend himself, and if he possessed armed superiority he was to send the captain and crew to Macao. Thus he would be exempted from Martínez's charges.

Now bullied by the Spaniards and cajoled by Kendrick, Douglas withstood a number of insults. He would have nothing to do with Martínez's undeclared ally Kendrick, whose complicity he rightly suspected. He objected to being ordered out of bed when he was sick and when the weather was poor. He objected to being incarcerated on board the *San Carlos*. Some of his personal effects were stolen, his officers detained, and half his crew divided between the two Spanish ships. He was given to understand that he and his ships would sail to San Blas under command of a Spanish captain, Don José Tobar. The Spaniards now completed the pillage, taking his provisions and all his trading goods—copper, iron, and manufactures.

These strange proceedings at Friendly Cove attracted the attention of the local Indians, who moved their lodges four miles away from Friendly Cove in order not to become involved in an Anglo-Spanish clash.[8] Martínez had forbidden Douglas and his men to approach the Nootka. The British nonetheless spoke to Maquinna and other chiefs about their arrest. The natives wanted to know if Douglas was not a "colt," that is, a slave. They claimed that as they were allies of "King George man" they would send canoes to carry Douglas safely out of Spanish hands.[9] Douglas asked the Indians to tell John Meares and Robert Funter of the *North West America* when they arrived not to enter Nootka Sound. Instead the Indians were to inform Meares and Funter that Douglas had been "cap chetld," that is, taken, which the Indians did. These developments seem to have been kept secret from the Spanish, who had failed to stop communication between the British and the Nootka.

On 22 May, Martínez ordered the *Iphigenia Nubiana,* recently caulked, to prepare to sail for San Blas. Handcuffs, conveniently crafted by Kendrick's armourer, were available to Martínez for use should Douglas prove obstreperous. A heated verbal exchange between Martínez and Douglas followed as the latter maintained that his papers did not imply the aggressions Martínez thought. "I told him," Douglas wrote, "if that was the only cause he had to allege against me, it would not be difficult for me to cast him in any court of justice in Europe." By now Martínez had taken everything out of the *Iphigenia Nubiana* that he wanted. As Douglas put it, the Spaniard had "robbed me of, in as gentle a manner as he possibly could."

However, at this stage, for reasons unknown, Martínez decided to return the *Iphigenia Nubiana* to Douglas and send her to the Hawaiian Islands rather than to Mexico. He insisted that Douglas sign a deposition which said that Martínez had found him at Nootka in a distressed condition and that although he had stopped his movements temporarily he had provided him with sufficient supplies to enable him to reach the Hawaiian Islands. Douglas might well have been content at having his freedom offered, yet he continued to be belligerent and stubbornly defiant. He refused to sign, on the grounds that the Spaniard had not only interfered with his progress but had seized his ship and taken possession of her contents. Again, Douglas argued that the Spanish could lay no claim to a port they had neither seen nor entered before. Finally, on the 26th, under pressure from English officers and men who wanted to return to the security of their own vessel, Douglas reversed his position and signed papers that admitted his guilt. Martínez now wanted Douglas to await the arrival of the *North West America* before sailing; that way he would be sure that neither ship would interfere with Spanish plans and that the *Iphigenia Nubiana* would not sail northward to trade. Douglas's reply, calculated to satisfy Martínez, was that he only had six weeks' provisions and that he would be obliged in any case to sail directly for Macao. Further, he said he had no trade items left with which to buy either sea otter skins on the Northwest Coast or provisions at the Hawaiian Islands. Martínez held a farewell dinner for Douglas on board the *Princesa* and on this occasion the invited guests, Kendrick and other Spanish and American officers, employed every subtle method to find out if Douglas intended to sail northward to trade. "I gave them the same answers as before," the wily Douglas recorded, "telling them I had no intention to throw away the lives of my people. On this day they drank my health, wishing me a good voyage to Macao, and accompanied it with thirteen guns."

After dinner Douglas gave orders to get his ship underway, and the *Iphigenia Nubiana,* still wearing Portuguese colours, passed by the Spanish port on Hog Island. The fort saluted with five guns but Douglas did not return this, begging a shortage of ammunition. The wind blew favourably from the north, and the *Iphigenia Nubiana* stood for the southward under full sail. By sunset the entrance to Nootka Sound lay seven or eight leagues away to the north-northwest, a sufficient distance, Douglas concluded in his journal with obvious relief, to be "out of the hands of my enemies."

The urgency of Douglas's movements and his belief in the legitimacy of his cause now become evident. He had no intention of running for Macao with only sixty or seventy sea otter skins. His crew, he wrote, were used to short allowance. He believed that the Spanish would not let Kendrick sail north to prosecute the fur trade north of Nootka Sound, and he knew that the *San Carlos* was not ready to sail northward from Friendly Cove to police the coast against foreign intruders. He accurately judged that the precious short interval belonged to him. At midnight he put his ship on the opposite tack and headed north. He hoped to meet the *North West America,* intending, if he did, to take her crew and cargo and destroy her by fire at sea if unable to keep her as his consort. He clearly had no intention of letting the valuable little schooner fall into rival hands, Spanish or American. He had won his freedom from Martínez, whose resolve had not yet been steeled.

Perhaps Douglas's return to the coast was inadvisable under the circumstances, for he had withstood the Spanish challenge once but might not succeed a second time. Perhaps, however, he felt that with the testy Meares likely to arrive he would be able to contest the Spanish claims to sole rights of navigation on the

Northwest Coast. Nonetheless, he was intent on completing his cargo of furs to make his passage to China profitable, especially if he could make the likely rendezvous with the *North West America*. If Kendrick's successful cruise southward in the *Lady Washington* from Nootka Sound provided any indication, further trade there could be highly profitable to the Meares syndicate. Douglas correctly predicted a bountiful commerce. During the following month he traded for seven hundred sea otter skins on the coast. However, he failed to sight the *North West America*, now coasting southward towards Nootka Sound, and he sailed to Canton with his cargo.

Meanwhile the *North West America* had put into her home port of Friendly Cove on 8 June. Her captain, Funter, had been looking for Douglas's *Iphigenia Nubiana*, expecting her to be there. Instead, to his surprise, he found Martínez and the two Spanish warships lying in wait for him. On the 9th, Martínez, having previously wined and dined Funter and his chief officer Thomas Barnett, searched the British schooner. They detained her on charges similar to those delivered to Douglas. The Spanish seized 207 sea otter pelts, incarcerated the crew on the Spanish ships, and beached the British ship for caulking in preparation for her use as a coastal exploration vessel they then needed.

Almost a week passed before the next English ship reached Nootka Sound. On 15 June a Spanish sentinel on Hog Island at the sound's entrance saw a ship approaching. Martínez hurriedly took two launches to bring in the visitor. She turned out to be yet a third Meares ship, the fifty-ton *Princess Royal*, a veteran in the trade on her third annual visit to the Northwest Coast, this time in command of Captain Thomas Hudson. The *Princess Royal* had been sent not only to trade but also to assist in the English colonization of Nootka Sound. The sight of two strange launches sailing out from Friendly Cove surprised Hudson. He hurriedly put his ship in the best state of defence time would permit. When the Spanish launches arrived just under cover of darkness, gun crews manned two cannon. From the launches a voice in English asked if Charles Duncan was still in command; no, a crew member shouted in reply, Hudson had succeeded Duncan as master. Some suspicious person on board the *Princess Royal* demanded to know if the launches were armed. "Just with a bottle of brandy!" a Spaniard replied in spirited fashion. To this Hudson obligingly replied, "come aboard, and about time!"[10] We can sense Hudson's astonishment when he found that his visitors were not his long-looked-for countrymen. Rather, they were rivals dressed in Spanish uniform about to subject him to the authority of Don Carlos III.

Hudson, however, did not bear the same papers as Douglas. What documents he possessed were neither Portuguese nor offensive to the Spanish. His plea, by now the standard explanation of being in distress after a 116-day stormy crossing from Macao and of needing repairs, water, and firewood, was made to the commandant. Martínez subsequently came to an understanding with Hudson that the *Princess Royal* would continue her voyage as soon as the British attended to these needs. Thus, while the *North West America* lay at Friendly Cove, detained by the Spanish, her sister ship the *Princess Royal* was able to put to sea, unmolested, on 2 July.

While the English sloop was sailing out of port, James Colnett's *Argonaut* was nearing Nootka Sound. Through the fog Colnett could see a vessel bearing away to the southward, but he could not be sure if it was Hudson's ship or the *Lady Washington*. Canoes came out to the *Argonaut,* and the Indians told Colnett numerous stories about the feverish activities of ships on the coast. But these were too confusing for Colnett to interpret with accuracy. Thus he proceeded towards Nootka Sound without proof that the Spanish were already there. Near the entrance to Nootka Sound a Spanish launch bearing Martínez approached, who delivered to Colnett a copy of Hudson's letter written the same day. This confidently indicated that if Colnett entered Friendly Cove Martínez would, in Hudson's words, "order every Assistance in his power as he has done me."[11] Colnett later regretted that Hudson had failed to take some precaution to warn him, such as by sailing northward after leaving Nootka Sound in keeping with his instructions.[12]

Colnett's account of the proceedings, understandably varying in content as well as in tone from that of Martínez, reveals his rising resentment against his Spanish rival. These two protagonists at Nootka Sound have been compared before. Certainly they make a curiously well-matched pair of agents provocateurs. Both were unbridled patriots. Both possessed a boundless attachment to duty in the names of their kings and countries. Both had a tendency to be heavy-handed. There the parallel ends. Martínez, desperately seeking to follow orders, at first hesitated but ultimately acted to avoid the censure of his superiors. Colnett was plagued by a tendency towards mental instability under stress. Both of these responses attract attention but mainly to the degree that they add to the understanding of the pressures under which each was living.

On his arrival at Nootka Sound in 1790 Colnett was in his thirty-eighth year. Plymouth-born, he had served with Cook as midshipman and had been in continuous sea service since 1770. Subsequently gunner and master, he became lieutenant on 4 February 1779. Twice, in 1787 and 1788, he had traded on the Northwest Coast for the Richard Cadman Etches concern in command of the *Prince of Wales*. A skilled and responsible sailor, he seemed the sort of commander Etches and Meares needed to superintend the building of their Nootka establishment.[13]

As Colnett had drawn closer to land he had suspected a Spanish trap. In fact, he had instructed his chief mate, Robert Duffin, to anchor outside Nootka Sound rather than sail past Hog Island into a roadstead where the Spanish might be the superior power and where the American ships also lay. Colnett went below deck expecting that Duffin would follow his instructions. When the noise of the ship's anchoring brought him again on deck he found to his mortification that the *Argonaut* lay within Friendly Cove. The *San Carlos,* lying off Hog Island, blocked any retreat to the Pacific. Duffin had either misunderstood or wilfully disobeyed Colnett's order. Colnett suspected that the mate intended to profit by a private and what, under terms of his articles for the voyage, would have been an illegal trade in skins.[14] Colnett, now trapped, determined to leave the port by getting to the mouth of the sound the next morning, from where he could sail to open waters. However, when Colnett received the copy of Hudson's letter his fears were allayed. Indeed, as yet no hint existed as to Martínez's designs.[15]

When "the Commandant," as Colnett frequently called Martínez, came on board the British ship, he told the Englishman that he could stay at Friendly Cove for some time. Colnett replied that he would, providing Martínez would give him leave to build the schooner *Jason,* the materials for which he had on board the *Argonaut* in frame. Martínez refused, for fear of being found at fault by the Viceroy. Colnett countered by saying that under these circumstances he could not stay but that he would supply the Spaniard with "all his Distresses which was the chief cause for my coming into port." Nothing could have been further from Colnett's intentions. His explanation to Martínez as to the reasons for his arrival were unabashedly false. Martínez said he would take little from the Englishman, for he intended to send an American ship to Monterey for supplies. Moreover, he expected the supply ship *Aranzazú* at any moment. The two ate and drank late, and in the early morning of 4 July Colnett accompanied Martínez at the latter's request on board the flagship *Princesa.* However, he was barred from entering Martínez's cabin, the first indication of trouble for Colnett.

In the morning Colnett was again on board the *Princesa,* this time to accept Martínez's offer of breakfast. They exchanged cordialities, first on board the *Princesa* and then on the *Argonaut.* But Martinez picked an argument when he discovered Colnett's boatswain to be a native of Gibraltar, and on demand Colnett freely gave him up to the Spaniard, agreeably offering other sailors to the Spanish, as he had plenty to spare. Colnett might have taken offence, because Gibraltar was then as now a British possession, and the boatswain was in debt to the *Argonaut.* Perhaps he wanted to avoid an altercation on this point, having more important things on his mind. But when he sought Martínez's help to get towed out of the cove, the commandant refused, saying he had not yet seen Colnett's papers.

In Martínez's cabin, the Spaniard produced for Colnett's inspection his printed book of regulations ordering the capture of all English vessels on the coast. "I calmly told him the service I had been in," Colnett righteously recorded,

and that I had served for upwards of 20 years for his Britannic Majesty which fully made me acquainted with his exalted station, at the same time requesting him to examine my papers which would inform him I had occupied for years past a very respectable station in the Royal Navy of Great Britain, and that he would also find, that I had his Majesty's permission for being in those seas, and to quit his service for that purpose, who had also furnished me with a Grant and a License for five years and that the papers were then on his Table, which I again and again entreated him to peruse.[16]

Martínez answered bluntly that not only were Colnett's papers forged but that he regarded him as a pirate.

Colnett now challenged Martínez about the legality of his detention. He told him that his actions were unbecoming an officer and described how the law of nations applied in such cases. He reminded Martínez of his earlier promise to let him quit port and told him it was ethically wrong to imprison a man who had put himself in the other's power. Martínez replied that he had not captured him but only detained him and that Colnett could not sail until he pleased. This, Colnett countered, was unprecedented. He told Martínez that he intended to sail even with his colours struck and even defenceless, "for I was not prepared for war having only two swivels mounted."[17]

At this, Colnett says, Martínez became outraged. He flew out of the cabin, brought in sailors armed with muskets, and confined the protesting Colnett to the cabin. Martínez's version is that as Colnett grew heated he two or three times placed his hand on his sword, thereby threatening the Spaniard in his own cabin, and insulted Martínez by shouting "God damned Spaniard."[18] Martinez subsequently seized the *Argonaut* against the protests of Chief Mate Duffin (who now charged that Colnett, by his intemperate actions, had prevented him from trading privately on the coast). A Spanish garrison was put on board and the main hold cleared of its cargo. Colnett again protested, saying that the Portuguese and American ships had been unmolested. Colnett eventually learned that these ships had no valuable cargo like the eighty-four sheets of copper that the *Argonaut* carried for the Indian trade. He also understood that the Spanish had entered into partnership with Kendrick in the maritime fur trade.[19] Colnett, now deranged by discomfort from five sleepless nights, continued his complaints against Martínez, who, he wrote, "still went on plundering and destroying."[20] On one occasion Colnett, acting as if he intended to urinate at the rail, attempted to jump overboard but was stopped by a guard. On another, he climbed through a port hole and dove into the icy water, but he was recovered, half-drowned, by the crew of a launch.[21]

Meanwhile, Colnett's *Argonaut* had been undergoing a refit for a voyage to San Blas for Colnett's trial by the Viceroy. On 14 July, under command of Tobar, she set sail for the Mexican naval base. The English sailors confined below her decks found this a tediously hot and uncomfortable passage. Some officers were kept in irons, but not Colnett and Duffin who remained under guard. Thoughts of retaking the ship raced through Colnett's mind, but Duffin, whom Colnett suspected of being in league with Martínez in order to claim part of the cargo at San Blas, failed to take advantage of good opportunities afforded by the constant drunkenness of the Spanish officers.[22] Colnett was in no condition to get up a mutiny: poorly fed and suffering from scurvy, he spent the thirty-two-day voyage in utter misery.

In mid-August the *Argonaut* came to anchor in the River St. Iago, the harbour of San Blas. The tepid climate, poor food, mosquitoes, and fever added to the Englishmen's misery. Eight British sailors died in this hell-hole, mostly of tropical ailments. In a fit of rage one of them slit his own throat with a razor. Though prisoners, they soon were given the run of the town. They were even given salaries equivalent to that of Spanish sailors. All the while they awaited the decisions of their captors. In mid-November authorities moved them inland to the upland town of Tepic, a comparatively temperate and healthy place. Here the English were amused by the actions of the local priest, who promoted Protestant-hating by staging a morality play called "Henry the Eighth" in the town plaza. Colnett and his fellow countrymen took it all in good humour. "We always attended ourselves and laugh'd at it," Colnett wrote,

> and explain'd the life of Henry, etc., which few of them knew. It had not the desired effect; and even the young lady that acted Ann Bullen prefer'd acting the more amorous part of Henry's Character with some of my Officers in Private to that in Public, and latterly refus'd to play at all without being better paid for it than an absolution of Sins from the Padre. When we left the Country she had grown very fat and was past playing.[23]

Nonetheless, the months passed slowly for the English at Tepic. Colnett appealed to the Viceroy in Mexico City, Count Revillagigedo, for justice. He and his men seemed resigned to their fate, depending on the intervention of Great Britain after news of their seizure at Nootka reached Canton through American traders.[24] Meanwhile the Spanish used the captured vessels to good effect. In the *Argonaut* they brought cannon from Acapulco; and they sent the *Princess Royal* (now the *Princesa Real* under Spanish colours) north to deliver supplies to Nootka and then to explore the Strait of Juan de Fuca.[25] Colnett objected to the use of these ships without restitution for damages sustained and without condemnation by a Spanish admiralty court. About the time he appealed to the Viceroy in Mexico City he met the new commandant of San Blas, Don Francisco de la Bodega y Quadra, a captain in the Spanish navy and an impressive and wealthy officer later to become known in the history of the Northwest Coast for his cordial relations with Captain George Vancouver at Nootka. Bodega told Colnett that soon he would be permitted to sail freely in the *Argonaut* without losing anything and, more significant, that he intended in a few days to order that the British declaration be taken against Martínez for "capturing and robbing us."[26] Colnett had found an unexpected ally, and subsequently Spanish authorities disavowed Martínez's acts at Nootka Sound.

Meanwhile, at Yuquot, Martínez had replaced the British flag with the Spanish standard and proclaimed that the coast from Cape Horn to 60°N belonged to his sovereign. In so doing, he reasserted Spanish claims to the west side of the Americas north as far as the Russian settlements on Kodiak Island. He had been sent, the English suspected, "for the purpose of reconnoitering the new establishments of the Russians in the North of this Continent." As correct as that might have been, they now knew that he aimed to give notice to Russians and others that the Northwest Coast from Monterey, the administrative capital of Alta California, to 60°N was closed to foreigners. This northern limit to Spanish aspirations, it may be noted, reflected Madrid's knowledge that Russia intended to develop a large naval station and commercial depot in the region of Cook Inlet. This was where Meares had discovered a small Russian entrepôt during his first voyage to the coast in 1786. By mid-1790 Britain knew that Russia acknowledged Spain's claim to exclusive sovereignty on the Northwest Coast as far as Cook Inlet and planned to build an organized settlement there. This project was completed shortly after the Anglo-Spanish crisis.[27]

At this same time in Europe, ministers of state and chargés d'affaires busied themselves with unravelling the details of the incident at Nootka Sound. They realized that they were not bargaining for a few yards of beach or a ship or two but for the future development of the Pacific and its resources. The Spanish government learned of the Nootka Sound seizures from the Mexican Viceroy long in advance of the information that leaked through to London from Canton via traders and shippers. The Spanish felt duly wronged and assumed the diplomatic offensive. In strong language that the English considered high-handed under the circumstances, they informed the British government of Spanish claims to 60°N and even to the southern extremity of Russian interests. This information reached the British ministry in mid-January 1790. The British cabinet quickly undertook to deal with the matter "with a high hand." The impatient Foreign Secretary, the Duke of Leeds, was evidently convinced of the strong possibility of war. He demanded that Spain immediately release the vessel *Argonaut* on the basis that until this was done no discussions about territorial claims could take place between the two nations. Shortly thereafter the Prime Minister, William Pitt, rebuked Leeds for his uncompromising stance. Pitt sought the maintenance of cordial relations with Spain, not war, for George III had no wish to break the peace. Moreover, Britain was then seeking a treaty of reciprocity to increase the sale of manufactured items in Spanish America through Spanish ports.[28] Thus if the British government could get its way by peaceful means all the better, but if war was the only alternative, Pitt knew that the Spanish had to be so warned. After his disagreement with Leeds, Pitt drafted most of the dispatches to Spain.

For two months the two governments disputed the issue, trenchantly clinging to their positions. Spain did not want war either, nor did she wish to admit Britain into her precious Pacific territory. In an attempt to appease the British, the Spanish foreign minister, Count Florida Blanca ordered the release of the *Argonaut,* trusting that compensation to the British for damages might be resolved later. But the British wanted recognition from Spain of the legality of their Pacific invasion and acceptance of British trade with Spanish America. The issues surrounding Nootka were important indeed. "Imagination refuses to picture nearly half the water surface of the world long barred to the shipping of all nations except the most reactionary powers of the Old World," J. Holland Rose wrote. "Yet that was what was at stake."[29]

The British ministry could not rely solely on the information that Madrid sent to London. Thus they patiently waited for full and accurate details from the Northwest Coast, information that would allow them to prepare a strong diplomatic counter-offensive against Spain. In early April, Meares arrived from China with documents that formed the basis for his celebrated *Memorial,* a document that listed Spanish insults to the British flag.[30] Meares told of the seizure of Douglas's *Iphigenia Nubiana,* and brought to London sworn testimony from Douglas concerning the Martínez affair. Now the government knew that four British ships had been molested and seized, three of which had lost their crews and cargoes to the Spanish. Moreover, the ministry learned of the seizure of Meares's shore establishment. Exaggerated rumours about Colnett's insanity as a result of Spanish brutality further seasoned British complaints against Spain.

The British ministry listened to Meares's complaints at a meeting of inquiry.[31] Pitt, William Grenville, Secretary of State, and Leeds all wanted satisfaction for Spain's interference with their nation's commercial interests. In addition, they wanted Spanish recognition of British commercial expansion in the Pacific. The British cabinet demanded an apology, compensation, and subsequent negotiations concerning territorial claims. The British government was in no position to back down in their demands. No British administration concerned with political stability and its future in office could shy away from such a situation. "Sixty years earlier, Sir Robert Walpole had ignored the excited resentment of merchants against the 'involence' of Spanish *guarda costas* and had refused to take official action when Capt. Jenkins had inflamed public opinion with his accounts of ill-usage and his exhibition of a severed ear; and in consequence Walpole had been driven into a war which had terminated his long and useful career. On the present occasion Meares had even more formidable propaganda material at hand than his predecessor: he represented more extensive claims; and the crisis came when the British were penetrating the Pacific from all sides."[32]

This data gave the British government precisely the fuel they needed to require from Spain "immediate and adequate satisfaction for the outrages" committed by Martínez. On 30 April the cabinet ordered a squadron of ships to be outfitted "in order to support that demand and to be prepared for such events as may arise."[33] The treasury allocated £1,000,000 for defence purposes. General preparations were made for war. Colonial governors received instructions to put local defences in order. On 5 May the King's message to Parliament explained the ministry's position. This seems to have been well received except by Charles Fox, who wondered why references to British territorial claims to Nootka Sound were not mentioned. And why, Fox asked, had Parliament not been informed what the British ships were doing there, "whether they were about to make an establishment, or whether Spain knew that we were about to make an establishment"?[34] This opposition forced Pitt to modify government policy but still keep a firm stance against Spain.

In the years of his ministry, Pitt had not neglected the British fleet. In 1783, Captain Sir Thomas Byam Martin, R.N., had complained that not a sound ship existed in the fleet; several men-of-war returning home from Newfoundland had foundered on the Grand Banks because of their "ill construction and rickety condition."[35] After the American Revolution, however, Britain's naval forces had been increased under Pitt's government. Decaying ships had been scrapped, others with life strengthened, and new ships' bottoms laid down. Using improved designs by the celebrated naval architect Sir Robert Seeping, public dockyards and private yards built better ships than before. During this reconstruction period Pitt held the comptroller of the navy, Sir Charles Middleton (the future Lord Barham), personally responsible for the conduct of this important national business and frequently visited Middleton's office to investigate the progress of the new construction.[36] Thus in the brief space of ten years the government had brought the Royal Navy to a highly prepared state.

Two days after the government had demanded "immediate and adequate satisfaction" from Madrid, the cabinet instructed the Navy Board to prepare a preliminary fleet of twenty-nine ships-of-the-line. Of these, fifteen were in service, while fourteen others, known as the guardships, needed only an increase in crews and stores to be ready for sea. Immediately, therefore, a nucleus force existed. Subsequently, fifteen frigates were also fitted out. The battleships, fit to stand in line against Spanish or French battleships, received priority.[37]

At the same time, the government issued orders to get seamen for these ships. The press began on 7 May and a bounty was offered to volunteers. But the newly impressed men and the recruits were frequently unsuitable: the commander-in-chief at Plymouth, Vice-Admiral Graves, thought many of them fit only for hospitals. Another admiral at Portsmouth, the Duke of Clarence, complained of "no provisions and very few men," though, "by scrapings and various other methods I have a few hundred shabby sheep." "Excepting the gunners and quarter masters," he wrote to the King, "I have not a man in the ship either as old as myself or has been long at sea. Another extraordinary circumstance is that none of the seamen have yet had the honour of serving your majesty."[38] As long as the new recruits could man the guns and tend the sails that was all that really counted, Admiral Samuel Barrington said with some frankness. Because haste mattered most in preparing for war with Spain, he ordered the fleet "to exercise without regard to form, but to perfect the men with the guns and sails."[39] Gradually, however, the number of seamen increased. Before the impressment order, the Navy had 17,340 seamen on wages. Within a month this had risen to 25,325 and in October it had grown to 55,508. A similar pattern is revealed for the Marines: in April there were 3,692; in October 5,337.[40]

By 24 June 1790, Barrington had assembled a sizeable fleet at Torbay on the English south coast, where it was hoped such a public display of force would be noticed by the sharp eyes of Spanish spies. This fleet, consisting of twenty-nine ships-of-the-line, nine frigates, two sloops, four cutters, and two fireships, formed the most powerful mustered by the Island Power up to that time.[41] During August and September this fleet, under Admiral Lord Howe, cruised at sea. Its station was thirty leagues west of Ushant between $49° 30'$ and $47° 35'N$, a latitude close to that of Nootka Sound but off a continental shoreline where the destiny of the Northwest Coast of North America was being determined through a cat and mouse game involving government stability, fleet diplomacy, and artful stratagems.

For weeks Howe's fleet patiently kept its position, signifying England's willingness to do battle if her demands over Nootka were unacceptable to Spain. From time to time Howe detached small ships to spy on French and Spanish port activities and to gather any information about rival preparations. Ultimately the Admiralty learned that the Spanish had thirty-one ships-of-the-line and nine frigates at sea, a force equal to that of the British.[42] In these tight circumstances, Howe sought clarification about what to do if he met with the Spanish fleet. The matter was sufficiently critical to warrant a cabinet meeting. Subsequently London instructed Howe that if he were to meet the rival fleet off Brest, the French naval base, he should tell the Spanish to return south and if they failed to comply to do battle. Furthermore he had instructions to use force if necessary to prevent any French fleet from joining their Spanish allies off Brest.[43] In other words, Howe's squadron was fully ready for battle at sea if Spain or France should contest the declared demands of Britain for Nootka and for the freedom of the south seas.

The Admiralty had long known that Spain's seaborne strength could not be discounted. In April and May, consuls at Cartegena and Cadiz reported active preparations. By early 1790 the Admiralty estimated Spanish strength at sixty-four ships-of-the-line with an additional seven under construction and forty-three frigates with an additional six under construction. Excellent maintenance facilities, especially at Cadiz, enabled Spain to get ships to sea quickly. She was less capable in her ship design, manpower, and supply system. Nonetheless, Britain had a healthy respect for the fighting capabilities of the Spanish; if the British had not neglected their fleet after 1783, neither had the Spanish.[44]

What the Spanish lacked, however, was a reliable alliance with France. For twenty-nine years since 1761, the two nations had been united by the Family Compact of the Royal House of Bourbon. Charles III had aided France during the last phase of the Seven Years' War. Similarly, when Louis XIV supported the rebellious Thirteen Colonies against Britain, Spain had followed its ally into war. During the Nootka crisis Spain naturally turned to France, expecting support against the inveterate enemy of both nations. She desperately needed a clear endorsement of the Family Compact against Britain's rising belligerence.

But in the summer of 1790, when Spain was in its greatest need, France was in no position to give immediate aid. Some months previously the National Assembly had authorized the armament of fourteen ships-of-the-line as a precautionary measure in view of English naval preparations. In the interim a protracted debate occurred in the Assembly on the question of whether the King or the Assembly had the right to declare war and peace. Ultimately this contentious issue for a nation in revolution was resolved in favour of the Assembly. This meant that it now had to approve Spain's urgent request. A six-week delay followed. The popular party remained stubbornly loath to support a foreign aristocratic government. Besides, Pitt had sent emissaries to influence the great orator Mirabeau, who denounced the compact as autocratic and declared that it must be replaced by a democratic one. Eventually, on 26 August, the Assembly decreed the equipping of an additional forty-five ships-of-the-line.[45] This brought vigorous protests from the British government. London was not about to be influenced by this weighty pressure. Leeds told Alleyne Fitzherbert, the Ambassador in Madrid, that he was to tell the Spanish court that the intervention of France would not make Britain abandon any of her present demands. He added sarcastically, "the sailing of a French squadron will be a tempting morsel to our hungry Tars."[46]

The Assembly also declared that France would not go to war to make conquests. Nor would she employ her armed forces against the liberty of a people. The implication was clear: by abandoning Spain the Family Compact was annulled. France weakened Spain's claims to Nootka and indeed to the sole trade and navigation on the west coast of the Americas. One historian has claimed that Mirabeau gave "Spanish Columbia" to England.[47] This is true in the sense that without France's aid Spain could no longer support her position through force. Now in uncomfortable isolation and facing British preponderance at sea and possible enemies in Britain's allies, Prussia and Holland, Spain backed down. The Spanish conceded that which they had so long opposed—"the buildings and tracts of land" in British possession in April 1789.

On 28 October representatives of the two kingdoms signed the Anglo-Spanish Convention in Madrid. Under this agreement Spain agreed to restore Meares's buildings and lands, to compensate Richard Cadman Etches, Meares, and their associates for their losses, to allow the British to trade without molestation and make establishments on the Northwest Coast, and to permit British whalers to sail the Pacific. For Britain's part, her whalers were not to sail within ten leagues of the west coast of the Americas, a measure designed to prevent illicit trade with Spanish settlements. Britain did not win from Spain a precise demarcation of the extent of Spanish dominion. What was the northern limit of the "Coast of California"? The British could get no satisfactory answer, but given their preference for commercial expansion, territorial ambition took a much lower position of importance, provided depots of trade could be established on the Northwest Coast. "We are not contending for a few miles, but a large world," Henry Dundas retorted to Opposition critics. "We did not insist on any right to invade the colonial rights of other nations in order to extend our Commerce; but the spirit of commercial adventure in this country was unbounded."[48]

This mobilization of the British fleet, the so-called "Spanish armament," had a decisive influence. As a later controller of the navy wrote, the armament afforded "proof of great exertions, and speaks volumes as to the opinions of Mr. Pitt with respect to the necessity of having the navy in great strength and ready for immediate action."[49] The exercise of "fleet diplomacy," which had its parallel in the Oregon Crisis of 1846, had served the British well.[50] The wisdom of having a strong navy, useful alliances, adequate finances, sufficient material and ample manpower, to say nothing of adroit statesmanship, had again been revealed to the nation.

In the Nootka Sound crisis Britain won a diplomatic victory important both for her Pacific trade and for the eventual extension of her North American dominions, although the full impact of the latter may not have been realized at the time. A chink had been made in the Spanish armour. Even so, at that time only a few far-seeing men such as Alexander Dalrymple, Hydrographer of the Admiralty, Sir Joseph Banks, botanist and President of the Royal Society, Alexander Mackenzie, the fur trader, and Sir John Simcoe, Lieutenant-Governor of Upper Canada, dreamed of transcontinental British North American dominion. Yet the origins of a Canada from sea to sea were born as a result of the Nootka Convention of 1790. What made this possible? British desires for commerce, a wish to remove Spanish pretentions and, lastly, the exercise, albeit peaceful, of British superiority at sea. The ancient Spanish obstacle to a British distant dominion of trade and sovereignty had been removed for all time, and it remained for Captain George Vancouver to explore the coast from Lower California to Cook Inlet. His discoveries destroyed the myth of the Northwest Passage in a southern latitude and gave the British a clear indication of the outline of the coast to which they had firm claim as a result of the Nootka Sound crisis.

10

The Surveyor-Diplomats

May Peace and Plenty on our Nation smile, And Trade & Commerce bless the British Isle.

"SUCCESS TO SHIP TRADE," ON A LATE
EIGHTEENTH-CENTURY JUG AT THE BRIGHTON PAVILION

On top of the parliament buildings in Victoria, the capital of British Columbia, stands the solitary and gilded figure of Captain George Vancouver, R.N. Holding the British flag and dressed in naval attire, he embodies the British presence on the Northwest Coast of North America in the late eighteenth century. He is perhaps second in importance to James Cook in defining the littoral of the North Pacific. There is no doubt that he ranks among the principal and founding figures in the modern history of Canada's west coast, for his surveys and, to a lesser degree, his diplomacy laid the basis for British dominion there. As his biographer, Admiral Bern Anderson, U.S.N., put it: "Without the solid foundation of Vancouver's monumental work as a basis for the British position, however, it is conceivable that the northern boundary of Oregon might have been fixed at latitude 54° 40′ North, and Canada today would have no Pacific shores."[1]

Vancouver's voyage, according to one of his contemporaries, was "the last important voyage of discovery, that will probably ever need to be undertaken in the Pacific ocean."[2] Commencing in 1791 and ending four years later, it was an arduous passage in small vessels to one of the most desolate and hazardous coasts in the world. Its achievements were of a high order: the non-existence of a Northwest Passage through the North American continent had been proved conclusively, the Northwest Coast had been more accurately defined than ever before, and the claims of the British crown to the region had been confirmed. Vancouver's voyage foreshadowed a permanent British presence on the coast.

Vancouver was to have sailed in H.M.S. *Discovery* towards the end of April 1790 as second officer to Captain Henry Roberts. This expedition was to expand British enterprises in the Pacific, in particular by encouraging whaling, building a settlement on the Northwest Coast, and fostering the maritime fur trade.[3] However, the government abruptly halted the expedition when John Meares arrived fresh from Nootka Sound with the alarming news that confirmed the rumour then afoot in London that the Spanish captain Martinez had seized British ships and shore establishments at Nootka Sound. Once the war clouds cleared away after the signing of the Nootka Convention with Spain in 1790, the government revived the project in an altered form. At that time Roberts was on service in the Caribbean and unable to command the *Discovery*. As the Northwest Coast expedition was a pressing business that could not await his return, the Lords of the Admiralty turned to Vancouver.

In 1791, Vancouver was only thirty-four years of age, but he was a seasoned and skilled mariner in the Cook tradition. Born 22 June 1757, in King's Lynn, Norfolk, then one of England's major ports, Vancouver was the sixth and youngest child and the third son of Bridget and John Jasper Vancouver, the latter a custom's officer and town dues collector of considerable prestige and local political influence.[4] As a boy Vancouver attended the local grammar school. Living in a bustling sea port, he could not fail to be marked by both the activity and the lure of the sea. Besides, there was a wider world to explore and a career to be made under Cook's tutorship, no small prospect for a son born into an ambitious middle class family. Twenty-nine years younger than Cook, Vancouver entered the navy in an altogether different way from his mentor, who served a hard apprenticeship in the coal trade before he received a commission in His Majesty's forces at age forty after thirteen years' service. By contrast, Vancouver became a "young gentleman of the quarterdeck" at fourteen and in 1771 began his apprenticeship for a commission in the navy by becoming a midshipman on board Cook's *Resolution*.

He was bound on a service as important in that age as putting a man on the moon has been in this century, the search for the fabled land of the ancients, Terra Australis Incognita, by circumnavigating the world as near as possible to the South Pole. By good fortune his schoolmaster was William Wales, one of the great astronomers of the age and discoverer of a method to determine longitude at sea. Wales taught Vancouver much, and he named an Alaskan headland Point Wales in honour of his teacher, whose instruction in astronomy and mathematics enabled him, he wrote later of the North Pacific, "to traverse these lonely regions." Young Vancouver also learned from others on board the *Resolution,* but from no one more than Cook. He mastered matters critical to distant voyaging such as rationing, disease prevention, ship maintenance, sketching, landfall identification, mapmaking, hydrographic surveying, and, of course, navigation. Above all he acquired from Cook an enthusiasm for exploration, an appreciation of the significance of discovery. It was not just youthful enthusiasm that had led him as a midshipman in January 1774 to mount the *Resolution*'s bowsprit just before she turned away from her deepest penetration towards the South Pole and cry "ne plus ultra." The young enthusiast was sharing the exploration of the unknown and in his own very personal way pushing back the frontiers of the world then known to mankind.

Vancouver had also gone with Cook on his third voyage to the Pacific and was thus no stranger to Nootka Sound and the Northwest Coast when he arrived there in 1791. In 1778 he had entered Nootka Sound, Cook Inlet, and Bering Sea. He had visited, among other places, the Hawaiian Islands, Kamchatka, and Macao and by the age of twenty-three had twice circled the globe. On 19 October 1780, two weeks after returning home from Cook's third voyage, Vancouver received his passing certificate as lieutenant in the Royal Navy.[5] From 1781 to 1789 he had further developed his skills as a surveyor during service in various royal ships stationed in that cockpit of imperial rivalries, the Caribbean. He also obtained the necessary experience at sea. And, not least, there he came under the watchful eye of Sir Alan Gardner, commodore of British warships in the West Indies, a man whose opinions bulked large in decisions made by the Lords of the Admiralty. Indeed, Gardner's concurrent rise to prominence in the naval affairs of the kingdom aided Vancouver's appointment as surveyor diplomat on the Northwest Coast.

The government assigned Vancouver a number of tasks. Two documents, the cabinet's directions to the Admiralty dated "February, 1791," signed by the Secretary of State, the Honourable W. W. Grenville, and the Admiralty's instructions to Vancouver of 8 March, tell at length of the British government's motives and expectations.[6]

The expedition's immediate purpose was to receive formally from Spanish authorities what the Anglo-Spanish Convention of 28 October 1790 called "the buildings and tracts of land, situated on the northwest coast of the continent of North America, or on islands adjacent to that continent" that had been seized by Martínez in 1789.[7] The British government remained uncertain as to the size of this property: Henry Dundas spoke in the House of Commons of a "few miles" of shoreline, a highly inflated perception of the small cove where Meares's house and breastwork had stood.[8] But Vancouver was being sent to obtain restitution of whatever had been British, a potentially difficult task if the Spanish proved obstinate.

Vancouver's second purpose was to survey and explore the whole coast of North America from lower California in about 30° to Cook Inlet in about 60°. The government, Grenville explained to the Admiralty, wanted "a more complete knowledge than has yet been obtained of the north-west coast of America." Vancouver's instructions specified that the principal objects of the examination were twofold: firstly, to acquire accurate information on any water communication existing between the Northwest Coast and British colonies or possessions on the other side of North America and, secondly, to ascertain as precisely as possible the situation and age of existing European settlements, especially Spanish, in the region between latitudes 30 and 60°N. Vancouver was to examine the general line of the sea coast and determine the direction and extent of inlets and rivers leading into the continent. He was given broad discretionary powers for the employment of his vessels, but his instructions were that "in order to avoid any unnecessary loss of time he should be directed not to pursue any inlet or river further than it shall appear to be navigable by vessels of such burthen as might safely navigate the Pacific Ocean.'' In other words, the passage had to be of sufficient size to be commercially or strategically useful.

Because the examination of such inlets might require the use of the *Discovery* in hazardous situations, the government advised Vancouver to employ her tender escort, the armed brig *Chatham,* for detailed work in the rivers and inlets. ''The particular course of the survey,'' Grenville's directive ran, ''must, of course, depend on the different circumstances which may arise in the execution of a service of this nature.'' Nonetheless, Vancouver was to pay particular attention to the coastline in the region between 48° and 49°N, where the British government had information from Meares that the American trading sloop *Lady Washington* had passed through the Strait of Juan de Fuca in 1789, and had come out again north of Nootka Sound. The government believed that such a sea passage, if it connected with the Lake of the Woods, would be particularly useful. However, even if no such communication existed, Grenville was optimistic that Cook Inlet, then thought to be a river, formed the mouth of a waterway rising in lakes known to fur traders from Canada and the Hudson's Bay Company. As he put it, ''it would in that case be material to ascertain with as much precision as the then existing circumstances of the expedition may allow. But the discovery of any similar communication more to the southward, should any such exist, would be much more advantageous for the purposes of commerce, and should therefore be preferably attended to.''

With respect to the question of ascertaining the extent, number, and situation of European, especially Spanish, settlements on the Northwest Coast, the government hoped to send more recent intelligence to Vancouver by way of the hired transport *Daedalus,* which was to take supplies from Port Jackson, New South Wales, to a rendezvous at the Hawaiian Islands. Evidently the ministry possessed little information on the extent of the British shore establishment at Nootka Sound at the time of capture and may have been reluctant to place too much credence on the data that they had, which was mainly Meares's sometimes inflated reports. If London failed to send these additional instructions, Vancouver was to act with all due caution, taking care not to give the Spanish any grounds for complaint or jealousy. He was to provide the commander of Spanish ships on similar service with whatever assistance and information he could. Vancouver was to engage with his opposite in the free interchange of ''plans and charts of discoveries made by them in their respective voyages.''

Such duties would require the ships to be on the coast for several years, and thus good relations with the native tribes would be both advantageous and necessary. The Admiralty provided presents for the Indians, these items to be disposed of by Vancouver according to Admiralty regulations applicable in similar cases. Sir Joseph Banks, the influential President of the Royal Society, seems to have been behind the choice of certain items of trade; and he acted through Archibald

Menzies, a determined Scot whom he had arranged to be the official naturalist to the Vancouver expedition.[9] This was done against the wishes of the commander, who objected to Banks's interference in his preparations and was opposed to non-service specialists on naval expeditions.

Yet Menzies had been on the Northwest Coast in a fur-trading vessel; consequently, he knew what trade items various Indian tribes would want. At Banks's request, he drew up a long list of trade goods. Copper would be needed at Nootka Sound, iron at Prince William Sound, and various metals at the Queen Charlotte Islands and Cape Edgecumbe. Menzies suggested that each vessel have two blacksmiths and a forge for fashioning gifts for the Indians. Some of the items he recommended for trade were frying pans, tin kettles, adzes, tinder boxes, pewter pots, fish hooks, old bayonets, tall caps covered with brass in the form of mitres, muskets, powder, beads, and even Scottish tartans.[10] By the time the *Discovery* was first ready to sail, that is before the Nootka crisis occurred, she carried 112 casks of nails and spikes, 354 cases of metals and articles of trade, 39 bales of woolens, and 20 half-barrels of gun powder.[11] Banks estimated the total weight of iron at fifty tons and the cost to British taxpayers at £6,848.10.0. These items, secretly consigned for the Northwest Coast in order that it could not be misconstrued that they were earmarked for Governor Phillip of New South Wales, were described by an official at the Home Office as "very necessary in the Settlement to be formed."[12] At the same time, he warned that the ships' officers, and not petty officers or sailors, should be in charge of these goods.[13] Vancouver made his own suggestions on the trade items and subsequently calicoes, copper, nails, vermillion, and red baize were added to the goods for the Indians.[14] The sum ultimately allowed by Parliament for "presents" carried out by Vancouver's ships to the Northwest Coast Indians totalled £10,329.15.4.[15]

The British government hoped to draw the Northwest Coast Indians into their trading orbit as the leading industrialized nation. If these were in fact "presents," perhaps tribes could be lured away from rival Spanish or even Russian traders.[16] The British were intent on developing commercial relations with Northwest America, and this was an underlying, even unwritten, assumption of the Vancouver voyage.

Another underlying motive of the expedition was scientific enquiry; and in this connection Sir Joseph Banks, at Grenville's request, wrote a lengthy memorandum of instructions to Menzies.[17] He was to investigate "the whole of the Natural History" of the places visited and to enquire into "the present state and comparative degree" of the various inhabitants of these countries. Such varied topics as soil, vegetation, produce, and climate were to be investigated. Banks also suggested that Menzies report on places suitable for settlement and locations where whales and seals were abundant. He was to gather specimens of curious or valuable plants for the national botanical collection at Kew Gardens. Banks and Menzies knew that the Northwest Coast Indians had unusual social mores of interest to the British, and Menzies had detailed instructions to make an ethnological study of unbounded dimensions. "At all places where a friendly intercourse with the Natives is established," they ran,

> you are to make diligent enquiry into their manners, customs, Languages and Religion, and to obtain all the information in your power concerning their manufactures, particularly the art of dyeing, in which Savages have been frequently found to excell, and if any of their conduct, civil, or religious, should appear to you so unreasonable as not to be likely to meet with credit when related in Europe, you are if you can do it with safety and propriety, to make yourself an Eyewitness of it, in order that the fact of its existence may be established on as firm a basis as the Nature of the enquiry will permit.[18]

Menzies, it seems, had the unfortunate duty of being the "complete scientist." A physician, surgeon, and botanist, he was a one-man scientific team working out of a small greenhouse designed by Sir Joseph Banks on the *Discovery*'s quarterdeck. His journal of the voyage indicates that he conducted his duties with a high degree of professional competence and in the fashion that was later to make him both a distinguished London doctor and president of the botanical collegium known as the Linnaean Society.[19] During the voyage he was highly useful to Vancouver in scientific matters and became surgeon of the *Discovery* in 1792 when the man he replaced in this capacity, Mr. Alexander Cranstoun, was invalided home. However, Menzies was not highly agreeable. As one historian has aptly put it, "There was a marked strain of the thistle in Mr. Menzies that reacted against—and upon—Vancouver's authoritarian tendencies. His reports to his patron [Banks] have done his captain's reputation no lasting good but they clearly require an index error. Menzies was not too easy a shipmate on an expedition of this kind."[20]

At last, at dawn on 1 April the two ships finally sailed from Falmouth, England, and one senses Vancouver's reluctance to be away on an extended voyage to distant parts. A war with France seemed in the offing and the thought of separation from England saddened him. As he wrote in his journal somewhat nostalgically: "The remote and barbarous regions, which were now destined, for some years, to be our transitory places of abode, were not likely to afford us any means of communicating with our native soil, our families, our friends or favorites, whom we were now leaving far behind."[21]

For nearly five years home to these sailors was His Majesty's ships *Discovery* and *Chatham,* now regarded as lengendary vessels in the maritime history of the Northwest Coast. They were particularly appropriate vessels for the service intended. The *Discovery,* not to be confused with Cook's consort which called at Nootka Sound in 1778, was a merchant ship being built on the Thames at the time of her purchase by the Admiralty in 1789. She measured ninety-six feet in length and 337 tons and drew fourteen feet of water. Originally she was shiprigged, that is, she bore three masts, all with square sails. She carried ten four-pounder short guns on carriages, ten half-pounder swivel guns, and four three-pounder brass guns which, as Vancouver specifically requested, had travelling carriages that would allow the guns to be used on shore if required. She had been coppered, sheathed with plank, and coppered again, an advance over the close-nailing treatment given Cook's ship against the teredo. Like the *Resolution* she had been given additional accommodation for captain, artists, and scientists. In her crowded quarters she carried nineteen officers, sixty-five seamen, and sixteen marines—one hundred in all.

Her tender, the *Chatham,* was eminently suitable for surveying in inshore waters and also capable of distant navigation. She was a small, two-masted, brig-rigged former merchant vessel purchased by the Navy from a Dover shipbuilder in 1788. She was registered as an armed tender and fitted in 1790 "for remote service." She measured only fifty-three feet in length and 131 tons. She mounted four three-pounder carriage guns and ten half-pounder swivels. She had a sizeable complement of fourteen officers and thirty-two men in extremely cramped quarters. Like the *Discovery,* she was copper-bottomed.

Vancouver's officers included, as first lieutenant, Zachary Mudge, and, as second and third, Peter Puget and Joseph Baker. Joseph Whidbey was the Master. All known and tried men, they had served with Vancouver in the Caribbean. In command of the *Chatham* was William Robert Broughton, then twenty-nine, five years Vancouver's junior. He had considerable service behind him on the North American and East Indies stations. He was a capable commander and surveyor who would himself complete much of the Admiralty chart of the Asian shoreline from 35°N to 52°N while in command of H.M.S. *Providence* in 1795-98. At the time of her departure the *Chatham*'s first lieutenant was James Hanson; her master, Mr. James Johnstone.[22]

The ships' complements contained a good number of "young gentlemen of the quarterdeck," that is master's mates and midshipmen, some hoping for advancement should a vacancy among the lieutenants occur during the voyage, meanwhile serving their time and learning the techniques of command. Several of them were to enjoy distinguished careers, including Sir Robert Barrie, Volant Vashon Ballard, and Peter Puget. But one, it may be mentioned here, was an exception. The Honourable Thomas Pitt (later Lord Camelford), a hot-tempered, quarrelsome youth closely connected to two of the nation's powerful political families, the Pitts and Grenvilles, was both young enough and foolish enough to create a general nuisance of himself on board the *Discovery.* This particular midshipman's conduct was Vancouver wrote, "too bad for me to represent in any one respect.'' He was insubordinate and was flogged on Vancouver's orders—an almost unheard-of act against a young gentleman even in that era of rigid, even brutal ship's discipline—and was sent home to England via the *Daedalus* in 1794. Later he challenged Vancouver to a duel and even once attacked him with a cane in a London street.

The Camelford affair shows Vancouver not to have been a tyrant or a brutal commander, as Camelford charged.[23] Rather, as Vancouver's recent biographer tells us, ''The record of the voyage shows Vancouver to have been an able and conscientious officer whose ill health and occasional outbursts of temper did not prevent him from working as hard as his men or from taking a personal interest in their health and welfare.''[24] Unsympathetic and austere as he was, it seems on balance that Vancouver demanded much of his men and gave a good deal. Would one expect less from a true disciple of Cook?[25] Camelford provided to be the exception rather than the rule in a long list of ''young gentlemen'' who went on to become themselves worthy leaders.

The *Discovery* and *Chatham* made their way to the Pacific by way of Tenerife, the Cape of Good Hope, and the western end of the south coast of Australia, where Vancouver surveyed some three hundred miles of coastline. Vancouver gave the name King George Sound to the only secure haven on that shoreline. Time did not permit him to determine, as the Admiralty wished, if Van Diemen's Land, now Tasmania, was separated from the continent. Vancouver next headed for Dusky Bay, New Zealand, which he reached on 2 November 1791. Here, for twenty days, a refit was carried out while boat parties surveyed the coast. Leaving Dusky Bay, the two ships reached Matavai Bay, Tahiti, in late December 1790. Two months later, on 1 March 1792, they were at Honolulu. The storeship *Daedalus* had not yet arrived at the rendezvous, and Vancouver, a month behind schedule, decided to leave a message for her captain. After watering his ships, Vancouver departed from the Hawaiian Islands. He set a course for the Northwest Coast, the principal geographical object of his voyage and a fabled place in English geopolitical thought since Drake's discoveries two centuries before.

On the afternoon of 18 April Vancouver made a landfall on the coast of Nova Albion, as English navigators remembering Drake still called it, in $39°\,27'$ longitude, that is, about 110 miles north of San Francisco Bay and slightly south of Cape Mendocino. On 19 April he passed this famous cape. The winds must not have been strong in that season, for Vancouver was able to keep quite close to land and observe the continental shore as he followed it steadily northward. At night the ships stood out to sea. At daybreak they returned to shore to recommence the survey at a distance of two to five miles from the coast. Sometimes the survey had to be broken off during storms, but Vancouver never failed to return to his point of departure. With the great deal of time at his disposal, he methodically charted the coastline with a fair degree of accuracy and thereby removed any misconceptions left from the English surveys of Cook and Meares.[26] During this phase of the voyage he named Cape Orford (now Cape Blanco) and recognized Meares's Cape Disappointment and Deception Bay.

The existence of a great western river in this latitude had been speculated by geographers, navigators, and explorers for two hundred years. In 1602 the Spaniard Martín de Aguilar reported the Strait of Anian in that locale. The early Canadian historian Charlevoix and French explorers of the Mississippi River Valley had called the often-heard-of stream the River of the West. Two colonial Americans, Major Robert Rogers and Jonathan Carver, linked it with various western rivers and called it the Ouragon or Oregon, a conjecture not disproved until the Nor'wester David Thompson discovered the true source of the Columbia in 1807. Bruno de Hezeta had sailed into its mouth in 1775, made astronomical observations to determine its precise location, and applied several place-names, no longer in use, to key topographical features.[27]

Certainly by the time Vancouver and Gray were on the coast, the honour of discovering the Columbia River mouth had already been won by Spain. Yet Hezeta had penetrated only the river's outer reaches, leaving its lower extremity virtually unexplored. The task of determining its size, course upstream, and navigability remained, an important mission in that age when river basins were keys to inland trade.

Despite his characteristic thoroughness in exploration, Vancouver missed the mouth of the Columbia. Perhaps he put too much emphasis on John Meares's claim that no such river existed. In July 1788, Meares had given the names Cape Disappointment and Deception Bay to coastal features where Spanish charts, especially that of Don Francisco Antonio Mourelle, indicated a river within what the Spanish had called Cape Saint Roc.[28] Meares's name for Cape Disappointment remains on the charts, designating a finger-like promontory enclosing within its reach the tricky entry to the great river. The dangerous and shoaling Columbia River bar, which made breakers across Deception Bay, had further deterred Meares's investigations.[29]

When Vancouver reached the river's mouth, the Columbia was in flood with spring freshets, making sighting the river all that more difficult. Vancouver recognized Meares's Cape Disappointment and saw that the sea changed from its natural colour to that of muddy water. This was, Vancouver reasoned, owing to some streams flowing into the bay or into the ocean to the north of it. "Not considering the opening worthy of more attention," he wrote, "I continued our pursuit to the N.W. being desirous to embrace the advantages of the now prevailing breeze and pleasant weather."[30]

It must be added here that Vancouver, like Cook, may have approached this section of the Northwest Coast with a bias against the possibility of a river waterway. Perhaps as a sceptic of the new age of scientific surveying he was too quick to pass judgment against the ancient claim by Juan de Fuca that a strait existed in that latitude. Vancouver, too, placed little credence on Alexander Dalrymple's claims that the strait coincided almost exactly with Hezeta's Columbia discovery. Vancouver disliked "closet philosophers" as he derisively called de Fuca, de Fonte, and others—voyagers of the Renaissance whose ideas, he later said, "have been adopted for the sole purpose of giving unlimited credit to the traditionary exploits of ancient foreigners and to undervalue the laborious and enterprising exertions of our own countrymen in the noble science of discovery."[31]

Vancouver's failure to discover the river plagued British diplomats, who in discussions with their American counterparts were obliged to base their priority of claims on the basis of the earlier, more cursory discoveries of Drake and Cook. American historians of the Oregon boundary dispute have tended to report Vancouver's omission in finding the Columbia's mouth as a major failure. However, his most recent biographer, Admiral Bern Anderson, himself familiar with the difficult entrance to the river, has ably come to the defence of his fellow seaman: "For even today, with the entrance to the river well marked and improved, ships treat it with deep respect when a heavy swell is running."[32] Two days after missing the river mouth, Vancouver, to his chagrin, learned from Captain Robert Gray of the Boston ship *Columbia* that the opening was indeed an important river and thus worthy of attention. Vancouver, however, did not enter the river, whose entrance Gray had found. Gray, by comparison, actually examined the river two weeks after meeting Vancouver. This fact distressed Vancouver, who later had Lieutenant Broughton of the *Chatham* survey the Columbia about 120 miles upstream in the hope of extending British claims inland.[33]

In the meantime, Vancouver had learned from Gray that the latter had not sailed around a body of land upon which Nootka Sound was situated, as Meares had reported. "It is not possible," he recorded, "to conceive any one to be more astonished than was Mr. Gray, on his being made acquainted that his authority had been quoted, and the track pointed out that he had been said to have made in the sloop *Washington*. In contradiction to which, he assured the officers that he had penetrated only 50 miles into the straits in question."[34] This gave Vancouver reason to be optimistic that he would make an extensive survey of the waters to the east of Cook's discovery, Cape Flattery. On 29 April, the same day he had met Gray, Vancouver sighted a pinnacle rock near the cape. This famous landmark he named Duncan Rock in honour of the British fur trader Charles Duncan. Then he proceeded into the Strait of Juan de Fuca past Neah Bay, where the Spaniard Quimper had previously been and made claims in July and August 1790.

Though Vancouver's primary interest was to delineate the shorelines of the inland straits and islands, he took pains, in keeping with his instructions and those to Archibald Menzies, to record details of native life. He knew that in 1788 John Meares's longboat under Robert Duffin's command had been attacked near Port Townsend. For this reason he was alert to the possibility of attack. However, the

Indians did not threaten and on one occasion paid no heed to the British warships. Near Cape Flattery he and his fellow officers compiled detailed reports of the Makahs' appearance, costumes, weapons, and implements. Further up the strait, near New Dungeness, Indian fishermen paid no attention to the passing ships, for the previous appearance of Spanish explorers and American and English fur traders had evidently satisfied the Salish curiosity about the intruders. At Discovery Bay, Protection Island, where the *Discovery* anchored for sixteen days, the British made detailed examinations of Salish and Klallam material culture. The artifacts collected at that time are in the British Museum in London and the University Museum in Cambridge, England. These items and the notes compiled by Vancouver, Menzies, Peter Puget, and others form a rich body of evidence for the reconstruction of these peoples at a time when a great cultural crisis was approaching them.[35] From New Dungeness, the *Discovery*'s cutter and the *Chatham*'s yawl were sent to examine the surrounding area. Later, at Protection Island, Vancouver himself landed and reported the surrounding landscape as "almost as enchantingly beautiful as the most elegantly finished pleasure grounds in Europe."[36] On 8 May, a small boat from the ships explored Admiralty Inlet, Puget Sound, and subsequently the surveying parties conducted a detailed examination of the waterways of the sound.

They found no Northwest Passage here; however, claims to British dominion were established on 4 June when Vancouver took formal possession of the territory at Tulalip. He recorded these proceedings as follows:

On Sunday all hands were employed in fishing with tolerably good success, or in taking a little recreation on shore; and on Monday they were served as good a dinner as we were able to provide them, with double allowance of grog to drink the King's health, it being the anniversary of His Majesty's birth; on which auspicious day, I had long since designed to take formal possession of all the countries we had lately been employed in exploring, in the name, of, and for His Britannic Majesty, his heirs and successors.

To execute this purpose, accompanied by Mr. Broughton, and some of the officers, I went on shore about one o'clock pursuing the usual formalities which are generally observed on such occasions, and under the discharge of a royal salute from the vessels, took possession accordingly of the coast, from that part of New Albion, in the latitude of $39°\ 20'$ north, and longitude $236°\ 26'$ east, to the entrance of this inlet of the sea, said to be the supposed straits of Juan de Fuca; as likewise all the coast, islands, &c. within the said straits, as well on the northern as on the southern shores; together with those situated in the interior sea we had discovered, extending from the said straits, in various directions, between the northwest, north, east and southern quarters; which interior sea I have honored with the name of the Gulf of Georgia, and the continent binding the said gulf, and extending southward to the 45th degree of north latitude, with that of New Georgia, in honor of His present Majesty.[37]

Surveying, important in its own right and yet extremely tedious, was unpleasant. In his journal, Menzies tells of the tiring effects of long hours at the oars in poor weather and the type of conditions which eventually led to the breakdown of Vancouver's health.

> . . . the weather was now become so cold wet & uncomfortable that the men were no longer able to endure the fatiguing hardships of distant excursions in open Boats exposd to the cold rigorous blasts of a high northern situation with high dreary snowy mountains on every side, performing toilsome labor on their Oars in the day, & alternately watching for their own safety at night, with no other Couch to repose upon than the Cold Stony Beach or the wet mossy Turf in damp woody situations, without having shelter sufficient to screen them from the inclemency of boisterous weather, and enduring at times the tormenting pangs of both hunger & thirst, yet on every occasion struggling who should be most forward in executing the orders of their superiors to accomplish the general interest of the Voyage.[38]

Meanwhile, Lieutenant Broughton in the *Chatham* had explored the intricacies of the San Juan archipelago, the British not knowing it had been charted in the previous year, 1791, by the Spanish expedition of Lieutenant Francisco de Eliza who called it "Isla y Archipelago de San Juan." Broughton's principal discovery, of immediate use to Vancouver, was that the archipelago lay south of "an extensive arm of the sea which stretched as far as the eye could see in a variety of branches to the northwest and to the north-northeast."[39] Could this lead at last to the Northwest Passage or, failing that, northward behind Nootka Sound to the Pacific?

By late afternoon of 11 June, the *Discovery* and *Chatham* had tacked north through Rosario Strait, passed Lummi Island, entered the Gulf of Georgia, now Georgia Strait, and anchored in a small bay on the continental mainland, now known as Birch Bay. Subsequently, the ships moved to another bay, within Point Roberts and near 49°N, now called Boundary Bay. From this place, Vancouver and Lieutenant Peter Puget took the yawl and launch north. At the same time, Joseph Whidbey, master of the *Discovery,* took the cutter and the *Chatham*'s launch south, where he found Bellingham Bay.

Vancouver made his way to Burrard Inlet, missing the Fraser River's mouth en route.[40] On 12 June 1792, he penetrated the narrows of Burrard Inlet on the shore of which the city bearing his name now stands. The British met fifty Capilano Indians in canoes who had previously heard rumours of strange monstrous vessels on the outer waters but hitherto had not been visited by a white man. Vancouver's visit has a distinct place in Capilano tradition. He later landed near the site of the present town of Port Moody. "The shores of this channel," Vancouver recorded, "which, after Sir Henry Burrard of the navy, I have distinguished by the name of Burrard's Channel, may be considered, on the southern side, of a moderate height, and though rocky, well covered with trees of large growth, principally of the pine tribe. On the northern side, the rugged snowy barrier, whose base we had now nearly approached, rose very abruptly, and was only protected from the wash of the sea by a very narrow border of low land."[41] Moving north, Vancouver got as far as Jervis Inlet, which to his disappointment offered no hope of a Northwest Passage.

On his return southward, near "Spanish Banks," Point Grey, at the entrance to Burrard Inlet, Vancouver met a Spanish brig, the *Sútil,* commanded by Alcalá Galiano, and a schooner, the *Mexicana,* commanded by Cayetano Valdés. These ships had left Acapulco on 8 March to make discoveries in the region. "It was the meeting of two destinies," Howay wrote, "the dawn of British rule, the setting of Spanish glory."[42] From the Spaniards Vancouver learned that Bodega was waiting for him at Nootka Sound to negotiate restoration of the place to the British crown. "Their conduct was replete with that politeness and friendship which characterizes the Spanish nation," Vancouver wrote in his *Voyages,* "but being intent on losing no time, I declined their obliging offers, and having partaken with them a very hearty breakfast, bade them farewell."[43] Returning to his ships, Vancouver sailed northwest through Georgia Strait with the *Sutil* and *Mexicana,* surveying the inland waters as they went.

Aided by his officers, Vancouver now conducted a thorough examination of Georgia Strait. One officer, James Johnstone, master of the *Chatham,* discovered a channel leading to the open sea, evidence that the land to the west was indeed an island, as the British had suspected. Then the ships sailed in turn through Discovery Strait, the turbulent and dangerous Seymour Narrows, Johnstone Strait, and Queen Charlotte Sound to the open Pacific. On the foggy afternoon of 6 August the *Discovery* grounded on a submerged rock in Queen Charlotte Sound, and on the following day the *Chatham* repeated the performance. However, neither ship was damaged. In subsequent days the waters of Queen Charlotte Sound were surveyed, particularly north of Cape Caution on the continental shore. While boats traced the shoreline north through Fitzhugh Sound to Menzies Point, that is, almost to the present town of Bella Bella, Vancouver, deterred by bad weather from continuing his own portion of the survey, waited at Safety Cove, Calvert Island, first used by Charles Duncan in 1788 and subsequently by other maritime fur traders. Here the *Venus,* a trading vessel, from Bengal brought him the news that the storeship *Daedalus* had at last reached Nootka Sound and confirmed that the Spanish commissioner eagerly awaited Vancouver's arrival.

Vancouver now broke off the survey, having completed 760 kilometres of the continental shore from the Strait of Juan de Fuca to a point midway between the north end of Vancouver Island and the southern tip of Alaska. In four short months he had proved that Vancouver Island was an island. He also had mapped a good portion of the present coastline of British Columbia. It had been painstaking work frequently conducted in difficult weather conditions. By 28 August both ships had reached Nootka Sound, where the exacting work of dealing with the Spanish began.

Vancouver's methods and facilities were superior to those of the Spanish. Not only was Galiano unable to keep pace with the British, owing to the unsuitability of the *Sútil* and *Mexicana* for surveying, but Lieutenant Peter Puget found that the Spanish investigation of the continental shore was inaccurate. Vancouver, it is true, did not discover the mouth of the Fraser River, which the Spanish had. However, Vancouver was searching for inlets that might form a northwest passage suitable for seagoing vessels. He could not, therefore, trust to Spanish findings on this critical subject, and in keeping with Puget's initiative he did not resume co-operative surveys with the Spanish. Nonetheless, he remained on good relations with Galiano and Valdés, naming two islands in Queen Charlotte Sound (now Hope and Nigei) after them.[44]

Bodega, commander-in-chief of the Spanish naval base of San Blas, was a man proud of his noble birth and Castilian blood. On instructions from Madrid, he placed a different emphasis on the matter of the restitution of property than Vancouver did: the Spaniard was prepared to cede what Vancouver described as "a small pittance of rocks and sandy beach" where Meares's fur post supposedly had been. Vancouver, for his part, demanded the return of Nootka and Clayoquot Sound and the recognition of Neah Bay on the south shore of the Strait of Juan de Fuca as a port open to both nations.

Neither Vancouver nor Bodega allowed acrimony to mar their delicate negotiations conducted at the end of the earth. With civility and ceremony they bargained amicably at Friendly Cove, exchanging pleasantries over the dinner table, though the *Discovery*'s simple fare became no match for the five course Spanish meals.[45] Royal salutes and toasts to the healths of the British and Spanish sovereigns became the order of the day. On the savage reaches of the Northwest Coast the strict decorum of Europe was being observed. Both officers knew how close their nations had come to war over this distant spot. Neither was foolish enough to become high-handed and upset the delicate balance of power in Europe. This was no time for an intemperate Martínez or a hot-headed Colnett; this was a time for diplomats. Vancouver and Bodega, mindful of the behaviour of their fellow countrymen three years earlier in the same cove, took pains to respect the position of the other and, ultimately, as gentlemen, agreed to disagree.

What divided the two emissaries was the extent of Spanish establishments on the Northwest Coast at the time of the signing of the Nootka Convention in October 1790. Bodega would only agree to the transfer of Meares's enclosure. The ''few miles'' of coastline that the British had reason to believe was rightfully theirs had now diminished to ''a small chasm,'' Vancouver wrote, ''not a hundred yards in extent in any one direction, being the exact space which the house and breastwork of Mr. Meares occupied.''[46] Aware of Bodega's intransigence, Vancouver could not press his point. Vancouver also was not prepared to admit Spanish claims based on expansion to Neah Bay after October 1790. As these matters could not be decided then and there, the two officers wisely referred the matter to their home governments for resolution.

The final stage of Nootka diplomacy was completed in Madrid on 11 January 1794 when representatives of the two powers, Lord St. Helens and the Duke of Alcudia, signed the Convention for the Mutual Abandonment of Nootka. By this document Britain and Spain bound themselves to a number of provisions respecting the future of the Northwest Coast in European hands. Subjects of either nation could erect temporary buildings at Nootka but not permanent establishments such as garrisons or factories. Moreover, neither nation could claim sovereignty to any territorial dominion at the other's expense. The two countries were also to maintain this free port against claims by any other power that might attempt to establish there any sovereignty or dominion. In other words, Nootka had become, irrespective of Indian interests, a free port to be maintained as such by an agreement of mutual exclusion.

Nonetheless, the nagging problem of restoring the lands and buildings at Friendly Cove to Britain still remained. The convention specified that the two governments would send new commissioners to Friendly Cove, where the Spanish officer would convey ''the Buildings and Districts of Land'' to the British officer. Subsequently the British officer would raise the Union Jack as a token sign of possession. Lastly, the officers of the two crowns would withdraw their subjects from Nootka Sound.[47]

As soon as possible, the two commissioners made their way to Vancouver Island. On 16 March 1795, Brigadier-General José Manuel de Alava, the governor of Nootka, and Lieutenant Thomas Pearce of the Royal Marines arrived at Friendly Cove in the Spanish brig *Activa* from Monterey. Pearce, Vancouver's successor as commissioner, had come from England by way of Havana and Mexico City to San Blas, where he embarked with Alava for Nootka. For twelve days he made his inquiries of Maquinna and the Nootka Indians, aided by the American trader John Kendrick, who served as interpreter. Pearce took pains to determine the precise extent of Meares's factory and, once satisfied, on 28 March the two commissioners went about their respective tasks of withdrawing.

Pearce's mission had a distinct imperial intent. He explained to Maquinna that his government had received many good reports of the Nootka Indians from Cook and from British traders. The British crown, Pearce told Maquinna, had decided to take the Nootka under its protective wing. "With this Account they all seemed much pleased," Pearce reported to London in self-congratulatory tones, "observing that the English had ever been their good Friends—but were very anxious to know if the Spanish should return, whether they were to be friends with them; from which I inferred that they had not been treated very kindly by them."[48] After the Spanish delivered over to Pearce the site of Meares's factory, Pearce ceremoniously raised and lowered the Union Jack on a flagpole and gave the flag to Maquinna for safekeeping, instructing him to hoist it whenever a ship appeared, a mark of confidence which gratified Maquinna very much, Pearce claimed. Pearce and Alava left letters in Maquinna's care to be shown to fur traders in order that the terms of evacuation could become known on the coast. Meanwhile the Spanish fort was dismantled on Alava's instructions, its guns and moveable property were stored aboard the *Activa* and the storeship *San Carlos,* and the Spanish abandoned the northernmost post of their American empire. The two commissioners exchanged documents verifying the restitution and mutual abandonment of Nootka and then sailed from the port, leaving it in Maquinna's peaceful possession.[49]

The natives soon demolished the village, carrying away everything of value to them, particularly nails and other pieces of metal that could be fashioned into implements or ornaments. They likewise ransacked the cemetery, taking nails from coffins. Within months the remnants of Spanish buildings had been replaced by Maquinna's lodges on the ancient site of his ancestors' dwellings, and Friendly Cove took on the appearance much like it had had twenty-one years previous, when the Spanish under Pérez had first anchored off the Sound.[50] A tide of empire had come and gone.

Subsequently neither Britain nor Spain attempted to violate the terms of the 1794 Convention. They undertook no settlements nor planned a settlement. Nonetheless, Spanish and British claims to sovereignty there were not forgotten by either nation. Britain's territorial ownership of Meares's land was significant in English claims to sovereignty used subsequently in diplomacy with Russia and the United States. Spain's claims to exclusive sovereignty at Nootka had been given up in 1794, but her territorial claims to the rest of the coast were not abandoned. She maintained a fragile presence on the coast, sending the *Sútil* expedition north to Nootka Sound in 1796 in response to fears that H.M.S. *Providence,* William Broughton commanding, might take aggressive action to secure a British beachhead on Vancouver Island.[51] When war broke out between Madrid and London in the same year, Spanish officials in Madrid and Mexico City ambitiously considered reoccupying Nootka, retaking Jamaica and Gibraltar from the ancient English rival, and taking offensive measures against the Russians in

Alaska. These schemes never reached fruition, for Spain did not possess the military capability either at home or abroad to defeat Wellington's armies and the British fleet. In any event, the main battleground of the Napoleonic Wars was Europe, and the alliances between Spain and Russia in 1801 removed Spanish complaints against the Tsar's aggrandizements on the Northwest Coast. Yet the loss of Nootka had become "a festering wound" to the Spanish, who did not easily give up the idea that they might regain it and recover their impetus for territorial expansion in northwestern America.[52] Not until 1819, by the Adams-Onis Treaty between the United States and Spain, did the latter power retreat from the contest for the Pacific Northwest. Henceforth, with the American republic inheriting Spanish historic claims to sovereignty between 42°N latitude, the present border of California and Oregon, and 54° 40′N, the coastal frontier between British Columbia and Alaska, Spain no longer took a role in imperial rivalry for the Northwest Coast. This left Britain and the United States to complete the final division of the Pacific Northwest by the Oregon Boundary Treaty of 1846.

Two and a half years before the restitution at Nootka Sound, on 12 October, Vancouver had left there with the *Chatham* and the *Daedalus*. He had sent the *Chatham* to examine the Columbia River, while he himself proceeded to San Francisco Bay and Monterey to meet Bodega and learn if the governments had sent instructions that would enable them to resolve their differences. None were received, so no progress could be made towards a diplomatic settlement. Vancouver sent Broughton to London by way of Acapulco and Santa Cruz with reports, charts, and plans for the British government, and Puget assumed temporary command of the *Chatham*. On 29 December the *Daedalus,* having supplied the *Discovery* and *Chatham,* sailed for Port Jackson, New South Wales, for further supplies, to be delivered to Nootka Sound by August 1793. Vancouver was in the Hawaiian Islands in February 1793, where he conducted a survey of the islands. The ships were again at Nootka Sound in the spring of the year; and in four months the two ships made surveys north to 56°N and then, in October, were back in Nootka Sound. During the winter months the *Chatham* surveyed Bodega Bay on the California coast while Vancouver was unsuccessfully dealing with Spanish authorities at San Francisco and Monterey. By 5 November he had resumed the survey, this time on the southern California coast south to 30°N, and by 8 January 1794 he had returned to Hawaii, where he met the *Daedalus* fresh with supplies from New South Wales.

Vancouver had now to complete his survey of the Northwest Coast in and around Cook Inlet. Throughout the summer the ships painstakingly worked the coast south and east to Admiralty Island. So thorough was this examination that he was able to report to the Admiralty of the absence of the Northwest Passage in those latitudes. As he wrote to a friend, he had proved "the non-existence of any water communication between this and the opposite side of America within the limits of our investigation beyond all doubt or disputation." Indeed, he admitted that he had written his *Voyages* to prove as conclusively as possible that a hyperborean or northern ocean between the Pacific and Atlantic did not exist.[53] While he exploded the myth of a Northwest Passage south of Alaska, the Admiralty was not deterred from sending expeditions during the years of peace after the Napoleonic Wars to search for a passage along the northern shores of North America. The idea of finding a navigable waterway to the Pacific died a slow and painful death in the minds of the British public and students of geopolitics.

Vancouver's voyage had lasted longer than expected. A three- or four-year passage had stretched into five. In September 1794, a young midshipman wrote home to a friend in frustrated tones: "I am afraid the pleasing prospect [of returning to England] is changed and we shall remain another year in these *damned* seas—while you and all your men at home are making your fortunes."[54] The strain had taken its toll on others. Surgeon Menzies complained at the same time of how long the expedition would remain "in this dreary Country, of which we are all heartily tired."[55] Vancouver, who had delayed leaving the Northwest Coast while awaiting orders from England, was of a like mind. He was, he wrote a friend, "entrapped in this infernal ocean." To his brother John he bemoaned his isolation in "these remote and uncouth parts," an isolation on secret national service that kept him from writing to friends and families in detail about places visited and persons met.[56] Such private views, expressed while on service in the Pacific and on the Northwest Coast, hardly accord with Vancouver's published views of the Puget Sound region. This was, he wrote, a beautiful park-like region with pleasing landscapes and fertile port that awaited only man's settlement and industry to make it "the most lovely country" imaginable.[57]

Distance and isolation taxed the patience, endurance, and health of these mariners, for shipboard life in a region unfrequented by European commerce posed special problems. The war against France then in progress lay tantalizingly beyond reach of officers seeking advancement or of seamen wanting less wearisome service. Occasional visits to Hawaii and California had broken the monotony, but still they had to face the long voyage home. In mid-October, Vancouver left Nootka Sound for Monterey, where he waited in vain for orders for yet another month. On 2 December, the *Discovery* and *Chatham* quit Monterey for Cape Horn, calling at various islands, Los Tres Marias, Cocos, Galapagos, and Juan Fernandez, for the purpose of watering and surveying. They called at Valparaiso to replace a sprung mast. At the end of April 1795, they began their last southerly leg, doubled Cape Horn in very heavy seas, and reached St. Helena on 2 July. There Vancouver afforded the British governor assistance by capturing the Dutch East India ship *Macassar,* then about to enter harbour, and helping secure the island colony against French or Dutch occupation. The *Discovery* and *Chatham* joined an East India convoy bound for the North Atlantic, and by September the ships had reached Shannon, Ireland. In a rare piece of comparative description midshipman Barrie wrote that Ireland was "a very wild place almost

as bad as the Northwest Coast of America and I can't understand the Natives."
"The Irish," he continued, "look at us with astonishment when they hear we
have been 5 years from a European port."[58]

By 15 October, the *Discovery* had reached Deal off the Kent coast, just a day
before the *Chatham* anchored at Plymouth. This brought to an end one of the
most notable British voyages to the Northwest Coast or, for that matter, any
other destination. It was the longest voyage on record both in time and distance.
The ships had been four years, six and one-half months at sea. In that time the
Discovery logged 120,000 kilometres, 16,000 more than the *Resolution* of
Cook's second voyage. To this might be added another 16,000 kilometres covered by the various boat expeditions during the survey.[59]

An epilogue to the Nootka crisis and Vancouver's voyage was the appearance
of the sixteen-gun British sloop-of-war *Providence,* Lieutenant Broughton commanding, on the Northwest Coast. She had been sent by the Admiralty to aid
Vancouver who, unknown to Broughton, had already sailed from Monterey.
From mid-March to mid-May 1796, Broughton made extensive repairs to his
ship at Nootka Sound. Maquinna told him that the dispute had been settled at
last. He then decided to sail for Neah Bay and San Francisco Bay and cross the
Pacific to survey the Asian shore from the China Sea north to the Kamchatka
Peninsula.[60] Misfortune overtook him in May 1797, when the *Providence* was
wrecked and the seas claimed her, though no lives were lost.

Vancouver's voyage to the North Pacific and Northwest Coast, and to a lesser
extent Broughton's, had important consequences for the development of British
interests there. Accurate surveys, so necessary for seaborne commerce, had been
made. By the end of the eighteenth century, also, British ambitions to expand
into the Pacific had been partially realized. After the Nootka Sound dispute British merchant adventurers were able to enter the maritime fur trade and to develop
other undertakings in the Pacific without fear of molestation from the Spanish. In
short, a wedge had been made into the Spanish hemispheric reserve: British
traders could use Nootka on a temporary basis, Canadian fur traders could now
move overland from the Athabaska country without fear of trespassing on foreign
soil, and English interests in the maritime fur trade and the whaling industry
could operate in the Pacific without fear of molestation.

11

The Overlanders

To secure to one's own people a disproportionate share of the benefits of sea commerce every effort was made to exclude others, either by the peaceful legislative methods of monopoly or prohibitory regulations, or, when these failed, by direct violence.

A. T. MAHAN, *THE INFLUENCE OF SEA POWER UPON HISTORY*

About the time that the Nootka convention recognized British rights to trade in the Pacific and to claim sovereignty over sections of the Northwest Coast not already occupied by European nations, traders of the North West Company were relentlessly pushing their commerce into every tributary of the Athabaska country east of the Rocky Mountains. West of the Rockies they were facing obstacles of distance no easier than the long, tenuous links by sea faced by maritime fur traders then frequenting the Northwest Coast. Westward from Fort Chipewyan, the hub of Athabaska trade, four immense mountain chains divided the prairie foothills from the Pacific. A maze of wildly turbulent rivers lay beyond the continental divide. The secrets of the streams that flowed to the Pacific lay hidden to Europeans until the explorations by Alexander Mackenzie, Simon Fraser, and David Thompson in the early years of the nineteenth century delineated the courses of the main rivers of the Pacific cordillera. Even then, they found no navigable artery except the lower Columbia River. This meant that to conquer distance and exploit the rich fur resources of the farthest west the Nor'westers would be obliged to use pack horses as well as canoes.[1]

Just as the maritime fur traders sought the riches of the China market, so did the Nor'westers. Their push to the Pacific was as much keyed to opening this new branch of commerce as it was to competing in the European market against their two great rivals, the Hudson's Bay Company and John Jacob Astor's American Fur Company.

In the search for profits in the China market, the North West Company had to observe mercantilist regulations emanating from London, not enjoying the munificent privileges of trade that their Hudson's Bay Company had possessed by charter since 1670.[2] And, as in the case of Meares and other British maritime fur traders, the Nor'westers had to resort to subterfuge in order to circumvent the powers of the East India Company. These two giant chartered companies and, to a lesser degree, the South Sea Company (which had some rights of licensing ships sailing in the Pacific between Cape Horn and the Cape of Good Hope), sought to keep rival British traders out of their precious trading preserves. Even though the East India Company allowed the North West Company to trade in China, stringent regulations were imposed. The monopolistic nature of British colonial and commercial policy hindered the growth of the company's trade to China. On the other hand, competition with the Hudson's Bay Company on its northern flank and with the Astorians on the south (both in the Old Northwest and on the Pacific slope) drew the Nor'westers westward. Essentially, they had to choose between expansion or elimination; and in their push to the Pacific the Nor'westers earned their motto, "Perseverance."

The Company's "Adventure to China" dates from the 1760's, shortly after Canada came under British control in the Treaty of Paris, 1763. In 1768, Sir Guy Carleton, Governor of Quebec, advised Lord Shelburne, President of the Board of Trade, that British traders should proceed across the continent to the Pacific Coast. There, Carleton wrote, they would select "a good port, take its latitude, longitude, and describe it so accurately as to enable our ships from the East Indies to find it out with ease, and then return the year following."[3] This was a concrete proposal for trans-Pacific trade emanating from the River St. Lawrence. At the same time two American colonists, Major Robert Rogers and Jonathan Carver, advanced schemes for finding a great northwest waterway that would permit commerce across the continent to a proposed post near the mouth of the legendary Strait of Anian. Carver believed that a British settlement on the Northwest Coast would aid trade, discovery, and communication with China and English settlements in the East Indies.[4]

Although the various partners and traders in the North West Company eventually undertook expansion towards the Pacific at their own cost, they never tired of sending memoranda to the home government for British support for their enterprises: this was especially true of the trader Peter Pond, who realized that Athabaska could be a base for a new trade to the Pacific Coast and the far east. Pond's map of 1785, his enduring contribution to the geographical knowledge of the North American interior, laid down the major drainage basins east of the Rocky Mountains and showed the relationship of these rivers to Cook Inlet, Prince William Sound, Bering Strait, and Nootka Sound. Much of his information was probably borrowed from the volumes about Cook's voyages, possibly W. Ellis's *An Authentic Narrative of a Voyage Performed by Captain Cook and Captain Clerke* (1782). On the basis of data obtained from Indians, Pond knew that Russians were already on the Northwest Coast and that American ships were fitting out to trade on the same coast. In 1785 he appealed to the government to assist the Nor'westers in developing their western operations "in order that trading posts may be settled and connections formed with the natives all over that country even to the sea coast; by which means so firm a footing may be established as will preserve that valuable trade from falling into the hands of other powers." He concluded that this extension of national interests would aid not only the British nation but Canada.[5]

Clearly Pond found stimulus in Cook's discoveries on the Northwest Coast. Might not the Athabaska River enter into Cook's "River," as Cook had called what later became known as Cook Inlet? Might not the Mackenzie River also flow to the Pacific? Or, might there not be another river coursing through the great mountains and leading to the distant ocean? Several Nor'westers speculated that the Slave River made its way to Prince William Sound, Cook's River, or some other destination on the Pacific Coast. In short, Pond's discoveries east of the mountains, matched with his and others' speculations about the topography west of the Rockies, again raised new hopes of a Northwest Passage. Pond's vision fired Alexander Mackenzie with the idea of setting out on voyages that would bring him in 1793 to the Pacific Coast.

Shortly after accounts of James Cook's last voyage had described the surprising demand for sea otter and other skins among the Chinese, the North West Company had begun its China trade via Montreal and London. The company did so through Moscow, Irkutsk, and thence to Peking. By the 1790's a quarter of all furs that came onto the English market were destined for Russia, and from there the largest portion were forwarded to China. Not only did the Nor'westers seek to expand this trade, but they wanted to trade directly with Canton. Thus, in 1792, they lobbied the government to request that Lord Macartney, the British emissary to Peking, negotiate with the Manchu emperor Ch'ien Lung for admission of furs to China. Macartney's mission was unsuccessful; he refused to kowtow, to bow in subjugation to the power of the Emperor of China. Consequently no direct trade could be established except through Canton or Kiahtka on the China-Russia border. The Nor'westers thus continued to conduct their trade via Russia, and during the period 1792-95 sent furs to the annual value of £40,000.

This method of trading with China seems to have terminated in 1797, by which time the company had found a less indirect, more lucrative way of doing business. In 1792 they began using American business connections in Canton. After the New York ship *Empress of China* had arrived in Macao in August 1784, several American ships had sailed for China from New York, Boston, and elsewhere on the eastern American seaboard. In 1788 the ships *Columbia* and *Lady Washington* solved the problem of the China trade by exchanging their cargoes of Northwest Coast pelts for tea and returning to Boston round the world. In Canton, recently arrived American agents received any furs, Canadian or other, that they could sell. This induced the Nor'wester partnership in Montreal of McTavish, Frobisher and Company to smuggle large quantities of furs across the border from Montreal to American ports to be forwarded to Canton. At Canton, agents effected sales wherever they could and arranged return cargoes. Gradually, the "Adventure to China" ran into trouble: by 1794 McTavish, Frobisher and Company had run up a deficit of £23,000 on their China account. As for the China trade via Russia, this proved similarly disappointing.[6]

While these difficulties were being encountered, Canadian traders pushed westward towards the Pacific, among them Peter Pond. He sold his interest in the North West Company in 1787, returned to Connecticut where he discussed his project for a fur empire of the West and a trans-Pacific commerce at Yale University and sought, unsuccessfully, the support of Congress. Meanwhile, the company deliberately took up his plan, which, as one historian deftly put it, "engrossed it for the rest of its career."[7] In particular, Alexander Mackenzie of Gregory, McLeod and Company, partners in the North West Company, prosecuted Pond's plan. In two major explorations—in 1789 and 1793—Mackenzie uncovered the principal geographical secrets of the Canadian far west. These were firstly that a great river, the Mackenzie, flowed northward to the Arctic Ocean and, secondly, that the Pacific could be reached by crossing the Rocky Mountains through the Peace River-Fraser River and West Road (Blackwater) River-Bella Coola River watersheds to Pacific tidewater at North Bentinck Arm.[8]

With a great deal of energy, Mackenzie now pressed on the government and public the necessity of developing the transcontinental trade route. In his book, *Voyages from Montreal,* first published in 1801 and for which he was knighted, Mackenzie put forward his suggestions, which deserve to be quoted at some length:[9]

The discovery of a passage by sea, North-East or NorthWest from the Atlantic to the Pacific Ocean, has for many years excited the attention of governments, and encouraged the enterprising spirit of individuals. The non-existence, however, of any such practical passage being at length determined, the practicability of a passage through the continents of Asia and America becomes an object of consideration. The Russians, who first discovered that, along the coasts of Asia no useful or regular navigation existed, opened an interior communication by rivers, and through that long and wide-extended continent, to the strait that separates Asia from America, over which they passed to the adjacent islands and continent of the latter. Our situation, at length, is in some degree similar to theirs; the non-existence of a practicable passage by sea, and the existence of one through the continent, are clearly proved; and it requires only the countenance and support of the British Government, to increase in a very ample proportion this national advantage, and secure the trade of that country to its subjects. . . . the Columbia is the line of communication from the Pacific Ocean, pointed out by nature, as it is the only navigable river in the whole extent of Vancouver's minute survey of that coast:[10] its banks also form the first level country in all the Southern extent of continental coast from Cook's entry, and, consequently, the most Northern situation fit for colonization, and suitable to the residence of a civilized people. By opening this intercourse between the Atlantic and Pacific Oceans, and forming regular establishments through the interior and at both extremes, as well as along the coasts and islands the entire command of the fur trade of North America might be obtained, from latitude 48 North to the pole, except that portion of it which the Russians have in the Pacific. To this may be added the fishing in both seas, and the markets of the four quarters of the globe.

Such would be the field for commercial enterprise, and incalculable would be the produce of it, when supported by the operations of that credit and capital which Great Britain so pre-eminently possesses. Then would this country begin to be remunerated for the expenses it has sustained in discovering and surveying the coast of the Pacific Ocean, which is at present left to American adventurers, who without regularity or capital, or the desire of conciliating future confidence, look altogether to the interest of the moment. They, therefore, collect all the skins they can procure, and in any manner that suits them, and having exchanged them at Canton for the produce of China, return to their own country. Such adventurers, and many of them, as I have been informed, have been very successful, would instantly disappear from before a well-regulated trade.[11]

In Mackenzie's scheme, oceanic trade via the Pacific would be less expensive and less difficult than overland trade through the St. Lawrence. Two trading stations, one at Cook Inlet and another at the southern limits of British trade, would secure the Pacific coastal trade, a commerce aided by a conciliatory native policy. The China trade would increase, a matter of importance to the East India Company, because importing furs would lessen the need for importing silver from India or England to China. British maritime interests would also advance with the development of trade via Hudson Bay, and in an emergency Upper Canada might be made more secure. In short, Mackenzie envisioned a dominion linking two great oceans.

He first pressed this plan on the government in Upper Canada, where he was a sometime member of the legislative assembly. He solicited the support of Colonel John Graves Simcoe, the lieutenant-governor of Upper Canada, who in turn submitted the project to the Board of Trade.[12] Mackenzie also brought his project before Sir Guy Carleton, now Lord Dorchester. In his capacity as Governor-in-Chief of British North America, Dorchester passed the information on to the British minister responsible for colonial affairs, the Duke of Portland.[13] It is clear that the advancement of trade and dominion was an idea to which Simcoe and Dorchester, but especially Simcoe, gave their support. However, Mackenzie's plan seems to have gathered dust in London. Cabinet ministers found the then critical affairs of Europe too pressing to divert their attention to a remote frontier of empire where rival claims were uncertain.

While Mackenzie was advancing his plan, the North West Company was effecting the grand design. In 1792, two years before Mackenzie met with Simcoe and a year before Mackenzie reached the Pacific Coast, the partnership of McTavish, Frobisher and Company, and possibly Astor, chartered the ships *Washington* and *America* to convey pelts to China via Cape Horn. The return cargo of yard goods, tea, and semi-porcelain purchased in Canton was sold to Astor.[14] This direct and profitable venture to China was followed by a second and more ambitious undertaking. The outlay for this was estimated at £279,894. The trade, involving the conveyance of 4,000 beaver pelts, was undertaken by an 800-ton vessel chartered in New York.[15]

The trade was given added impetus when Mackenzie, now a principal partner in McTavish, Frobisher and Company, implemented his plan. He was "confirmed in his view that the salvation of the fur trade lay in the north-west, in access to the Pacific and in the absorption of the Hudson's Bay Company's rights; not in collaboration with the Americans."[16] Having convinced his partners to extend their capital outlay, Mackenzie went to New York in 1798 where he purchased in the name of William Seton and William Magee Seton, citizens of the United States and residents of New York, the 340-ton ship *Northern Liberties*. He had her coppered and fitted out. He also convinced Messrs. Seton and Maitland & Co. of New York to invest $25,000 in the project.[17] He had the venture insured for the total cost, $115,000, and for a voyage from New York to Canton and thence to any European port with leave to call at Falmouth, England, for goods marked "American property."[18] Thus was the subterfuge of using foreign ships complete.

The success of this voyage encouraged the Nor'westers whenever possible to consign first-quality furs to China. Unfortunately, however, the company did not have enough of them for both the London and Canton markets: in consequence, the former began to suffer, much to the regret of the London partners. Thus the Montreal interests soon were at odds with their London counterparts; the "Canadians" (McTavish, Frobisher) wanted to extend the new commerce, while the "British" (McTavish, Fraser) warned that that would weaken their position on the London market in relation to the Hudson's Bay Company, to say nothing of running afoul of East India Company regulations and French warships at large on the high seas. McTavish and Frobisher were now obliged to "juggle the demands of the Far East with those of Europe and somehow to retain both."[19]

This extension of markets naturally tied in with Mackenzie's strategy of extending company trade across the continent. Athabaska was the farthest west from which furs could, with profit, be sent east to Montreal and then to markets.

Why not send the Athabaska returns westward to the Pacific? Here was the origin of what later became known as the "Columbian enterprise." At this germinal stage, Mackenzie was pressing for a division of company exports: on the one hand, pelts could be sent via Hudson Bay (thus avoiding the expensive Montreal route); on the other, western furs could be taken to the Pacific, where company ships would transport them to China ports.

In global terms Mackenzie was thinking of how he could outflank the East India, South Sea, and Hudson's Bay companies. He reasoned, rightly, that the North Pacific Coast fishery had immense commercial possibilities. He planned to set up a new company, "The Fishery and Fur Company." Whale ships would take trade items to the Northwest Coast. An entrepôt of trade and a main base of coastal operations would be built at Nootka Sound, with smaller posts on the Columbia River in the south and at Sea Otter Harbour in latitude 55°N.

In January 1802, Mackenzie laid his plan before the Secretary of State for War and the Colonies, Lord Hobart, under the title, "Preliminaries to the Establishment of a Permanent Fishery and Trade in Furs etc. in the Interior and on the West Coast of North America."[20] Eight months later, on 25 October 1802, Mackenzie again appealed to the Colonial Office for support—this time military—for the building of an establishment on the Northwest Coast and for forestalling foreign rivals.[21]

When the government again failed to act, the Nor'westers were obliged to counter the steady expansion of Astor's trade on the southern frontiers of North West Company influence. In 1806 Mackenzie and his associates formed the Michilimackinac Fur Company to forestall Astor in the Old Northwest, between the Great Lakes and the Mississippi. But more than this, the rise of Astor's larger intentions of trade to the Pacific alarmed the Nor'westers. They did not wish to see their Columbia enterprise, as first described by Mackenzie, pre-empted. They refused to agree to Astor's 1809 proposal that the Canadians buy one-third of the stock in his own Pacific plan. They preferred to go it alone. However, five disgruntled Nor'westers, dissatisfied with the company reorganization in 1804, fell in with Astor and were included in the Pacific Fur Company trade agreement of 23 June 1810.[22] Thus was born the American company which sent the *Tonquin* to the Northwest Coast (she arrived at the mouth of the Columbia 22 March 1811), built Astoria, and stopped the Nor'westers at the very mouth of the Columbia River.

Until 1813 and the British purchase and occupation of Astoria (Fort George), the Astorians proved that the "golden round"—from Europe, eastern North America, the Northwest Coast, and Canton—was highly profitable.[23] What Mackenzie had warned of, and in fact proposed for British commerce as late as 1809, had been achieved.[24] No doubt some Nor'westers must have been greatly concerned that the British government failed to heed the appeal of their London agent, Simon McGillivray, dated 10 November 1810, to send a British warship and to build a military fort or settlement at the mouth of the Columbia, thereby giving Great Britain rights of possession.[25] That, however, was a development the government, in conjunction with the company, would pursue during wartime and pursue in 1813 with success.[26]

In the meantime, beginning about 1800, the Nor'westers had been extending their operations to the Pacific slope.[27] Mackenzie's route to North Bentinck Arm was patently unsuitable for trade, and the Nor'westers continued to search for a navigable river to the Pacific. By the winter of 1807-8, William McGillivray could write that the company had "commenced a project for extending their researches and trade as far as the South Sea" and that it intended to "form an establishment for the trade of that country on the Columbia river, which . . . receives and conducts to the Ocean all the waters that rise West of the Mountains."[28] In keeping with these objectives, David Thompson, geographer extraordinaire, crossed the Rockies to set up the Columbia trade. During 1808, Simon Fraser, under instructions to determine the course and character of the Columbia, followed the river bearing his name. The company built a number of posts west of the Rockies, including Fort St. James and Fort Fraser in 1806, Fort George and Kootenai House in 1807, Kullyspell House in 1809, Spokane House in 1810 or 1811, and Fort Thompson in 1812. The company was there because it had to be; as Mackenzie noted in 1812, the Pacific cordillera was "our only remaining Beaver country." The scarcity of beaver, he lamented, "has been so much felt for the last two years that the country in its present state cannot support our establishment of partners, clerks and canoemen, so that there is a necessity for extending the field, were there no intruders in the country to menace us."[29] There were, of course, "intruders" in the north country. Fraser had learned from the Carrier Indians at Fort St. James on Stuart Lake that they were obtaining trade goods from American ships trading at the mouth of the Skeena and Nass rivers. Fraser's plan to develop the posts of the northern interior was designed to undercut American rivals on the coast.

Because of the nature of the Pacific Coast drainage basin with its short, swift rivers, the company had to develop a practicable link between the interior, which Fraser called New Caledonia, and the sea. Over a decade, they developed the Okanagan Trail, which went from Alexandria on the Fraser to Kamloops and through the Okanagan Valley to the Okanagan River, a tributary of the Columbia. In 1813, traders left Fort St. James on Stuart Lake and found a trail to Kamloops. As one Nor'wester wrote, "we shall, for the future, obtain our yearly supply of goods by that route, and send our returns out that way, to be shipped directly for China."[30]

The ultimate destination of these land brigades was the mouth of the Columbia River. Not only was it a place where furs were collected for export, but it also served as the entrepôt where supplies and trade items for the vast interior were received. In short, it was the linchpin of the transcontinental-trans-Pacific fur trade. Rivalry with the Astorians, the military assistance of Britain during wartime, the westward expansion of the Canadian fur trade had all brought the Nor'westers to Pacific shores in 1813. There they were some 4,800 kilometres from Montreal overland and, some 29,000 kilometres from London via long, tenuous sea lanes. Directly across the Pacific, some 13,000 kilometres, was the lucrative China market.

Though the North West Company's fortunes continued to expand in the first decade of the nineteenth century, the lack of a charter prevented any great advance in company trade. It repeatedly pressed the government to issue such a charter.[31] At one time, in 1812, the Board of Trade came very close to granting one to the company for the rights of trade to the Mackenzie River watershed and the Pacific slope.[32] Evidently it was not granted because the full extent of American interests and claims on the Northwest Coast was unknown. Certainly the British ministry knew of Lewis and Clark's penetration to the Pacific and of the role of the United States government in that expedition. With characteristic caution they were ready to grant such a charter only provided it did not interfere with United States claims to territories on the Northwest Coast, the limits of which were not precisely defined.[33]

The plight of the Nor'westers was somewhat relieved when they entered into an arrangement with the East India Company. How this came about seems to be as follows. On 13 July 1811, when the Nor'westers were at their Fort William rendezvous on Lake Superior, discussion centred on correspondence with the British ministry and the East India Company "relative to a licence solicited from the latter on the part of the North West Company—to enable them to dispose of such Furs and Skins in China as they might collect in course of their intended trade on the North West Coast of America." Three days later they resolved to enter "into adventure and a Trade from England, and China to the North West Coast of America," if a suitable licence could be acquired from the East India Company. This application was successful, much to the satisfaction of the North West Company. "We are happy to hear," wrote the North West partners to William McGillivray, "that part of the difficulties that existed between us and the East India Company are done away."[34]

How did this change come about and how did it benefit the Nor'westers? Maybe because the government could not grant a charter to the Nor'westers, they may have prevailed upon the East India Company to ease its restrictions.[35] The principal, perhaps sole, concession from the East India Company seems to have been that the Nor'westers were assured of getting dollars rather than Oriental products in exchange for beaver skins.[36] This they preferred because dollars gave them an immediate freedom from competition with the East India Company.

Immediately the Montreal agents learned the good news, they instructed their London associates that a ship, the *Isaac Todd,* would be sent from Montreal to London and then to the Columbia and Canton. They acquired naval support, with the result that H.M.S. *Racoon,* a sloop-of-war mounting 26 guns, reached Fort George on 30 November 1813 and the *Isaac Todd* on 23 April 1814.[37] The *Isaac Todd* subsequently took *all* the Columbia furs from Fort George to Canton and returned to England with tea on account for the East India Company.[38] Evidently the venture did not meet expectations, for in reference to the trader Angus Bethune, who had gone with the *Isaac Todd* to Canton, one Nor'wester wrote to another: "Bethune is returned from China where he sold his furs, but not at a flattering price."[39] The total value of furs sold on this occasion amounted to $101,155.40.[40]

This first legitimate trans-Pacific, Anglo-Canadian trade from the Columbia to Canton was followed by a venture in 1814 by a schooner aptly named the *Columbia* which twice conveyed Northwest Coast furs to Canton.[41] Certainly, information from "the Gentlemen of the Columbia" indicated that the state and resources of the Columbia region were highly satisfactory.[42] Not only did the *Columbia* trade with China, she initiated the Canadian company's trade with the Spanish in Alta California, the Russians at Bodega Bay, the Hawaiians at Kailua, and with the Russians again at Sitka.[43] The "golden round" depended not only on British manufactures, Northwest Coast furs, and Chinese tea. Such items as sandalwood, rum, livestock, tallow, provisions, naval stores, and tobacco were conveyed by the *Columbia* within the broad confines of the Pacific rim. A third company ship, the *Colonel Allan,* visited Fort George and took furs and specie to China in 1816.

Nonetheless, for reasons of cost after these three vessels were sent, the company reverted to having an American house facilitate their business in China.[44] Such an arrangement, which lasted through 1821, involved a partnership with the firms of Perkins & Co. of Boston and J. and J. N. Perkins of Canton.[45] Five or six ships sailed under this arrangement from 1815 to 1821.[46] To make this trade more legal and circumvent the East India Company monopoly, in 1817 the company considered the Oregon territory to belong to the United States.[47] In a peculiar way American independence favoured the company's achievement.

With the merger of the North West Company and the Hudson's Bay Company in 1821, Company ships continued to send supplies from London to Fort George on the North Pacific Coast, supplanted in 1825 by Fort Vancouver, and to new entrepôts such as Fort Simpson and Fort Victoria. Furs from the Columbia Department were invariably sent to the London auctions by return ship. Until 1828 at least, the Company continued to sell high-quality furs to Canton, though with some difficulty, especially because of the East India Company's tenacious position regarding their rights in the China trade.[48] The Company continued to trade throughout the Pacific rim, at such diverse places as San Francisco Bay, Bodega Bay, Sitka, and Honolulu.

The North West Company's "Adventure to China" proved to be a success, if qualified. They overcame almost insurmountable obstacles of topography and distance in order to market Columbia furs in Canton by the thousands, for instance, 98,240 pelts in 1817[49] and 21,826 in 1820.[50] Their achievement reflected the strategy they employed in carrying on trade through American corporate auspices in order to avoid British, mainly East India Company, restrictions.[51] Further, it demonstrated their ability to determine market needs, to obtain capital, and by no means least to ensure cheap bulk transportation.

Cook had thought trade in furs in the North Pacific too distant from England to be profitable. Yet in fact this became a paying proposition with respect to the China market. As in some other trades of this sort, past and present, it brought forth smuggling and flags of convenience, subterfuges, and surreptitious arrangements. The British had pioneered the maritime fur trade, the Americans later had acquired ascendancy, and the North West Company had begun the Columbia enterprise and "adventure to China." The Nor'westers, who accepted the legacy for trade and dominion given the British under terms of the Nootka convention, came to the Northwest Coast first by land and then by sea. They employed direct and indirect trading links with China. Frequently they found it best to deal through London and New York rather than sending their peltry directly to Canton. In this way the North Atlantic Triangle played its own distant role in the opening of the China trade, in the promotion of commerce beyond the great southern capes, and in the development of the Northwest Coast.

Epilogue

Francis Drake's 1579 approach to the Northwest Coast had shown other mariners the difficulties of sailing the northeastern Pacific, and for nearly two centuries few ships had reached the Northwest Coast via the southern capes. In the mid-eighteenth century Russia approached the coast from Siberia and Kamchatka. At the same time Spain pressed north and west from Mexico into Alta California. Yet not until the British and the Americans in their wake conquered the watery wastes did the Northwest Coast between California and Alaska become profitable for European enterprise. Cook's third voyage placed Nootka Sound on world maps for the first time, and although his charts of the North Pacific gave mariners a rough idea of the ocean's littoral, they contained yawning blanks suggesting unknown islands and reefs, harbours, and hazards. Subsequent trading voyages by Meares, Duncan, Barkley, and others provided further details, and as a result of Vancouver's survey the main features of the coastline had been duly determined and charted.

Drake, Cook, and Vancouver all had been entrusted by their government with the same objective, to find a northwest passage linking the Atlantic with the Pacific. This waterway eluded each of them. In the case of Cook and Vancouver, inshore coastal exploration was needed to seek the passage, from which the British gained a comprehensive understanding of the intricate coastline. They compiled charts and views published by the government, navigational aids which were made available without restriction to mariners of other nationalities. Freedom of navigation on the high seas formed a tenet of Britain's maritime predominance, and the charts completed after Cook's and Vancouver's voyages enabled ships of any flag to approach the Northwest Coast. As a result of these two probes the chart showed not a vague shoreline stretching north and west from California to Alaska, but several large islands flanking the coast, including Vancouver and the Queen Charlottes, an entry into an inner passage from Cape Flattery via the Strait of Juan de Fuca, and an extensive arm of sea, Puget Sound, that would become in time a focal point of Pacific Northwest development. The chart also showed a maze of islands and channels separating Vancouver Island from the continental shore, numerous inlets penetrating eastward into the coastal mountains, and northward, beyond Cape Caution on the mainland towards the Gulf of Alaska islands, countless passages, and inlets.

Cook and, to a greater degree, Vancouver had shown how complex the coastline was between $49°$ and $60°N$. It was a unique blend of offshore islands, straits, and mountains quite unlike any other habitat on the west side of the Americas. These two great mariners had proven that the Strait of Juan de Fuca was not the legendary Strait of Anian, that no great river of the west drained out of Athabaska to the Gulf of Alaska, and that the great lone land of Alaska was not an island but part of the American continent. In other words, their discoveries suggested that the Northwest Passage to the Atlantic might lie north of Bering Strait along the northern shoreline of the American continent. Had they found a navigable waterway to Hudson Bay, they would have ended the comparative isolation of the Northwest Coast from Europe. As it was, until the completion of the Panama Canal, the shortest sea link between Britain and British Columbia remained the passage by way of Cape Horn.

Even so, the voyages of Cook and Vancouver heralded a vast influx of irrepressible white men—fur traders, whalers, administrators, visitors, missionaries, miners, botanists, and sailors—men of every class and distinction. They came to conquer the Pacific, its islands, and its continents for "God, gold, and glory." They brought with them their morals, ideologies, knowledge, technology, plants, and animals. They also brought diseases, rum, and guns. They brought with them powers to build and powers to destroy.

The western invasion of the Pacific and its littoral came by sea and by land. It brought the British and others in touch with the entire Pacific in a dramatic surge in the late eighteenth century. Almost concurrently, the invaders expanded trade in China, established garrisons in California, built posts in Alaska, made contact with the island peoples of Hawaii, Tahiti, and elsewhere in Oceania, claimed Australia and New Zealand, and established a trading relationship with the Northwest Coast Indians.

The British were not the sole participants in this process but were clearly the leaders. In the years following the American Revolution, British interests shifted perceptibly to eastern seas, and in this process the commercial ambitions of the first industrial nation found ample vent in the new carrying trades of eastern seas. The need for bases of trade, for naval stores, for new markets and products, and for penal settlements drew the British to the Pacific. In the process new commodities gained the attention of merchant adventurers. The sea otter and beaver, two prime furs of the Northwest Coast, were only two of the new luxuries. Tortoise meat and shell, the sea slug known as *bêche-de-mer* or trepang, edible birds' nests, pearls and pearl shells, arrowroot, flax, sandalwood, timber, ginseng, tea, silk, whale oil, guano, hides, and tallow were other trade items that brought the British in touch with Pacific peoples and made the Pacific a hunting ground for the merchantman. Many of these products found their way to Canton, in the late eighteenth century the commercial hub of the Pacific. The logbooks of the seaborne pioneers tell of the new links of trade within the Pacific: the ship's entry via Cape Horn, a call at the Galapagos for tortoise, a visit to Hawaii for provisions, a voyage to the Northwest Coast for sea otter, a stop at Hawaii for sandalwood, and passage to Canton to unload valued peltry and take on tea, silk, and porcelain for the homeward track to the North Atlantic.

To make a profitable commercial circumnavigation on each stretch of the voyage was the aim of every British merchantman who sailed the Pacific. But the restrictive charter of the East India Company and, to a lesser extent, that of the South Sea Company, stood in the way of entrepreneurs such as John Meares and Richard Cadman Etches. The strangling tentacles of monopoly prevented them from unrestricted trade. They were obliged to sail under foreign flags of convenience or to pay heavy licensing fees in order to traffic in waters hitherto the prerogative of these companies. After the 1790 Nootka Convention with Spain, the government pressured the East India Company to make concessions. In 1790, the government received from the company the hollow offer that traders from the Northwest Coast could sell their furs at Canton provided that they return directly from whence they came or that they carry a limited quantity of China goods to Europe on company accounts.[1] This was hardly a concession to the fur traders and left them no better off than before. The government countered by sending Lord Macartney to Peking to gain access to north China ports and crack the Canton monopoly, but the mission was coldly received and the government was unable to modify the company's position. Thus, when Parliament renewed the company's charter in 1793, no material change to the provisions regulating trans-Pacific commerce was made.[2]

In these circumstances, the British maritime fur trade began to fall off dramatically, especially after 1796. In the period 1797 to 1820, only 26 British vessels visited the Northwest Coast. By contrast, 238 American vessels were in the same trade.[3] Thus while a valuable commerce was kept up by the Americans, the British, hamstrung by regulation, lost an important branch of trade to a rival nation. Wars with France and the United States also affected the nature of overseas commerce in these years. Moreover, the decline in abundance of the sea otter made the trade less lucrative. Yet at the bottom of British failure in this trade lay the inability of government to modify the company monopoly. Thus, until the New Englanders in turn gave way to the Nor'westers trading in pelts of land animals, the Americans held commercial ascendancy on the coast.

The rise of the continental fur trade, however, buttressed the British Empire's claim to the Northwest Coast. The occupation of sites for trading purposes throughout the Pacific cordillera from Alaska to California strengthened the British claim to sovereignty in the farthest west. It gave reality to Francis Drake's Nova Albion. A new continental empire of commerce had been formed across Canada. Although American rivals in the form of John Jacob Astor and Company offered competition from 1806 through 1813, the Nor'westers, backed by the Royal Navy during the War of 1812, gained sole control of the mouth of the Columbia River, the new Nootka of the continental fur trade.

Even so, the East India Company still barred the door, and while schemes were made by the North West Company to join with the East India Company in common ventures to exploit the trans-Pacific trade, the East India Company remained adamantly opposed to any arrangement that would threaten their precious preserve. Because of this the North West Company never reached its destiny in oriental trade, a factor which led to its impoverishment and eventual merger with its rivals from the Bay in 1821. Statesmen such as George Canning knew that the trans-Pacific trade was the most promising commerce of the future. Until government modified the East India Company's charter in 1833, no British ship could sail from the Columbia River or elsewhere on the Northwest Coast to Canton without the company's permission.

Though the maritime fur traders suffered from the neglect of government, whaling interests made rapid gains in the Pacific after the Nootka Convention of 1790. In that year Britain led all nations in the search for oil on the high seas. Of the forty-one ships whaling in the Pacific in 1790, twenty-three were of British registry and the so-called Southern Whale fishery had become far more profitable than the ancient Greenland fishery.[4] Ships from London, Bristol, and Liverpool were doubling Cape Horn and pressing north into the Pacific's whale grounds with great success but not without rivalry from Nantucket, Dunkirk, and Boston sailors. Like the Nor'westers they faced discriminatory restrictions at home. The British Arabs of the Pacific, the Enderbys, the Champions, and the St. Barbes, demanded that the government free them from the restrictions of the South Sea Company and the East India Company. Lord Hawkesbury at the Board of Trade readily responded by pressing these companies to loosen their requirements and allow whalers to enter their waters. Consequently, in 1793 whalers were allowed to fish in Australian waters, and in 1802 the old bugbear of licences was lifted against whalers.[5]

The Nootka Convention gave Britain the right to whale in eastern seas provided British subjects did not interfere with Spanish trade and colonial control in the Americas. To encourage this new branch of commerce, in 1792 the government lent H.M.S. *Rattler* to the Enderbys and their London associates for the purpose of discovering and charting islands off the west coast of South America that would serve as bases to repair ships and refresh crews. The *Rattler* was commanded by none other than Captain James Colnett who, with his ship *Argonaut,* had been seized by Martínez at Nootka three years before. In 1793 and 1794, Colnett cruised the southeastern Pacific, putting in at such places as Juan Fernandez and the Galapagos, making important charts and discovering harbours suitable for whalers. Colnett had not forgotten his incarceration at Spanish hands, and in his recommendations for the expansion of whaling his patriotism and abhorrence of the Spanish remained unbridled. He foresaw a new British dominion of trade in the Pacific. He envisioned a Latin America liberated from Spanish imperialism, a whaling base at the Galapagos, an interconnected trade in whales, seals, and sea otter up to the North Pole, and a settlement at Nootka Sound that would serve the twofold purpose of securing the trade of the whole Northwest Coast from the Russians and taking the sea otter trade out of the hands of natives, whom he thought a lazy and unproductive lot.[6] He also foresaw a commerce in spars from the Northwest Coast to Europe, a new trade with Japan, and an interest in the Hawaiian Islands as the key to succouring British merchant and naval ships in the Pacific. In all this, Colnett was clearly an imperialist and an able visionary of how the Pacific eventually would develop as an economic unit. Indeed, he stood at the forefront of a successful British commercial thrust into the Pacific.

The rising tide of empire represented by the maritime fur traders and whalers affected the Northwest Coast Indians in a number of ways. It increased their wealth by drawing their native economies into a worldwide trading network. The Indians of the coast found that their peltry was highly prized by the maritime fur traders who were, after all, only middlemen in the trade to Canton. The Indians were crafty traders, skilfully bargaining for the highest price. The Moachat Nootka were the first to enjoy the influence that trade gave them in relation to their neighbours. As white traders ranged up and down the coast, other tribes such as the Clayoquot, the Makah, the Newitty Kwakiutl, and the Haida also increased their wealth. Some, such as the Nootka and Haida, grew aggressively commercial in the search for power and prestige. Trade links with the wider world stimulated their ancient customs based on clan and chieftainship. Their newly acquired wealth enabled them to intensify their gift-giving to rival chiefs at their potlaches. In general, many facets of Indian culture and life-style were affected by the veneer of European civilization brought by Cook and his followers to the Northwest Coast, where the resulting modifications have left a legacy that can be seen today.

On the other hand, the European presence on the coast brought features of a cultural impact that were to be so apparent elsewhere in the Pacific, notably in Polynesia. Cook and Vancouver had Admiralty instructions to be conciliatory and friendly in their dealings with natives, but these strictures did not extend to the maritime fur traders, British or otherwise. Traders disregarded Indian codes of conduct and mistreated native women. They also offended the dignity of chiefs and acted barbarously towards people they regarded as primitive. Whites brought with them rum and guns, two potent and dangerous additions. On the Indian side, the natives invariably retaliated as they did against James Hanna at Nootka Sound in 1785. White traders acquired a healthy respect for the military capabilities of the Northwest Coast Indians and increased their defences. Trade was so competitive that violence frequently occurred on the coast. In 1794, Vancouver believed that he had been sent none too soon to survey the coast. The unjustifiable conduct of the fur traders had so provoked the animosity of the Indians that he felt that in another year he would not have had sufficient force on board his ships to repel their attacks.[7]

One of Vancouver's officers, Joseph Whidbey, thought that trade on the Northwest Coast would "prove a new source of wealth to Great Britain little short of any she at present had."[8] The British did not covet land in the far off seas but broad fields for maritime and commercial endeavour.[9] As Lord Shelburne said in 1783 with respect to British policy in North America, "We prefer trade to dominion." The British prized a trading post at a remote spot such as Nootka Sound. If necessary, they were prepared to go to war to defend their rights of trade on the high seas. In the late eighteenth and early nineteenth century, British ministers were interested in empire as a means rather than an end in itself. Commerce remained the life blood of the nation, and the pursuit of profit on the Northwest Coast formed a small artery contributing to the healthy condition of the nation. Yet, in time, trade spelled dominion. As Russia, Spain, and the nascent United States intensified their respective interests in the farthest west, and as Canadian and British fur traders penetrated overland to Pacific tidewater, British interest in the Northwest Coast increased. By the mid-nineteenth century, the question of sovereignty of the Pacific cordillera from $49°$ to $54°$ $40'$ latitude and of the southern tip of Vancouver Island had been resolved in Britain's favour.

In retrospect, by the second decade of the nineteenth century the Northwest Coast had been brought within the limits of European influence. In the course of the previous two and a half centuries, explorers and traders had garnered reasonably accurate data concerning a shoreline that was the most remote and least accessible from Europe. The three-masted ship perfected during the late eighteenth century had given the leading maritime nations, especially Britain, the deepwater capability to extend their influence to the uttermost quarters of the navigable oceans. This tool of empire brought the Northwest Coast within the orbit of world commerce and ended forever its quiet isolation. But by no means was the Northwest Coast, as it would become, a thriving and productive area of millions of people exploiting in the industrial age the great mineral, agricultural, and forest resources of the Pacific cordillera. Yet the promise of its future had been given—the first wave of exploiters had appeared, greedily taken its wealth, changed beyond measure the culture of its Indian peoples, and fomented an international rivalry for the last unclaimed quarter of North America.

Abbreviations

Adm.	Admiralty Papers, P.R.O.
A.R.S.	Archives of the Royal Society, London
B.T.	Board of Trade Papers, P.R.O.
B.L.Y.U.	Beineke Library, Yale University
B.L.	British Library, London
C.O.	Colonial Office Papers, P.R.O.
F.O.	Foreign Office Papers, P.R.O.
H.B.C.A.	Hudson's Bay Company Archives, Winnipeg
H.M.S.	Home Miscellaneous Series, I.O.L.
H.O.	Home Office, P.R.O.
I.O.L.	India Office Library, London (in Commonwealth Office Library)
M.M.B.C.	Maritime Museum of British Columbia, Victoria
O.H.S.	Oregon Historical Society, Portland
P.A.B.C.	Provincial Archives of British Columbia, Victoria
P.A.C.	Public Archives of Canada, Ottawa
P.C.	Privy Council Papers, P.R.O.
P.L.D.U.	Perkins Library, Duke University, Durham, North Carolina
P.R.O.	Public Record Office, London
R.C.S.	Royal Commonwealth Society, London
S.P.	State Papers, P.R.O.

Notes

NOTES TO CHAPTER ONE: TYRANNY OF DISTANCE

1. N. W. Jones, "Account of Chinese Voyages to the Northwest Coast of America," *Indian Bulletin for 1868* (New York, 1869), p. 8.
2. Alan Moorehead, *Darwin and The Beagle* (London: Hamish Hamilton, 1969), p. 218. See also Harry Morton, *The Wind Commands: Sailors and Sailing Ships in the Pacific* (Vancouver: University of British Columbia Press, 1975), p. 166.
3. Small merchantmen seldom attempted the Horn even in the 1780's. In 1786, the 50-ton sloop *Princess Royal,* Master Charles Duncan, R.N., commanding, made a remarkably easy passage round the Horn that was for some time the talk of mariners on the west coast of the Americas.
4. See Matthew F. Maury, *Explanations and Sailing Directions to Accompany the Wind and Current Charts . . .,* 8th ed., 2 vols. (Washington, 1858-59), pp. 764-67. By 1869 enough was known concerning winds and currents to enable Maury to list the following distances for sailing ships: England to San Francisco, 130 days; Shanghai to San Francisco, 45 days; San Francisco to Shanghai, 64 days; New South Wales to San Francisco, 43 days; New South Wales to the eastern seaboard of the United States or Europe, 110 days; London to New South Wales via Cape of Good Hope, 124 days. See winds and routes map in Matthew F. Maury, *Physical Geography of the Sea and Its Meteorology,* new ed. (London, 1869), plate 8.
5. Important mid-eighteenth-century advances in scientific navigation were: Hadley's reflecting quadrant, Campbell's sextant, Bird's astronomical quadrant, Knight's azimuth compasses, Ramsden's theodolites, and Harrison's chronometers. See R. A. Skelton, "Captain James Cook as a Hydrographer," *Mariner's Mirror* 40 (1954): 95.
6. The 1795 regulation may have sufficed for the Royal Navy, but it did not always meet all dietetic needs. Even early in the twentieth century the causes and prevention of scurvy were still being debated. (see "Discussion on the Prevention of Scurvy," *British Medical Journal,* 4 October 1902, pp. 1023-24). On this subject generally, see Christopher Lloyd, ed., *The Health of Seamen* (London: Navy Records Society, 1965), vol. 107. Also, Barbara Burkhardt et al., *Sailors & Sauerkraut* (Sidney, B.C.: Gray's Publishing, 1978), pp. 23-26.
7. Admiral G. A. Ballard, "Cape Horn," *Mariner's Mirror* 3 (1945): 144.
8. Morton, *Wind Commands,* p. 3.

NOTES TO CHAPTER TWO: PACIFIC PROBES

1. William Camden, *History* (1675 ed.), p. 255 (quoted in Sir William Foster, *England's Quest of Eastern Trade* [London: A. & C. Black, 1933], p. 64).
2. Gregory King, "The Naval Trade of England, 1688," in *Two Tracts by Gregory King,* p. 31 (quoted in K. G. Davies, "Joint-Stock Investment in the Late Seventeenth Century," *Economic History Review,* 2d ser. 4 [1952]: 285).
3. A. P. Newton, "The Beginnings of English Colonization, 1569-1618,"

Cambridge History of the British Empire, 24 vols. (Cambridge: University Press, 1929), 1: 53. A specific link between Dee and Drake is postulated in Richard Koebner, *Empire* (New York: Grosset and Dunlap, 1965), p. 62.

4. Privateering was so extensive that by the early 1580's, when England and Spain were at war, a hundred English private armed vessels were sailing under royal commission. The Spanish ambassador wrote with alarm from London, "with the great profit they make by the Spanish trade, and in confidence that it will continue, they are building ships without cessation, and they are thus making themselves masters of the seas" (Mendoza to the King, 9 January 1581, *Calendar of State Papers; Spanish,* 3: 72 (see also, Kenneth R. Andrews, *Elizabethan Privateering* [Cambridge: University Press, 1964], passim).

5. Newton, "English Colonization," pp. 58-59. See E. G. R. Taylor, *Tudor Geography, 1485-1583* (London: Methuen, 1930), pp. 113-17.

6. Zelia Nuttall, ed., *New Light on Drake: A Collection of Documents Relating to His Voyage of Circumnavigation, 1577-1580* (London: Hakluyt Society, 1914), p. 241.

7. W. S. Vaux, ed., *The World Encompassed by Sir Francis Drake, Being His Next Voyage to that to Nombre de Dios, Collated with an Unpublished Manuscript of Francis Fletcher, Chaplain to the Expedition* (London: Hakluyt Society, 1854), p. x; Kenneth R. Andrews, "The English in the Caribbean, 1560-1620," in *The Westward Enterprise: English Activities in Ireland, the Atlantic, and America, 1480-1650,* ed. Kenneth R. Andrews et al. (Liverpool: Liverpool University Press, 1978), p. 114.

8. Quoted in Admiral Sir Herbert Richmond, *Statesmen and Sea Power* (Oxford: Clarendon Press, 1946), p. 7.

9. Quoted in Vaux, *World Encompassed,* p. ix.

10. Nuttall, *New Light on Drake,* pp. xxxii-xxxiv.

11. E. G. R. Taylor, "The Missing Draft Project of Drake's Voyage of 1577-80," *Geographical Journal* 75 (January 1930): 44-47.

12. Nuttall, *New Light on Drake,* pp. xxxii-xxxviii, 318-19, 386.

13. Kenneth R. Andrews, *Drake's Voyages: A Re-Assessment of Their Place in Elizabethan Maritime Expansion* (New York: Scribner, 1967), p. 76.

14. Vaux, *World Encompassed,* p. 113.

15. Ibid.

16. R. P. Bishop, "Drake's Course in the North Pacific," *British Columbia Historical Quarterly* 3 (1939): 151-82, esp. 173.

17. Vaux, *World Encompassed,* p. 115.

18. Raymond Aker, *Report of Findings Relating to Identification of Sir Francis Drake's Encampment at Point Reyes National Seashore: A Research Report of the Drake Navigators Guild* (Palo Alto, Calif.: Drake Navigators Guild [c. 1976]), ch. 4, p. 244a. John Drake's deposition is in Nuttall, *New Light on Drake,* p. 50.

19. Edward P. Von der Porter, "Drake's First Landfall," *Pacific Discovery* 28 (1975): 28-30. See also, Aker, *Report,* ch. 5.

20. Vaux, *The World Encompassed,* p. 115.

21. I support the contention of numerous scholars and sailors, including George Davidson, Chester Nimitz, Samuel Eliot Morison, Alan Villiers, and Frank Carr, that Drake's anchorage was Drakes Bay. Morison's conclusion is given in *The European Discovery of America: The Southern Voyages, A.D. 1492-1616* (New York: Oxford University Press, 1974), pp. 669-73. On 25 November 1976, I visited Drake's Estero within Drakes Bay, Point Reyes National Seashore, in order to examine the waters and compare the insert of Hondius' Portus Novae Albionis with the topographical features of the Estero. When Drake sailed south past Point Reyes looking for a safe harbour, even assuming excellent visibility, he could not have seen the entrance to San Francisco Bay, then 26.5 nautical miles away. The entrance would have been closed to him and perhaps not even visible over the horizon. There can be no doubt that the insert and the Estero resemble each other (see N.B. Martin, "*Portus Novae Albionis:* Site of Drake's California Sojourn," *Pacific Historical Review* 48

[1979]: 319-34). Two detractors from this important finding of the Drake Navigators Guild have sought without success to correlate the Hondius insert with Bolinas Lagoon ten nautical miles northwest of the Golden Gate and San Quentin Cove in the Bay of San Francisco. On this, see *California Historical Quarterly* 53 (1974): passim.

22. A replica of this plaque was found near San Quentin in 1936. It may have been a joke played by some of Professor H. E. Bolton's students on their University of California, Berkeley, history teacher. In any case, for 41 years the plaque provided a constant focus for a controversy surrounding its authenticity. It has now been proven beyond doubt that it is a fake (see *Plate of Brass Reexamined: A Report Issued by the Bancroft Library, University of California, Berkeley, 1977* [Berkeley: Bancroft Library, 1977]). The distinguished English scholar Vincent Harlow investigated the authenticity of the plate in 1937 and concluded that "the worthy professor . . . has been deceived" (Harlow to M. Powicke, 22 June 1937, copy in author's possession).

24. During the mid-nineteenth-century international rivalry for the Pacific Northwest, Drake's claims formed the foundations of the English position. See, for instance, Sir Travers Twiss, *The Ore-*

gon Question Examined, in Respect to Facts and the Law of Nations (London, 1846).

25. For Anson's instructions and other information on the Manilla galleon, see Glyndwr Williams, ed., *Documents Relating to Anson's Voyage Round the World, 1740-1744* (London: Navy Records Society, 1967) pp. 3-44, 109-11, 183-225.

26. Raymond H. Fisher, *Bering's Voyages: Whither and Why* (Seattle: University of Washington Press, 1977), pp. 158-60; John Dunmore, *French Explorers in the Pacific. Volume I. The Eighteenth Century* (Oxford: Clarendon Press, 1965), passim; W. P. Morrell, *Britain in the Pacific Islands* (Oxford: Claredon Press, 1960), p. 29; A. P. Nasatir, *French Activities in California* (Palo Alto: Stanford University Press, 1945), pp. 1-2.

27. Secret orders and instructions to Captain the Honourable John Byron, 17 June 1764, Adm. 2/1332, pp. 99-108.

28. See Robert E. Gallagher, ed., *Byron's Journal of His Circumnavigation, 1764-1766* (Cambridge: Hakluyt Society, 1964), pp. xlvi-1. For a concise account of Byron's voyage as it relates to the Falkland Islands, see Vincent T. Harlow, *The Founding of the Second British Empire, 1763-1793*, 2 vols. (London: Longmans, Green, 1952), 1: 22-28.

NOTES TO CHAPTER THREE: COOK'S RECONNAISSANCE

1. 16 Geo. 3, c. 6, succeeding 18 Geo. 2, c. 17.

2. See Glyndwr Williams, *The British Search for the Northwest Passage in the Eighteenth Century* (London: Longmans, Green, 1962), p. 167.

3. The pamphlets were later republished (Daines Barrington, *Miscellanies, by the Honourable Daines Barrington . . . London . . .* [London, 1781]).

4. Minutes of the Council of the Royal Society, 10 and 17 February 1774, A.R.S., 6, pp. 214, 216.

5. Dr. M. Maty to Admiralty, 17 February 1774, ibid., p. 216; see also Williams, *British Search*, p. 166.

6. D. Barrington to Royal Society, 30 March 1774, A.R.S., 6, p. 227.

7. Glyndwr Williams, "Myth and Reality: James Cook and the Theoretical Geography of Northwest America" (typescript, 1978). For an assessment of Stählin's theory, see John C. Beaglehole, ed., *The Journals of Captain James Cook on His Voyages of Discovery*, Vol. 3, *The Voyage of the "Resolution" and "Discovery," 1776-1780* (Cambridge: Hakluyt Society, 1967), part 1: pp. 1xi-1xiv.

8. Hearne's discoveries were first made public in 1784 when they were incorporated in a map accompanying the offi-

cial published account of Cook's third voyage (see J. B. Brebner, *The Explorers of North America* [New York: Macmillan, 1933], p. 397).

9. James Cook, "An Observation of an Eclipse of the Sun at the Island of Newfoundland, August 5, 1776," *Philosophical Transactions of the Royal Society,* 58 (1767): 215-16.

10. "The method taken for preserving the Health of the Crew of His Majesty's Ship the Resolution . . . by Captain James Cook, F.R.S.," ibid., 66 (1776): 402-6.

11. These views are quoted in Skelton, "Cook as Hydrographer," p. 119, and John C. Beaglehole, *The Life of Captain James Cook* (London: Hakluyt Society, 1974), p. 474.

12. Skelton, "Cook as Hydrographer," p. 107; see also Beaglehole, *Life of Cook,* p. 445.

13. Rear-Admiral P. W. Brock, H.M.S. *Resolution* dossier, M.M.B.C.

14. Short biographies of these and others in the two ships are given in Beaglehole, *Cook's Journals,* 3: part 2, app. 4.

15. Secret instructions to Capt. James Cook, 6 July 1776, Adm. 2/1332, pp. 284-96 (printed in Vincent Harlow and Frederick Madden, eds., *British Colonial Developments, 1774-1834: Select Documents* [Oxford: Clarendon Press, 1953], pp. 1-4).

16. Ibid.

17. Instructions to Lieut. R. Pickersgill, 14 May 1776, Adm. 2/101, pp. 89-90.

18. Instructions to Lieut. W. Young, 13 March 1777, Adm. 2/1332, p. 322.

19. Beaglehole, *Cook's Journals,* 3: part 1, p. 286.

20. Ibid., pp. 289n2, 293.

21. Ibid., pp. 293-94.

22. Ibid., p. 294n1.

23. Skelton, "Cook as Hydrographer," p. 92.

24. The Cape Flattery lighthouse on Tatoosh Island first shone in 1858, but the Strait's entrance still proved troublesome. As a Royal Navy lieutenant wrote: "All high northern latitudes are peculiarly liable to sudden changes of weather, and in entering the Strait of Fuca all the knowledge and experience of which the navigator is master will often be called into requisition" (R. C.

Mayne, *Four Years in British Columbia and Vancouver Island* [London, 1862], p. 19).

25. In 1774, for instance, Martínez, bound southward on the Pérez expedition, saw the strait's entrance. He did not investigate it until 1778, by which time Charles Duncan had made more particular discoveries. (Henry R. Wagner, "Apocryphal Voyages to the Northwest Coast of America," *Proceedings of the American Antiquarian Society,* 41 [1931]: 215-16). Duncan's *Sketch of the Entrance to the Strait of Juan de Fuca . . . 15 August 1788* (1790) is reproduced in Warren L. Cook, *Floodtide of Empire: Spain and the Pacific Northwest, 1543-1819* (New Haven: Yale University Press, 1973), facing p. 304.

26. Beaglehole, *Cook's Journals,* 3: part 2, p. 1088.

27. Ibid., 3: part 1, 294. James K. Munford, ed., *John Ledyard's Journal of Captain Cook's Last Voyage* (Corvallis: Oregon State University Press, 1963), p. 69.

28. Beaglehole, *Cook's Journals,* 3: part 1, pp. 294-95; part 2, p. 1393.

29. Interview with Winifred David, 24 August 1977; copy in Aural History Archives, P.A.B.C.

30. Beaglehole, *Cook's Journals,* 3: part 2, p. 1088.

31. *Piceaexcelsa, Pseudotsuga menziesii,* and *Cypressus thyoides,* respectively.

32. Beaglehole, *Cook's Journals,* 3: part 2, pp. 1096-97, 1329, 1323.

33. Ibid., part 1, p. 300.

34. James Cook and James King, *A Voyage to the Pacific Ocean . . .* 3 vols. (London, 1784), 3: 285. "Spars, of every denomination, are constantly in demand here," Meares's instructions said. "Bring as many of those as you can conveniently stow." He did, and he wrote, "Indeed the woods of this part of America are capable of supplying with these valuable materials, all the navies of Europe" (John Meares, *Voyages Made in the Years 1788 and 1789, from China to the North-West Coast of America* [London, 1790], p. 224, appendix).

35. The beer was made from Sitka Spruce (*Picea Sitchensis*); Beaglehole *Cook's Journals,* 3: part 1, p. 310n3. The In-

dians' uses of this tree for medicinal, artistic, and religious purposes were many (see *Davidsonia* 4 [1973]: 41-45).

36. Beaglehole, *Cook's Journals,* 3: part 2, pp. 1103, 1324, 1410. Munford, *Ledyard's Journal,* p. 70.

37. In a proper native orthography, the name is written mukwina, meaning possessor of pebbles (*Dictionary of Canadian Biography* [Toronto: University of Toronto Press, 1979]), 4:567. But his name has been variously spelled—Macuina, Maquilla, Muquinna, and Maquinna, the last of which is customary locally and is used herein on editorial advice.

38. Beaglehole, *Cook's Journals,* 3: part 1, p. 295.

39. Thomas Edgar, Logbook, 20 April 1778 (Add. MS 37,528, B.L.); Beaglehole, *Cook's Journals,* 3: part 1, p. 298.

40. *Cook's Journals,* 3: part 1, 298.

41. Ibid, 3: part 2, pp. 1398, 1350-51.

42. Munford, *Ledyard's Journal,* p. 72.

43. Beaglehole, *Cook's Journals,* 3: part 1, p. 295n5. An analysis of Riou's account of the Nootka is given in Erna Gunther, *Indian Life of the Northwest Coast of North America as Seen by the Early Explorers and Fur Traders during the Last Decades of the Eighteenth Century* (Chicago: University of Chicago Press, 1972), p. 24.

44. An excellent Spanish ethnological account (though of a slightly later date) is by José Mariana Moziño, published as *Noticias de Nutka: An Account of Nootka Sound in 1792,* trans. and ed. Iris Higbie Wilson (Toronto: McClelland and Stewart Ltd., 1970).

45. See Plate 11.

46. Beaglehole, *Cook's Journals,* 3, part 2, p. 1401.

47. Father A. J. Brabant, who lived on the west coast near Nootka Sound during the late nineteenth century, vehemently maintained that the word *Nootka* existed in the language of the people. This was used to counter the opinion, mainly from Spanish sources, that the natives did not understand the term (A. J. Brabant to J. Walbran, 31 October 1896, Brabant Misc. Papers, P.A.B.C.). See Moziño, *Noticias de Nutka,* p. 67, for the view that the native term was unknown.

48. ". . . when they were satisfied or pleased with anything, they would with one voice call out Wak'ash wak'ash." Beaglehole, *Cook's Journals,* 3: part 1, 323.

49. In 1975 the British Columbia Historical Society, in seeking to visit the historic site (now an Indian reserve), found their way blocked by Indian militants on the local federal wharf. Yuquot, the present spelling, should actually be *yukwzt*; John E. Mills, "The Ethnohistory of Nootka Sound, Vancouver Island" (Ph.D. diss., University of Washington, 1955), p. iv.

50. Quoted in Beaglehole, *Life of Cook,* p. 588.

51. Ibid., p. 589.

52. Beaglehole, *Cook's Journals,* 3: part 1, pp. 307-8.

53. For full details on de Fonte and his influence, see Williams, *British Search,* passim.

54. Beaglehole, *Cook's Journals,* 3: part 1, p. 335.

55. Ibid., p. cxxxviii.

56. Ibid., p. 470.

57. Ibid., pp. cliv-clvii.

NOTES TO CHAPTER FOUR: SPANNING THE PACIFIC

1. Beaglehole, *Cook's Journals,* 3: part 2, p. 1396; Robin Fisher, "Cook and the Nootka" (typescript, 1978), p. 9.

2. Beaglehole, *Cook's Journals,* 3: part 1, p. 302.

3. Ibid.

4. Christopher Lloyd and R.C. Anderson,

ed., *A Memoir of James Trevenen* (London: Navy Records Society, 1959), p.28.

5. Beaglehole *Cook's Journals,* 3: part 1, p. 296n. Cook and his crew sometimes called them the "sea beaver," taking the term from the Russian *bobri morski.*

Actually, they were sea otter *(Enhydra lutris)*, which resemble the land otter *(Lutra canadensis)* in appearance. The sea otter attained a mature size of from 4 to 5 feet in length and 80 pounds in weight.

6. Karl W. Kenyon, *The Sea Otter in the Eastern Pacific Ocean* (Washington: Government Printing Office, 1969) and T. A. Rickard, "The Sea Otter in History," *British Columbia Historical Quarterly* 3 (1947): 15-31.
7. Munford, *Ledyard's Journal*, p. 70.
8. Ibid.
9. Beaglehole, *Cook's Journals*, 3: part 1, pp. 349-51.
10. Ibid., p. 371.
11. Michel N. Pavlovsky, *Chinese-Russian Relations* (New York: Philosophical Library, 1949), pp. 22-24.
12. Ibid., p. 452. For the Russian side of these meetings, see Eleanor Liever, ed. and trans., "The English in Kamchatka, 1779," *Geographical Journal* 84 (1934): 417-19; and [Ya. M. Svet], *Cook and the Russians* (London: Hakluyt Society, 1973), pp. 3-9.
13. Munford, *Ledyard's Journal*, p. 99.
14. Beaglehole, *Cook's Journals*, 3: part 1, p. 433n.
15. Ibid., p. 371.
16. Beaglehole, *Cook's Journals*, part 1, p. 653n; part 2, pp. 1243, 1260.

17. John Meares, *Voyages made in the Years 1788 and 1789, from China to the North West Coast* (London, 1790), p. lxxvi.
18. As Meares put it, "Various are the oppressions which afflict our commerce in this part of the East" (ibid., p. lxxv).
19. Harlow, *Founding of the Second British Empire*, I: 65-67.
20. John Gore to Committee of Supercargoes, 3 December 1779, Canton Factory Records, MS/52, I.O.L. (micro. 1573, reel 6, O.H.S.).
21. Committee of Supercargoes to Gore, 5 and 30 December 1779, Adm. 55/120.
22. Consultation Committee of Supercargoes, 22 December 1779, Committee of Supercargoes to John Gore, 12 December 1779, and Gore to Committee of Supercargoes, 9 December 1779, MS/52, I.O.L. (micros. 1573, reel 6, O.H.S.).
23. Cook and King, *A Voyage . . .*, 3: 430.
24. Ibid., p. 431.
25. Ibid., p. 437.
26. Lloyd and Anderson, eds., *A Memoir of James Trevenen*, p. 28.
27. Ibid., pp. 21-22.
28. Cook and King, *A Voyage . . .* 3: 437-40.
29. Ibid., 3, p. 437.

NOTES TO CHAPTER FIVE: THE FORTUNE SEEKERS

1. Robert K. Buell and Charlotte N. Skladal, *Sea Otters and the China Trade* (New York: David McKay, 1968), pp. 50-51.
2. The Manila galleon's voyage lasted 4 months in each direction and its success depended on a good knowledge, acquired through seasoned experience, of the Japanese Current and the wind patterns of the Pacific. The Manila galleon dates from 1565. Manila was the halfway house between Mexico and China until late in the eighteenth century (W. L. Schurz, *The Manila Galleon* [New York: Dutton, 1939], pp. 26-31). On Spain and the sea otter trade, see Adele Ogden, *California Sea Otter*

Trade, 1784-1848 (Berkeley: University of California Press, 1941).
3. Nathaniel Portlock, *A Voyage round the World* (London, 1789), pp. ix, 1-2.
4. James King's scheme is given in Cook and King, *A Voyage . . .*: 3: 437-40.
5. W. Bolts to J. Johnstone, 31 Aug. 1872, enclosing Bolts to Menzies, Leith & Co., 31 July 1782, Add. MSS 223, B.L. Louis Dermigny, *La Chine et l'Occident: La Commerce à Canton en XVIIIe Siècle, 1719-1833*, 3 vols. (Paris: S.E.V.P.E.N., 1964), 3: 1154-55; Norman L. Hallward, *William Bolts: A Dutch Adventurer under John Company* (Cambridge: University Press, 1920), pp. 1-5, 190-95.

6. Minutes, Court of Directors, 29 April 1785, H.M.S. 494(5), pp. 359ff., I.O.L.; Portlock says the Bolts project led "British subjects who were settled in Asia" to adopt King's suggestion. Portlock, *Voyage round the World*, pp. 1-2.

7. "The weather for a long time," Hanna wrote on 31 July, "has been as warm as Europeans can wish, the sea commonly smooth and Winds moderate, but then, it is so thick, wet and hazey or foggy, that since the 14th. May we have not had a clear sky or opportunity of observing for Long either by night or day, which certainly is a great loss, as well as an unhappiness to me" (J. Hanna, MS journal, AA 20.5, Se 1H, P.A.B.C.). See also, William Beresford, *A Voyage round the World* (London, 1789). pp. 316ff., and Meares, *Voyages*, p. lii.

8. *DCB* 4:325.

9. "I believe," wrote a seasoned fur trader, "I am the only man living who has a personal knowledge of those early transactions and I can show *that in each and every case* where a vessel was attacked by them [the Indians of the region], it was in direction retaliation for some life taken or some gross outrage committed against *that tribe*" (S. W. Jackman, ed., *The Journal of William Sturgis* [Victoria: Sono Nis Press, 1978], p. 15). See also, F. W. Howay, "Indian Attacks upon Maritime Traders of the Northwest Coast," *Canadian Historical Review* 6 (1925): 287-309.

10. Beresford, *Voyage*, pp. 316-17; Derek Pethick, *First Approaches to the Northwest Coast* (Vancouver: J. J. Douglas Ltd., 1976), p. 80.

11. For an account of these arrangements, see Harlow, *Second British Empire*, 2: 420-25.

12. F. W. Howay, ed., *The Dixon-Meares Controversy* (Toronto: Ryerson Press, 1929), p. 61; and Vincent Harlow and Frederick Madden, eds., *British Colonial Developments, 1774-1834: Select Documents* (Oxford: Clarendon Press, 1953), pp. 29-30.

13. Howay, *Dixon-Meares Controversy*, p. 134.

14. Portlock, *Voyage round the World*, p. 382.

15. F. W. Howay, "Four Letters from Richard Cadman Etches to Sir Joseph Banks, 1788-1792," *British Columbia Historical Quarterly* 6 (1942): 127.

16. Portlock, *Voyage round the World*, p. 4.

17. George Taswell, a Madras merchant, warned Lord Sydney at the Home Office on 25 March 1785 that an expedition should be sent via Magellan Strait to the Northwest Coast as soon as possible to take advantage of the season and forestall the French, then known to be preparing at Brest an elaborate expedition to the Pacific under La Pérouse (Taswell to Sydney, 25 March 1785, H.M.S., v. 190 [13], 617). Strange was not to trade in Spanish territories but rather north of them. ("Instructions to James Strange . . .", ibid., v. 494 [5], 422-27).

18. Instructions to James Strange, 7 December, 1785, H.M.S., 494 (5), 422-27. See also, A. V. Ayyar, "An Adventurous Madras Servant: James Strange, 1753-1840," *Proceedings of the Indian Historical Records Commission* 11 (1928): 22-29.

19. Alexander Walker, "An Account of a Voyage to the North West Coast of America with Observations on the Manners of the Inhabitants and on the Production of that Country in 1785 and 1786," MS. 13778, N.L.S., preface and introduction. The original was lost and this manuscript was prepared during Walker's first period of retirement, probably between 1815 and 1821. On Walker, see below, n.24.

20. Scott to Strange, 1 September 1785, H.M.S., 494 (5), 419-22.

21. Walker Journal, 7 July 1786, N.L.S., and *James Strange's Journal and Narrative of the Commercial Expedition from Bombay to the Northwest Coast of America* (Madras: Government Press, 1928), p. 21.

22. *Strange's Journal*, p. 28.

23. Ibid., pp. 20-28.

24. Alexander Walker (born 12 May 1764) was the eldest son of the minister of Collessie, Fife. In 1780 he was appointed a cadet in the East India Company Service and went to India in that year. An ensign in 1782, he fought in the Company army at Mangalore, Malabar. He left Bombay with the James Strange expedition on 8 December 1785

and on his return in 1786 joined the grenadier battalion in garrison at Bombay. Successively Lieutenant (1788), Captain (1797), deputy Auditor-General (1798), political resident at Baroda (1802), Major (1803), and Lieutenant-Colonel (1809), he served in various active military and political functions, returning to England in 1810 and retiring in 1812. Called from retirement in 1822, with the rank of Brigadier-General, he was appointed Governor of St. Helena, then under Company control. He made several improvements in agriculture, horticulture, schools and libraries and introduced the culture of silkworms. Soon after retiring he died in Edinburgh 5 March 1831. His valuable collection of Arabic, Persian and Sanskrit manuscripts, gathered in India, is in the Bodleian Library, Oxford. *Dictionary of National Biography,* 59 (London, 1899), 42-43.

25. Walker Journal, entry for 14-19 July 1786, N.L.S.
26. Ibid., 27 and 28 June 1786.
27. Ibid., p. 42.
28. Ibid., pp. 37 ff.
29. Ibid., entry for 14-19 July 1786.
30. Ibid., marginal notation at entry for 22 July 1786.
31. Also spelled Mackey, M'Key and McKay (by Walker). I have used Strange's spelling, Mackay.
32. R. C. Etches to N. Portlock, 3 September 1785, in Howay, *Dixon-Meares Controversy,* p. 61.
33. Strange believed, mistakenly, that Mackay was forcibly taken from Nootka Sound to Canton by Portlock in the *King George* (John Hosie, "James Charles Stuart Strange and His Expedition to the Northwest Coast of America in 1786," *Fourth Report and Proceedings of the British Columbia Historical Association,* [1929], p. 49).
34. John T. Walbran, "The Cruise of the Imperial Eagle," *Victoria Colonist,* 3 March 1901, Beresford, *Voyage,* pp. 232-33, W. K. Lamb, "The Mystery of Mrs. Barkley's Diary," *British Columbia Historical Review* 6 (1942): 41; F. W. Howay, "The Voyage of the *Captain Cook* and the *Experiment,* 1785-8," ibid. 5 (1941): 286, 292.
35. Walbran, "Cruise," and Beresford, *Voyage,* p. 233.

36. Walker Journal, marginal note at entry for 23 July 1786, N.L.S.
37. *Strange's Journal,* p. 29.
38. Ibid., p. 32.
39. Ibid., p. 37.
40. Ibid.
41. Reported in William Coxe, *Account of the Russian Discoveries between Asia and America* (London, 1780), p. 251.
42. East India Company Factory Records, China 2, vol. 16. p. 1 (4 April 1787); quoted in Howay, "*Captain Cook* and the *Experiment,*" p. 288.
43. Strange to Sir Archibald Campbell, 22 February 1788, in *Proceedings of the Indian Historical Records Commission* 11 (1928): 29-34.
44. Harlow, *Second British Empire,* 2:431.
45. In 1787, Charles Barkley of the *Imperial Eagle* named Cape Beale for his ship's purser; Meares claimed it for his Canton associate Daniel Beale. Meares failed to credit Barkley with being first to enter the Strait of Juan de Fuca (Lamb, "Mystery of Mrs. Barkley's Diary," pp. 31-32). His quarrel with Dixon over the latter's aid given at Prince William Sound was conducted in a pamphlet war in 1790 and 1791 (Howay, *Dixon-Meares Controversy,* passim).
46. *Official Papers Relative to the Dispute between the Courts of Great Britain and Spain [on] Nootka Sound* (1790), p. iv.
47. John T. Walbran, *British Columbia Coast Names 1592-1906* (Ottawa: Government Printing Bureau, 1909), pp. 33-35; Lamb, "Mystery of Mrs. Barkley's Diary," 31-47; F. W. Howay, ed., "Letters Concerning Voyages of British Vessels to the Northwest Coast of America, 1787-1809," *Oregon Historical Quarterly* 29 (1938): 307-13.
48. Privy Council evidence, 8 February 1791, in P.C. 2/135.
49. Harlow, *Second British Empire,* 2:434 and Beresford, *Voyage,* pp. 154-58.
50. The *Felice Adventurer* was, in fact, Meares's *Nootka* under a new name. Harlow, *Second British Empire,* 2: 435n31.
51. Pierce ed., Howay's *List of Trading Vessels,* p. 7.
52. Meares's instructions, 24 December 1787, in Meares, *Voyages,* app. 1.
53. *Prince of Wales* Journal, 16 October 1786 to 7 November 1788, Adm.

55/146 (micro. A250, University of Washington Libraries, Seattle).

54. See George Dixon, *Further Remarks on the Voyages of John Meares* (London, 1791), pp. 20-31, for Duncan's cruise between the Queen Charlotte Islands and the continental shore. Duncan's chart and views are in Cook, *Floodtide of Empire,* facing p. 304. See also Williams, *British Search,* pp. 219-20 and 242-43; and Howard T. Fry, *Alexander Dalrymple (1737-1808) and the Expansion of British Trade* (Toronto: University of Toronto Press, 1970), p. 220.

55. Harlow, *Second British Empire,* 2: 436ff.

56. Meares, "Statement of the Value of Furs Exported from the Northwestern Coast of America by British and Foreign Ships Previous to the Year 1790," 20 May 1790, H.O. 42/16 (24). This does not include the British snow *Lark,* William Peters master and owned by the East India Company, which sailed from Bengal in March 1786 with a crew of seventy but was wrecked on Copper or Bering's Island with the loss of all but two hands.

NOTES TO CHAPTER SIX: BEACHHEAD OF EMPIRE

1. Meares, *Voyages,* p. 2.
2. Ibid.
3. Ibid., p. 113.
4. Ibid., pp. 115-16.
5. Frederic W. Howay, ed., *Voyages of the "Columbia" to the Northwest Coast 1787-1790 and 1790-1793* (Boston: Massachusetts Historical Society, 1941), p. 48.
6. Meares, *Voyages,* pp. 88-89.
7. Ibid., p. 212.
8. Meares (ibid., p. 220) claimed that the house and schooner displayed the English ensign. See also Duffin's Journal, in Meares, *Voyages,* app. 4. Compare Haswell's claim that the *Iphigenia Nubiana* and *Felice Adventurer* wore Portuguese colours, with Meares's own admission, as he told Duncan, that he had "a small vessel on the stocks at Nootka; where he had a fort, guns mounted, and *Portuguese colors* flying" (Cook, *Floodtide of Empire,* pp. 141-42).
9. Meares's instructions to Captain Douglas, 20 September 1788; in Meares, *Voyages,* app. 5.
10. Howay, *Voyages of the "Columbia,"* p. 49.
11. Ibid.
12. Ibid., pp. 52, 54.
13. Ibid., p. 55.
14. Tofino was perhaps then known as Oakamin or Okeamin (ibid., p. 70n1).
15. "Fort Defiance" is now in a 135-acre archaeological and historical site at Adventure Cove, on Meares Island, off Lemmens Inlet. The site was discovered in 1966. See Edmund Hayes, "Gray's Adventure Cove," *Oregon Historical*

Quarterly 68 (1967): 101-10. Friendly Cove, within Indian reserve land, is out of bounds to government historical preservation or restoration.

16. Meares, *Voyages,* pp. 216-17. See also instructions to Douglas, 20 September 1788 (ibid., app. 5).
17. Instructions to Douglas, 20 September 1788 (ibid., app. 5).
18. Ibid.
19. These claims are in John Meares's *Memorial* (London, 1790). They cannot be supported by his *Voyages* except in reference to Nootka. Graham's confirmation is in ibid., enclosure 6, with Meares's *Memorial,* appendix to *Voyages;* Duffin's deposition is in Adm. 1/2628, f. 640r. See also George Vancouver, *Voyage of Discovery to the North Pacific Ocean and around the World,* 3 vols. (London, 1798), 2: 370-72.
20. Cook, *Floodtide of Empire,* pp. 138-39.
21. Ibid., p. 139.
22. Vancouver, *Voyages,* 2: 335ff.; William Ray Manning, *Nootka Sound Controversy* (Washington, D.C.: American Historical Association, 1905) pp. 290-91.
23. The account of Meares's plans is taken from *Argonaut's* Sailing Orders, 3 April 1789; in F. W. Howay, ed., *The Journal of Captain James Colnett Aboard the "Argonaut" from April 26, 1789, to November 3, 1791* (Toronto: Champlain Society, 1940), pp. 19-23, 25-27; also, Cook, *Floodtide of Empire,* p. 144.

NOTES TO CHAPTER SEVEN: IMPERIAL DREAMS AND FALSE STARTS

1. This chapter and the next owe much to Harlow, *Founding of the Second British Empire*, 2, ch. 7.
2. The most recent study is A. G. L. Shaw, *Convicts and the Colonies: A Study of Penal Transportation from Great Britain and Ireland to Australia and Other Parts of the British Empire* (London: Faber and Faber, 1966).
3. K. M. Dallas of Tasmania has written that England needed a sea base and refitting port in the East, that Botany Bay offered such a site, and that trade in China tea, northwest coast furs, seals and whales, and Spanish loot from Mexico, South America, and the Philippines would be aided by it. Since the Cape was in Dutch hands, Mauritius under French control, and Cape Horn under Spanish influence, England needed a base to protect her envied trade in India and China. With the Northwest Passage deemed unnavigable since Cook's voyage, an alternative route to the Pacific in southern latitudes would need a supply base—Botany Bay—astride that approach (K. M. Dallas, "The First Settlement in Australia: Considered in Relation to Sea-Power in World Politics," *Tasmanian Historical Research Association, Proceedings, for 1952*, pp. 4-12). See also Michael Roe, "Australia's Place in the 'Swing to the East,' 1788-1810," *Historical Studies* 8 (1958): 202-13.
4. Geoffrey Blainey, *The Tyranny of Distance: How Distance Shaped Australia's History* (Melbourne: Macmillan, 1968), p. 37.
5. See Banks, "Evidence before Committee of the House of Commons, 1 April 1779"; in Harlow and Madden, *British Colonial Developments*, pp. 426-28. Etches called Banks "so warm a Promoter of my first expedition to the Northwest Coast." Banks had named the *Queen Charlotte*—as had George Rose, Treasurer of the Navy, the *King George*—before the departure of these ships from London (R. Cadman Etches to Sir Joseph Banks, 19 May 1792, Sutro Branch, California State Library; in F. W. Howay, ed., "Four Letters

from Richard Cadman Etches to Sir Joseph Banks, 1788-92," in *British Columbia Historical Quarterly* 6 [1942]: 137).
6. Matra, "Proposal for Establishing a Settlement in New South Wales," 23 August 1783; in Harlow and Madden, *British Colonial Developments*, pp. 428-30.
7. Young's plan is in *Historical Records of New South Wales*, Vol. 1, part 2 (Sydney: Government Printer, 1892-1901), p. 12ff. See also Barbara Atkins, "Australia's Place in the Swing to the East—An Addendum," *Historical Studies, Australia and New Zealand* 8 (1958): 315-18.
8. Alexander Dalrymple, *A Serious Admonition to the Public on the Intended Thief Colony at Botany Bay* (London, 1786), pp. 22-25; quoted in Shaw, *Convicts and the Colonies*, p. 50.
9. Etches to Banks, 17 July 1788, quoted in Howay, "Four Letters," p. 132.
10. See Richard H. Dillon, "Convict Colonies for the Pacific Northwest," *British Columbia Historical Quarterly* 19 (1955): 93-102.
11. Capt. George Dixon to Evan Nepean (Home Office), 14 July 1789, Q/49, p. 354, P.A.C., printed in *Report of Canadian Archives, 1887* (Ottawa: Queen's Printer, 1890), p. 29.
12. "Memorandum by Alexander Dalrymple on the route for Discoveries, 2 February 1790, Q/49, p. 368, P.A.C.; printed in *Report on the Canadian Archives, 1889* (Ottawa: Queen's Printer, 1890), pp. 32-35.
13. Ibid.
14. "Captain Holland's Plan to Explore from Quebec [1790]," with lists of expenses and instruments, ibid., pp. 36-37; Fry, *Alexander Dalrymple*, pp. 202ff.
15. *Alexander Dalrymple, Plan for Promoting the Fur-Trade, and Securing It to This Country, by Uniting the Operations of the East India and Hudson's Bay Companys* (London, 1789), p. 31. See also his "Trade to the Northwest Coast of America [1791]," H.M.S. 494 (5).
16. 26 Geo. 3, c. 50, "Act for Encourage-

ment of the Southern Whale Fishery," commonly known as the Fishery Bill. In 1802 by statute British-built ships in the fishery no longer had to carry licences from the East India Company. See Edouard A. Stackpole, *Whales and Destiny: The Rivalry between American, France and Britain for Control of the Southern Whale Fishery, 1785-1825* (Amherst: University of Massachussets Press, 1972), pp. 155ff. See also G. S. Graham, "The Migrations of the Nantucket Whale Fishery: An Episode in British Colonial Policy," *New England Quarterly* 8 (1937): 179-202.

17. Quoted in David MacKay, "British Interest in the Southern Oceans, 1782-1794," *New Zealand Journal of History* 3 (1969): 131.
18. Ibid., pp. 132-33.
19. Chairman and Deputy Chairman of the East India Company to Lord Hillsborough, October 25, 1781, H.M.S. 154/6 (Harlow and Madden, *British Colonial Developments*, p. 6).
20. J. H. Parry, *Trade and Dominion: The European Overseas Empires in the*

Eighteenth Century (London: Cardinal, 1974), p. 349.
21. W. W. Grenville to Governor Arthur Phillip, March 1790 (*Historical Records of Australia*, ser. 1, vol. 1 [Sydney, 1914], pp. 161-63).
22. Grenville to Governor Phillip, New South Wales, March 1790 (George Godwin, *Vancouver: A Life, 1757-1798* [New York: D. Appleton and Company, 1931], pp. 189-91).
23. Gordon Greenwood, *Early Australian-American Relations, from the Arrival of the Spaniards in America to the Close of 1830* (Melbourne: Melbourne University Press, 1944), p. 88.
24. See Mackay, "British Interest," pp. 135-36.
25. "Heads of Instructions for an Expedition to the Northwest Coast of America, Secret, February 1790," H.O. 42/16 (10).
26. Etches to Banks, 17 July 1788, printed in Howay, "Four Letters," p. 131.
27. Vancouver, *A Voyage of Discovery to the North Pacific Ocean and Round the World*, 3 vols. (London, 1798), 1: x.

NOTES TO CHAPTER EIGHT: CONFLICTS OF AMBITION

1. As Commodore J. Blankett, R.N., had advised London to take the Cape of Good Hope in 1795 (Vincent Harlow and Frederick Madden, eds., *British Colonial Developments, 1774-1834: Select Documents* [Oxford: Clarendon Press, 1953], pp. 19-21).
2. Quoted in M. B. R. Cawkwell, D. H. Maling, and E. M. Cawkwell, *The Falkland Islands* (London: Macmillan, 1960), p. 14.
3. Quoted in Nicholas Tracy, "The Falkland Islands Crisis of 1770: Use of Naval Force," *English Historical Review* 90 (1975): 40.
4. In 1780 the Spanish destroyed the British buildings. For 50 years thereafter, British authority was not maintained, which caused Charles Darwin to lament: "Here, we, in dog in the manger fashion seize an island and leave to protect it a Union Jack" (Cawkwell et al., *Falkland Islands*, p. 44).

5. Quoted in Tracy, "Falkland Islands Crisis," p. 72.
6. The usage here is by the First Lord of the Admiralty (Memorandum by Earl of Egmont, 20 July 1765, S.P. 94/253, f. 228).
7. Harlow, *Second British Empire*, 1:52.
8. See B. G. Corey, ed., and trans., *The Quest and Occupation of Tahiti by Emissaries of Spain during the Years 1772-1776*, 3 vols. (London: Hakluyt Society, 1913-19), 1: 108.
9. I owe much of the following account of Spanish motives and activities to Cook, *Floodtide of Empire*, pp. 54-69, 88-134; Michael E. Thurman, *The Naval Department of San Blas: New Spain's Bastion for Alta California and Nootka, 1767 to 1798* (Glendale, Calif.: Arthur H. Clark, 1967), pp. 257-76; and Christon I. Archer, "The Spanish Reaction to Cook's Third Voyage" (typescript, 1978).

10. Bucareli to Julián de Arriaga, 27 July 1773; in Cook, *Floodtide of Empire*, p. 55.
11. Cook, *Floodtide of Empire*, p. 67.
12. Ibid., p. 69.
13. Ibid., pp. 90-91, which reviews Bucareli's dilemma.
14. Ibid., pp. 97-98.
15. France had sent La Pérouse to complete Cook's work. With respect to the Northwest Coast he was to inquire into the prospects of the maritime fur trade north of Spanish possessions, claim a bay suitable for a depot for French traders, and find the western entrance to the Northwest Passage. La Pérouse claimed Lituya Bay, near Yakutat or Bering Bay, known locally as Frenchmen's Bay until the early twentieth century. Port des Français, as La Pérouse called it, remained the only French claim on the Northwest Coast until 1790, when Captain Etienne Marchand left Marseilles in the *Solide* on a private project to visit the Northwest Coast for furs (see John Dunmore, *French Explorers in the Pacific* (Oxford: Clarendon Press, 1965), 1: 262-63, 1:266-68, 1:342-53).
16. Thurman, *Naval Department*, p. 259.
17. James R. Gibson, *Feeding the Russian Fur Trade: Provisionment of the Okhotsk Peninsula, 1639-1856* (Madison: University of Wisconsin Press, 1969), pp. 16-17.
18. Ibid., p. 17. See also, James R. Gibson, *Imperial Russia in Frontier America: The Changing Geography of Supply of Russian America, 1784-1867* (New York: Oxford University Press, 1976), pp. 3-5.
19. Descriptions of Billings' voyage can be found in H. H. Bancroft, *Alaska, 1730-1885* (San Francisco, 1886), ch. 13, and Raisa V. Makarova, *Russians on the Pacific, 1743-1799*, trans. and ed. by Richard A. Pierce and Alton S. Donnelly (Kingston: Limestone Press, 1975). In 1790 Billings met the Spaniard, Salvidor Fidalgo, near Kodiak, but this encounter of rival imperial interests had no immediate political consequences owing to the then present state of the Nootka crisis. An Anglo-Russian alliance against Spain in the North Pacific, California, and Spanish America with a view to conquests was considered but never came to anything. R. A. Humphreys, "Richard Oswald's Plan for an English and Russian Attack on Spanish America, 1781-82," *Hispanic American Historical Review* 18 (1930): 95-101.
20. Manning, *Nootka Sound*, pp. 300-301. López de Haro's estimate of 462 Russians is more accurate; see Thurman, *Naval Department*, pp. 272-73.
21. Ibid. Martínez to Flores, 5 December 1788 (Manning, *Nootka Sound*, pp. 300-301).
22. Ibid.
23. Flores to Valdés, 23 December 1788 (Cook, *Floodtide of Empire*, p. 130).
24. Christon I. Archer, "The Transient Presence: A Re-Appraisal of Spanish Attitudes towards the Northwest Coast in the Eighteenth Century," *BC Studies* 18 (Summer 1973): 20.
25. Meares complained of "a prodigious number of otter skins" brought to Manila by the galleon and thence to China. He thought they had not been obtained on the Northwest Coast north of 46°N, for nowhere during his voyages had he met with Spanish trade items (Meares to Douglas, 20 September 1788, in Meares, *Voyages*, app. 5).

NOTES TO CHAPTER NINE: DEALING WITH THE DONS

1. See F. W. Howay, "A List of Trading Vessels in the Maritime Fur Trade 1785-1794," *Transactions of the Royal Society of Canada*, 3rd ser. 24, section 2 (1930): 113-19, for an enumeration of British and American vessels for these years. John Meares, *Memorial* (London, 1790), includes estimates for the commercial value of this commerce to Britain.
2. Douglas's instructions (Howay, *Colnett Journal*, pp. 28-39). Douglas's account of his proceedings is in Meares, *Voyages*, app. 12.

3. She was not the only ship in the sound, the *Columbia* then being at Mahwhinna, five miles from Friendly Cove. Howay, *Columbia*, p. 474.
4. Gray and Ingraham to Bodega, 3 August 1792 (ibid., p. 475).
5. Quoted in Cook, *Floodtide of Empire*, pp. 151-52.
6. Ibid., p. 152. Martínez's motivation was legally dubious. On the one hand, a defence of the Spanish actions can be based in the Treaty of Madrid of 1670 and the Treaty of Paris of 1763, whereby territorial rights of each nation were to be recognized and the British were not to visit or trade in Spanish ports in the New World. On the other, Martínez was actually violating instructions from his Viceroy. To subjects of other nations he had been ordered to explain Spanish claims with "prudent firmness" and not to take actions that would cause displeasure, but rather to avoid a clash unless the foreigners attempted to use force.
7. Douglas, "Extract of the Journal of the *Iphigenia Nubiana*," in Meares, *Voyages*, app. 12.
8. Father Sanchez, however, says the move was owing to a shortage of food nearby (Cook, *Floodtide of Empire*, p. 153-54). This seems unlikely, not only because Yuquot was their regular summer village but also because the Nootka were highly mobile by canoe and could reach nearby fishing locales with ease.
9. Douglas Journal, in Meares, *Voyages*, app. 12.
10. Based on Thomas Hudson, "Relacíon de sur apresamiento" (San Blas, 1789), as in Cook, *Floodtide of Empire*, p. 161.
11. Hudson to Colnett, July 3, 1789 (Howay, *Colnett Journal*, p. 55).
12. Ibid., pp. 57-58.
13. Colnett, in fact, commanded both the *Prince of Wales* and the *Princess Royal*. When the *Prince of Wales* sailed from Canton to London with a cargo of tea on consignment for the East India Company, Colnett took command of the snow *Argonaut*. It was owned by the "Associated Merchants," that is, Meares and Etches and Co. Concerning these arrangements, see above, ch. 6.

14. Howay, *Colnett Journal*, p. 56.
15. "I learnt when it was too late that a Young Man in C[ommodore] M[artínez's] employ had a letter from Captain Hudson to be left with the Indian Chief [Maquinna] and which he was to have given this Day but had not done it and was also so thoughtless as not to bring it on board when he came off in the first boat. This letter Captain Hudson informed me afterwards would have saved my vessel had I received it" (ibid., p. 57).
16. Ibid., p. 59. Colnett was referring to his commission as Lieutenant, R.N. (he was then on half-pay) and to the South Sea and East India Company permits to trade. Ibid., app. 1 and 2.
17. Ibid., p. 60.
18. Martínez Diary, 3 July 1789; in ibid., p. 312.
19. Howay, *Colnett Journal*, p. 61. Colnett's charge can be substantiated only in some details. Martínez entrusted to Kendrick 137 sea otter skins to be sold on his account in China.
20. Ibid.
21. Martínez Diary, 9 and 11 July 1789; and ibid., p. 315.
22. Ibid., pp. 65-66.
23. Ibid., p. 126.
24. Ibid., p. 78.
25. Which she did as far as the San Juan Islands and Haro Strait under Manuel Quimper in 1790.
26. Howay, *Colnett Journal*, p. 82.
27. Harlow, *Second British Empire*, 2: 443.
28. Ibid., p. 445.
29. J. Holland Rose, "Sea Power and the Winning of British Columbia," *Mariner's Mirror* 7 (1921): 78.
30. The *Memorial* was dated 30 April 1790 and was addressed "to the Right Honourable William Wyndham Grenville, one of His Majesty's Principal Secretaries of State." It was ordered to be printed 13 May 1790, and was included in Great Britain, Parliament, House of Commons *Journals*, 45 (21 January-10 June 1790): 463-84.
31. Meares's evidence before the Privy Committee for Trade, 27 May 1790, B.T. 5/6, pp. 230-3.
32. Harlow, *Second British Empire*, 2: 448. On British political stability and its rela-

tion to the crisis, see John Norris, "The Policy of the British Cabinet in the Nootka Crisis," *English Historical Review* 70 (1955): 562-80.

33. Cabinet minute, 30 April 1790, F.O. 95/7, fol. 295.
34. *The Parliamentary History of England from the Earliest Period to the Year 1803* 28 (London, 1816): 773.
35. Sir Richard Vesey Hamilton, ed., *Letters and Papers of Admiral of the Fleet Sir Thomas Byam Martin, G.C.B.,* vol. 3 (London: Navy Records Society, 1901), p. 380.
36. John Holland Rose, *William Pitt and National Revival* (London: G. Bell, 1912), pp. 210-11 and 567-68.
37. Paul Webb, "The Naval Aspects of the Nootka Sound Crisis," *Mariner's Mirror* 61 (1975): 135.
38. Quoted in ibid., p. 136.
39. Quoted in ibid.
40. Ibid. The number of seamen voted continued to fluctuate after the crisis: in 1792, 16,000; in 1793, 45,000; in 1794, 85,000; and when peace was signed with France in 1802, 135,000 (Cdr. Charles N. Robinson, *The British Fleet* [London, 1894], pp. 434-45).
41. W. Laird Clowes, *The Royal Navy: A History,* 7 vols (London: Sampson, Low and Marston, 1897-1913), 4: 107.

42. Webb, "Naval Aspects," p. 144.
43. Cabinet minutes of 29 July 1790; in A. Aspinall, ed., *The Later Correspondence of George III,* Vol. 1, no. 617 (Cambridge: University Press, 1962); also Grenville to Admiralty, 30 July 1790, Adm. 1/4155, and secret order, 3 August 1790, Adm. 2/1343.
44. Webb, "Naval Aspects," pp. 136, 138-39.
45. Howard V. Evans, "The Nootka Sound Controversy in Anglo-French Diplomacy—1790," *Journal of Modern History* 46 (1974): 623.
46. Leeds to Fizherbert, 1 September 1790, Add. MSS 28,066, fols. 241-2 B.L.; ibid.
47. Charles-Marie Boissonnault, "Mirabeau donne la Colombie espagnole à l'Angleterre," *Transactions of the Royal Society of Canada/Mémoires de la Société royale du Canada,* 4th ser. 10, section 2 (1972): 110-11.
48. *Parliamentary History,* 38, 979.
49. Hamilton, *Martin Journals,* 3: 382.
50. Barry M. Gough, *The Royal Navy and the Northwest Coast of North America, 1810-1914: A Study of British Maritime Ascendancy* (Vancouver: University of British Columbia Press, 1971), pp. 50-83.

NOTES TO CHAPTER TEN: THE SURVEYOR DIPLOMATS

1. Bern Anderson, *The Life and Voyages of Captain George Vancouver, Surveyor of the Sea* (Seattle: University of Washington Press, 1960), p. 231
2. D. Macpherson, *Annals of Commerce,* 4 vols. (London, 1804), 4: 356.
3. Draft instructions from Grenville to Phillip, March 1790, printed in Godwin, *Vancouver,* pp. 189-91, and Harlow, *Second British Empire, 1763-1793,* 2: 440-41.
4. Anderson, *George Vancouver,* p. 6.
5. Ibid., pp. 10, 26-28, 44.
6. Lord Grenville to Lords Commissioner of the Admiralty, 11 February 1791, draft, in H.O. 28/8, pp. 17-24; George Vancouver, *A Voyage of Discovery to the North Pacific Ocean and Round the*

World, 3 vols. and atlas (London, 1798), 1: xvii-xxiii.
7. Harlow, *Second British Empire,* 2: 479.
8. Ibid.
9. See Banks to Nepean, 20 February 1791, with enclosures, H.O. 42/18 (33).
10. "List of Articles Best Calculated for Trading with the Natives on the N.W. Coast of America," in Archibald Menzies to Sir Joseph Banks, 4 April 1790, H.O. 42/16 (15).
11. "Treasury Letter to Customs," November 1790, H.O. 42/17 (76).
12. See unsigned minute [probably by Grenville], n.d. [early 1790], H.O. 42/16 (18).

13. Ibid.
14. Alexander Davidson to E. Nepean, 10 January 1791, H.O. 42/18 (9).
15. 32 Geo. 3, c. 35; Macpherson, *Annals of Commerce*, 4: 356.
16. See Banks to Nepean, 25 February 1791, H.O. 42/18 (35).
17. Sir Joseph Banks to Mr. Archibald Menzies, 22 February 1791, printed in *Report of the Provincial Archives . . . of British Columbia for . . . 1913* (Victoria, B.C.; King's Printer, 1914), pp. V40-41.
18. Ibid.
19. See *Menzies' Journal of Vancouver's Voyage, April to October 1792*, ed. with botanical and ethnological notes by C. F. Newcombe, and a biographical note by J. Forsyth (Victoria, B.C.: Archives of British Columbia Memoir No. 5, King's Printer, 1923).
20. Rear-Admiral P. W. Brock, "H.M.S. *Discovery*, 1789-1834" (typescript [1967], M.M.B.C.), p. 4. Compare Anderson, *George Vancouver*, p. 46.
21. Quoted in Godwin, *Vancouver*, p. 36.
22. Details of ships and complements from Brock, "H.M.S. *Discovery*" and "H.M.S. *Chatham*," dossiers, M.M.B.C.
23. Anderson, *George Vancouver*, ch. 15.
24. Ibid., p. 223.
25. Brock, Vancouver biography, p. 2, in H.M.S. *Discovery* dossier, M.M.B.C.
26. Anderson, *George Vancouver*, pp. 69-75.
27. Hezeta concluded that the river mouth corresponded to the position of de Fuca's strait. See his journal in Thomas C. Russell, ed., *Voyage of the Sonora . . . by F. A. Mourelle*, trans. by the Hon. Daines Barrington (1920; reprint, New York: Kraus Reprint Co., 1975), p. 87. Hezeta was convinced that the entrance was that of a river, not a strait. Ibid.
28. Meares, *Voyages*, pp. 167-68.
29. Broughton's 1792 sketch of the river entrance reveals a very narrow channel, a tricky entrance for any sailing vessel, as the number of shipwrecks in the early nineteenth century testify. Broughton's sketch is reproduced in Godwin, *Vancouver*, facing p. 63.
30. Vancouver, *Voyage*, 1: 210.
31. Quoted in Fry, *Alexander Dalrymple*, p. 221.

32. Anderson, *George Vancouver*, p. 74.
33. Ibid., p. 75. Frederick W. Howay, ed., *Voyages of the "Columbia" to the Northwest Coast, 1787-1790* (Boston: Massachusetts Historical Society, 1941), p. 396.
34. Quoted in Godwin, *Vancouver*, p. 65. For a detailed account of Vancouver's discoveries in the Strait of Juan de Fuca and Puget Sound, see Robert Ballard Whitebrook, *Coastal Exploration of Washington* (Palo Alto: Pacific Books, 1959), pp. 70ff.; see also Edmond S. Meany, *Vancouver's Discovery of Puget Sound* (Portland: Binfords and Mort, 1942).
35. Charles Read, "An Account of a Collection of Ethnographical Specimens Formed during Vancouver's Voyage to the Pacific Ocean, 1790-1795," *Journal of the Royal Anthropological Institute of Great Britain and Ireland* 21 (1891-92); O. M. Dalton, "Notes on an Ethnographical Collection from the West Coast of North America . . . 1790-1795," *Internationales Archiv für Ethnographic* 10 (1897); Erna Gunther, "Vancouver and the Indians of Puget Sound," *Pacific Northwest Quarterly* 51 (1960): 1-12; and Bern Anderson, ed., "The Vancouver Expedition: Peter Puget's Journal of the Exploration of Puget Sound, May 7-June 11, 1792," ibid. 30 (1939): 195-205.
36. Quoted in Whitebrook, *Coastal Exploration*, p. 72.
37. Ibid., p. 81. Subsequently the Gulf of Georgia became known as the Strait of Georgia, for it led north as well as south to the sea.
38. *Menzies' Journal*, p. 103.
39. Meany, *Vancouver's Discovery*, p. 137. See also J. Neilson Barry ed., "Broughton's Reconnaissance of the San Juan Islands in 1792," *Washington Historical Quarterly* 21 (1930): 55-60.
40. With respect to the first European discovery of the Fraser River, José María Narvaez "sailed for two leagues through water more sweet than salt . . . There must be some copious river there" *(Relacion del Viage Hecho por las Goletas Sutil y Mexicana en el ano de 1792 para Reconocer el Estrecho de Fuca . . .* [Madrid, 1802]) in July 1791, a year before Vancouver. On 14 June 1792, two days after Vancouver, Ga-

liano and Valdés entered and anchored in the north arm of the Fraser River. Vancouver found them near the river mouth on 15 June, thus indicating that the Spanish and British explorers did not meet "off" Spanish Banks as has been usually claimed but "near" Spanish Banks, as I have stated.

41. Vancouver, *Voyage,* 2: 189-94. Charles Hill-Tout, *The Far West: The Home of the Salish and Dene* (London: Archibald Constable, 1907), p. 19.

42. F. W. Howay, *Captain George Vancouver* (Toronto: The Ryerson Canadian History Readers, [1943]), pp. 19-20.

43. Quoted in Whitebrook, *Coastal Exploration,* p. 89.

44. Peter Puget, Log of the *Discovery,* 29 April, 22 and 29 June 1792, Adm. 55/27. See also Lalla Rookh Boone, "Captain George Vancouver on the Northwest Coast" (Ph.D. diss., University of California, Berkeley, 1939), pp. 43-45.

45. Godwin, *Vancouver,* pp. 74-75.

46. Quoted in Harlow, *Second British Empire,* 2: 479.

47. *Nootka, Acuerdo o' Convenio entre Espania e Inglaterra* . . . , trans. in Bancroft, *Northwest Coast,* 1: 300-301. See also Duke of Portland to Pearce, draft instructions, 31 March 1794, F.O. 95/7.

48. Pearce to the Duke of Portland, 25 April 1795, *London Gazette,* no. 13813 (12-15 September 1795); reprinted in J. Forsyth, ed., "Documents Connected with the Final Settlement of the Nootka Dispute," *B.C. Historical Association Second Annual Report* (1924): 33-35.

49. Christon I. Archer, "Retreat from the North: Spain's Withdrawal from Nootka Sound," *BC Studies* 37 (1978): 19-36.

50. F. W. Howay, "The Spanish Settlement at Nootka," *Washington Historical Quarterly* 8 (1917): 170.

51. Cook, *Floodtide of Empire,* pp. 426-28.

52. Ibid., pp. 430-32.

53. Autograph of George Vancouver, Nootka, 2 October 1794, encl. to Cole to H. U. Addington, 1 January 1846, F.O. 5/459. Vancouver, *Voyage,* 1, intro.

54. Robert Barrie to a friend, 7 September 1794, Sir Robert Barrie Papers, P.L.D.U.

55. Menzies to Sir Joseph Banks, 1 October 1794, Botany Library of National History Museum, London; quoted in G. P. V. Akrigg and Helen B. Akrigg, *British Columbia Chronicle, 1778-1846: Adventurers by Sea and Land* (Vancouver: Discovery Press, 1975), p. 97.

56. Vancouver to a friend, 2 October 1794, Nootka, encl. in R. Cole to H. U. Addington, 1 January 1846, F.O. 5/459; printed in *Washington Historical Quarterly* 18 (1927): 55-56. See also Vancouver to John Vancouver, 8 September 1794, attached to end papers, *Voyage,* 1, copy in B.L.Y.U.

57. Vancouver, *Voyage,* 1, 259.

58. Barrie to his mother, 1795, Barrie Papers, P.L.D.U.

59. Anderson, *George Vancouver,* p. 213.

60. Broughton, *Voyage,* passim.

NOTES TO CHAPTER ELEVEN: THE OVERLANDERS

1. Each of the following include material on the western advance, by sea and land, of the Nor'westers: L. R. Masson, ed., *Les Bourgeois de la Compagnie du Nord-Ouest: récits de voyages, lettres et rapports inédits relatifs au nord-ouest canadien,* 2 vols. (Quebec, 1889, 1890); Gordon C. Davidson, *The North West Company* (Berkeley: University of California Press, 1918); W. S. Wallace, ed., *Documents Relating to the North West Company* (Toronto: Champlain Society, 1934); Marjorie Wilkins Campbell, *(The North West Company* (Toronto: Macmillan of Canada, 1957); E. E. Rich, *Montreal and the Fur Trade*

(Montreal: McGill University Press, 1966); E. E. Rich, *The Fur Trade and the Northwest to 1857* (Toronto: McClelland & Stewart, 1967); E. E. Rich, *The History of the Hudson's Bay Company, 1670-1870*, Vol. 2 (London: Hudson's Bay Record Society, 1959), ch. 5-16, passim; and Harold A. Innis, *The Fur Trade in Canada: An Introduction to Canadian Economic History* (rev. ed., New Haven, Conn.: Yale University Press, 1962), sec. 3.

2. The first reference to their corporate name seems to be 1776. Wallace, *Documents Relating to the North West Company*, p. 5. The syndicate may well have been formed before that time, however.

3. Sir Guy Carleton to Lord Shelburne, Quebec, 2 March 1768 (Lawrence J. Burpee, *The Search for the Western Sea*, 2 vols. [Toronto: Macmillan of Canada, 1935], 1: 303).

4. Ibid., 1: 289-90. Also, Major Rogers's Instructions to Captain Tate . . . for the Discovery of the North West Passage, 12 September 1766, Baby Collection, M.G. 24, L3, vol. 40, P.A.C.

5. Memorial by Peter Pond, 18 April 1785, Q/24-2, p. 418 P.A.C.; also in *Report on Canadian Archives, 1890* (Ottawa, 1891), pp. 52-54. At this time, the North West Company was seeking a 10-year monopoly in the Northwest. Ibid., pp. 403, 405. H. A. Innis, *Peter Pond: Fur Trader and Adventurer* (Toronto: Irwin and Gordon Ltd., 1930), pp. 124-43.

6. Davidson, *North West Company*, pp. 195-97. Rich, *History of the Hudson's Bay Company*, 2: 206-7.

7. Rich, *Montreal and the Fur Trade*, p. 86.

8. See W. Kaye Lamb, ed., *The Journals and Letters of Sir Alexander Mackenzie* (Cambridge: Hakluyt Society, 1970), p. 373.

9. *Voyages from Montreal, on the River St. Laurence, through the Continent of North America, to the Frozen and Pacific Oceans; in the Years 1789 and 1793, with a Preliminary Account of the Rise, Progress and Present State of the Fur Trade of that Country* (London and Edinburgh, 1801).

10. Here the reference is to the voyage of exploration of Capt. George Vancouver,

R.N., 1791-95. Mackenzie is confusing the Columbia with the Fraser. At that time the courses of these two rivers had not been delineated.

11. Lamb, ed., *Journals and Letters of Sir Alexander Mackenzie*, pp. 415, 417-18.

12. Simcoe's report to the Lords of the Committee of the Privy Council, for Trade and Foreign Plantations, 1 September 1794, encl. in Simcoe to the Hon. Henry Dundas, 11 September 1794, C.O 42/318, pp. 227, 266-69 (P.A.C. microfilm reel B-281); printed in Brig. Gen. E. A. Cruikshank, ed., *Correspondence of Lieut. Governor John Graves Simcoe, 1789-1796*, 5 vols. (Toronto: Ontario Historical Society, 1923-31), 3: 68-69.

13. Mackenzie to Lord Dorchester, 17 November 1794, C.O. 42/101.

14. Campbell, *North West Company*, pp. 89-90.

15. Ibid., p. 90.

16. Rich, *History of the Hudson's Bay Company*, 2: 210-11; Lamb, ed., *Journals and Letters of Sir Alexander Mackenzie*, p. 28.

17. Simon McGillivray later wrote that the North West Company had an arrangement with Messrs. Nicklin and Griffiths of Philadelphia and then Messrs. Seton, Maitland & Company of New York to ship at least $100,000 annually to China. By the new agreement (1804), no shipments were sent. Memorandum of Simon McGillivray, 1 September 1823, A.7/1, fols. 38 d.-39, H.B.C.A.

18. Mackenzie to McTavish, Fraser & Co., London, 10 March 1798, in Lamb, ed., *Journals and Letters of Sir Alexander Mackenzie*, p. 470.

19. Campbell, *North West Company*, pp. 115-16.

20. Encl. in Mackenzie to Hobart, 7 January 1802, C.O. 42/120. This project, Mackenzie knew, had two legal obstacles: (1) getting rights of fishing and navigation from the East India Company and South Sea Company (which commerce neither company had exercised); (2) obtaining a licence of transit for trade goods through Hudson Bay and Rupert's Land. Ibid.

21. Sir Alexander Mackenzie to John Sullivan (for Lord Hobart), 25 October 1802, Q/293, p. 225, P.A.C.; printed in

Report on Canadian Archives, 1892 (Ottawa: Queen's Printer, 1893), pp. 150-51.

22. Masson, ed., *Bourgeois de la Compagnie du Nord-Ouest,* 2: 482-99, and Wallace, ed., *Documents Relating to the North West Company,* pp. 143-57. They were Alexander McKee, Donald McKenzie, Duncan McDougall, David Stuart, and Robert Stuart.

23. See W. Kaye Lamb, ed., *Journal of a Voyage to the North West Coast of North America during the years 1811, 1812, 1813 and 1814 by Gabriel Franchère* (Toronto: The Champlain Society, 1969), intro. Also, Peter Corney, *Early Voyages in the North Pacific, 1813-1818* (Honolulu, 1896; reprint, Fairfield, Wash.: Ye Galleon Press, 1965), pp. 93-98.

24. Mackenzie's last appeal to the Board of Trade, probably in 1809, is considered in Campbell, *North West Company,* pp. 176-77. On this occasion, Mackenzie proposed to pay a reasonable rent for the East India Company's exclusive right of trade to the Orient.

25. S. McGillivray to Lord Liverpool, 10 November 1810, M.G. 11, Q/113, pp. 221-23, P.A.C.

26. Gough, *Royal Navy and the Northwest Coast,* pp. 12-28.

27. In that year, 1800, Simon McTavish and Duncan McGillivray undertook an abortive expedition to open trade west of the Rockies. Wallace, ed., *Documents Relating to the North West Company,* p. 19. Perseverance ''paid off.'' For a description of the establishment of posts west of the continental divide, see Innis, *Fur Trade,* pp. 203-4.

28. William M'Gillivray [?], ''Some Account of the Trade Carried on by the North-West Company,'' fol. 20, R.C.S.

29. Quoted in Roy Daniells, *Alexander Mackenzie and the Northwest* (London: Faber and Faber, 1969), pp. 189-90.

30. Quoted in Donald W. Meinig, *The Great Columbia Plain: A Historical Geography, 1805-1910* (Seattle: University of Washington Press, 1968), pp. 53-54.

31. One such appeal originated in Montreal. See McTavish, McGillivrays & Co., John Ogilvy, Thomas Thain to McTavish, Fraser and Co., Inglis, El-lice & Co. and Sir Alexander Mackenzie, 23 January 1810, M.G. 11, Q/113, pp. 228-30, P.A.C. For subsequent appeals, see Davidson, *Northwest Company,* pp. 124-32.

32. Report to Privy Council, 16 November 1812, B.T. 5/22, pp. 17-19.

33. The United States was similarly aware of the relation of the Pacific Northwest to the commercial potential of the Orient. See R. W. Van Alstyne, *The Rising American Empire* (Oxford: Basil Blackwell, 1960), pp. 93-96, 124-46. There can be no doubt that the push towards Oregon and California in the 1840's was tied to the lure of China markets. See Charles Vevier, ''American Continentalism: An Idea of Expansion, 1845-1910,'' *American Historical Review* 65 (1960): 323-25, and Norman A. Graebner, *Empire on the Pacific: A Study in American Continental Expansion* (New York: Ronald Press, 1955), passim.

34. Wallace, ed., *Documents Relating to the North West Company,* pp. 266-68. North West Company partners to William McGillivray, 18 July 1812, Selkirk Papers, M.G. 19, El, vol. 28, p. 8627, P.A.C. The date of permission is probably 1811. See Davidson, *North West Company,* p. 130n37.

35. For evidence of opposition to the East India Company in the Cabinet, see Viscount Melville to Earl Bathurst, 6 April 1812, encl. G. Rose to Melville, 3 April 1812, in Historical Manuscripts Commission, *Report on the Manuscripts of Earl Bathurst, Preserved at Cirencester Park* (London, 1923), pp. 170-72.

36. Wm. McGillivray to Wintering Partners, 9 April 1812, M.G. 19, El, 1(30), p. 9123, P.A.C. This was a removal of a barrier which McGillivray previously considered ''insurmountable.''

37. Gough, *Royal Navy and the Northwest Coast,* pp. 20-24.

38. A. Macdonnel to J. Severeght, 6 March 1815, Selkirk Papers, M. G. 19, El, vol. 30, p. 9022, P.A.C.

39. J. Haldane to J. Leith, 21 February 1816, vol. 29, p. 8843, ibid.

40. ''Canton Sales, 1815,'' vol. 31, pp. 9209-10, ibid.

41. Marion O'Neil, ''The Maritime Activi-

ties of the North West Company, 1813 to 1821," *Washington Historical Quarterly* 21 (1930): 254-63. This vessel, under consignment to the company, was owned by her captain, Robson.

42. Wallace, ed., *Documents Relating to the North West Company*, p. 283.

43. The *Columbia*'s voyage is recounted in Corney, *Early Voyages in The North Pacific*, pp. 93-188.

44. Wallace, ed., *Documents Relating to the North West Company*, p. 283.

45. "Diary of Nicholas Garry . . . 1821," *Proceedings and Transactions of the Royal Society of Canada*, ser. 2, vol. 6 (1900), sec. 2, p. 81.

46. For an account of these "Boston Ships," see O'Neil, "Maritime Activities of the North West Company," pp. 265-67.

47. Inglis, Ellice & Co. to Messrs. Sir Alexander Mackenzie and Co., 5 November 1817, Baby Collection, M.G. 24, L3, vol. 16, P.A.C. "Memo of Simon McGillivray, 1 Sept. 1823," A. 7/1, fol. 39, H.B.C.A.

48. See H. A. Innis's introduction in R. Harvey Fleming, ed., *Minutes of Council, Northern Department of Rupert's Land, 1821-31* (London: Hudson's Bay Record Society, 1940), pp. xxx-xxxi, lxx.

49. "Importation into Canton in 1817," A. 7/1, fol. 27, H.B.C.A.

50. Compiled from J. G. McTavish to Agents and Proprietors of the North West Company, 22 April 1821, C.O. 40/367.

51. The East India Company privileges were suspended by an Act of Parliament in 1833. From 1821 to 1833 the restrictions had handicapped expansion of commerce from the Northwest Coast to China. This and related matters are considered in Frederick Merk, ed., *Fur Trade and Empire: George Simpson's Journal, 1824-1825* (rev. ed., Cambridge, MA: Harvard University Press, 1968), pp. 71, 78-86, 120; John S. Galbraith, *The Hudson's Bay Company as an Imperial Factor, 1821-1869* (Berkeley and Los Angeles: University of California Press, 1957), pp. 123-24 and 447n36; Frederick Merk, *The Oregon Question: Essays in Anglo-American Diplomacy and Politics* (Cambridge, MA: Harvard University Press, 1967), pp. x, 142-46, 157-59; and Edward J. Stapleton, ed., *Some Official Correspondence of George Canning*, 2 vols. (London, 1887), 2: 71-116.

NOTES TO EPILOGUE

1. J. H. Parry, *Trade and Dominion: European Overseas Empires in the Eighteenth Century* (London: Cardinal, 1974), p. 353.

2. The Charter Act of 1793 (33 Geo. 3, c. 52, sec. 78) permitted ships to sail from the Northwest Coast "direct to the Isles of Japan and the Coasts of Korea and Canton" and to dispose of their cargoes and return directly to the Northwest Coast, but this was hardly a concession given the government ambitions to free the trade. These ambitions are spelled out in "Review of Charters and Acts of Parliament Governing the East India, South Sea and Hudson's Bay Companies and Southern Whale Fishery," prepared by

F. Russell, India Board, 28 March 1791 [for Henry Dundas], Hargrave MSS 494, 7, ff. 66-98, B. L., and "Heads of the Proposed New Bill," 28 March 1791, B. T. 6/95. For political reasons, Pitt and his colleagues did not press their case in Parliament against the chartered companies. See Harlow, *Second British Empire*, 2: 325.

3. See "Nationality of Vessels Visiting the Northwest Coast, 1774-1820," Cook, *Floodtide of Empire*, app. E.

4. Edouard A. Stackpole, *Whales and Destiny*, pp. 386-87, 398-9.

5. Harlow, *Second British Empire*, 2: 326.

6. "If we do not sooner or later they [the

Russians] will have that Fur Trade entirely in their own hands, which now is the time to prevent. The Indians of the NW are an Idle Lazy set of People, will not kill more sea-otter or seals than they can dispose of or to supply their own wants which are small; Europeans I am sure can do twice as much as them at best, and assisted by Sandwich Isle Indians might take what Sea-otter they please when sleeping on the water gorged with food . . . the NW Natives finding we could do without them, would seek to obtain only the most valuble Furs and Barter them for usefull articles only, particularly woollen & hardware.'' Lieut. James Colnett, ''A Voyage for Whaling and Discovery . . .,'' Add. MSS 30,369, B. L., p. 358 (O.H.S. Micro. No. 138).

7. Vancouver, *Voyage to the North Pacific Ocean,* 3: 306-7. See also F. W. Howay, ''Indian Attacks upon Maritime Traders of the North-West Coast, 1785-1805,'' *Canadian Historical Review* 6 (1935).

8. Joseph Whidbey to ?, 2 January 1793, in Hardin Craig, ed., ''A Letter from the Vancouver Expedition,'' *Pacific Northwest Quarterly* 41 (1950): 353.

9. In 1841, during a review of British ambitions on the Northwest Coast, the British government remained doggedly reluctant to expand its liabilities there. At the Admiralty, the permanent secretary Sir John Barrow opposed placing Britain again in a ''wasp's nest'' as at Nootka Sound. The United States and Russia had established themselves on the coast, he said, and Britain should avoid a predicament based on territorial claims. He believed that a port near the Columbia River's mouth would be advantageous to national maritime enterprise. Thus the 1841 government opposed ''any *new* acquisitions at present . . . either on the Shores, or among the Islands of the Pacific.'' Sir John Barrow to James Stephen, 11 February 1841, C.O. 42/482, and Stephen to John Pelly, draft, 16 February 1841, C.O. 42/485.

Note on Sources

The manuscript and printed sources for this book are numerous and varied, as indicated by the notes to the text and the acknowledgements to libraries, archives, and respositories given in the preface. Therefore a long list of sources of marginal importance is redundant. Due reference to these and other sources is given in the notes. However, in the Public Record Office, London, I made particular use of the Admiralty Papers and the Home Office Papers; in the old India Office Library (now the Commonwealth Relations Office Library) the records of the East India Company; and in the Provincial Archives of British Columbia, originals or copies of pertinent letters and journals. A convenient and comprehensive list of printed voyages and accounts relating to the early maritime history of the northwest coast is given in Gloria M. Strathern's *Navigations, Traffiques & Discoveries, 1774-1848: A Guide to Publications Relating to the Area Now British Columbia* (Victoria, B.C.: Social Sciences Research Centre, 1970). The following bibliography is therefore select, and I have listed sources in four categories: (1) manuscripts, (2) printed accounts: journals, voyages and letters, (3) monographs: books and articles, and (4) Dissertations, theses and unpublished reports.

Select Bibliography

1. Manuscripts

Public Record Office, London (P.R.O.)

Admiralty Papers (Adm.)
- 1/2628. Duffin Correspondence
- 14155. Correspondence with Cabinet
- 2/101. Instructions to Lieut. R. Pickersgill, 14 May 1776
- 2/1332. Instructions to Captain the Hon. John Byron, 17 June 1764, Captain James Cook, 6 July 1776, and Lieut. W. Young, 13 March 1777.
- 2/1343. Secret Orders
- 55/27. Peter Puget's Log, 1792
- 55/120. Gore, Correspondence with East India Company, China
- 55/146. *Prince of Wales* Journal, 1786-88

Board of Trade (B.T.)
- 5/6. Meares's evidence before Committee of Trade, 27 May 1790
- 6/95. "Heads of the Proposed New Bill," 28 March 1791

Colonial Office (C.O.)
- 42/101, 120. Mackenzie correspondence
- 42/318. Simcoe correspondence
- 42/482, 485. Barrow, Stephen and Pelly correspondence

Foreign Office (F.O.)
- 5/459. Correspondence re: Oregon, including Vancouver material
- 95/7. Cabinet Minutes, 1790 and Draft Instructions to T. Pearce, 31 March 1794

Home Office (H.O.)
- 28/8. Grenville's Instructions to Admiralty.
- 42/13(57). "Re: Important Discoveries Made by Captain Duncan on the N.W. Coast of America, 1787-8"
- 42/16 (10). "Heads of Instruction for an Expedition to the Northwest Coast of America, Secret, February 1790."
- 42/16 (15, 18). Correspondence with J. Banks re: *Discovery* voyage
- 42/16 (24). J. Meares, "Statement of the Value of Furs Exported to the Northwestern Coast of America by British and Foreign Ships Previous to the Year 1790."
- 42/17 (76). Treasury Correspondence re: *Discovery* voyage on "Secret Service," November 1790.
- 42/17 (89). Memo from Mr. Nepean re: Sending 2 ships to Coast of N.W. America, 1790
- 42/18 (9, 33, 35, 56). Correspondence re: *Discovery* voyage.

Privy Council (P.C.)
- 2/135. Privy Council Evidence, 1791.

State Papers (S.P.)
- 94/253. Memorandum by the Earl of Egmont, 20 July 1765.

India Office Library (I.O.L.) [now Commonwealth Office Library], London
- MS/52. Canton Factory Records, 1779.

H.M.S. (Home Miscellaneous Series)
- 494 (5). Minutes, Court of Directors, 1785
  Orders to J. Strange from D. Scott, 1 September 1785.

"Trade to the Northwest Coast of America [1791],"
[by Alexander Dalrymple.]
Instructions to J. Strange, 7 December 1785
190 (13). Correspondence re: R. C. Etches' proposed expedition
494 (5). Papers re: fur trade between Northwest Coast and China and Japan, 1785-1791.
800 (1). Narrative of James Strange, 1 January-15 November 1786.

Archives of the Royal Society, London (A.R.S.)
vol. 6 (1774). Minutes of Council and Correspondence, February-March

British Library, London (B.L.)
Add. MSS
223. W. Bolts Correspondence
28, 066. Leeds Correspondence
30, 369. Lieut. James Colnett, "A Voyage for Whaling and Discovery."
37, 528. Thomas Edgar, Log book
MSS 494. Hargrave Correspondence

Royal Commonwealth Society, London (R.C.S.)
"Some Account of the Trade Carried on by the North-West Company"
[by William M'Gillivray?]

Hudson's Bay Company Archives, Winnipeg (H.B.C.A.)
A.7/1. "Importation into Canton, 1817."
"Memorandum of Simon McGillivray, 1 September 1823."

Provincial Archives of British Columbia, Victoria (P.A.B.C.)
Aural History Archives. Interview with Winifred David, 24 August 1977
Manuscript Collection
A. J. Brabant Miscellaneous Papers.
A A 10, C 78.9. James Cook, miscellaneous documents, including list of ships logs
A A 10.1, Sp 12. Correspondence between the Court of Spain and Great Britain relative to the settlement of the Nootka Controversy and claims arising therefrom, 1789-1798.
A A 20.5, Se 1H. J. Hanna, "Journal of a Voyage from Macao towards King George's Sound in the Sea Otter, Capt. Hanna, Commander [1785]."
A A 40, C77T. James Trevenen, Notes on Cook's voyage
A A 40, V28M. George Vancouver, miscellaneous papers.

Public Archives of Canada, Ottawa (P.A.C.)
M.G. 11
Q/24-2. Memorial by Peter Pond, 18 April 1785
Q/49. Dixon to Nepean Correspondence, 1789.
A. Dalrymple, "Memorandum . . . on the Route of Discoveries . . .," 1790.
"Captain Holland's Plan to Explore from Quebec [1790]."
Q/113. North West Company Correspondence with British Government
Q/293. Mackenzie Correspondence with British Government
M.G. 19. E1 Selkirk Papers, vol. 28, North West Company papers
M.G. 24 L3 Baby Collection, vol. 40.

Perkins Library, Duke University, Durham, North Carolina (P.L.D.U.)
Sir Robert Barrie Papers, 1794-95
George Vancouver, Correspondence with John
Vancouver, 1794, attached to end papers of
Vancouver's *Voyage* (1798), vol. 1.

2. Printed Accounts: Journals, Voyages, and Letters

Anderson, Bern, ed. "The Vancouver Expedition: Peter Puget's Journal of the Exploration of Puget Sound, May 7-June 11, 1792." *Pacific Northwest Quarterly* 30 (April 1939): 195-205.

Barry, J. Neilson. "Broughton on the Columbia in 1792." *Oregon Historical Quarterly* 27 (December 1926): 397-411.

―――. "Broughton up Columbia River, 1792." *Oregon Historical Quarterly* 27 (December 1931): 301-12.

―――. "Broughton's Reconnaissance of the San Juan Islands in 1792." *Washington Historical Quarterly* 21 (January 1930): 55-60.

Beaglehole, John C., ed. *The Journals of Captain Cook on His Voyages of Discovery: The Voyage of the "Resolution" and "Discovery," 1776-1780.* Vol. 3, 2 pts.; Cambridge: Hakluyt Society, 1967.

[Bell, Edward]. "A New Vancouver Journal." *Washington Historical Quarterly* 5 (April 1914): 129-37; 5 (July 1914): 215-24; (October 1914): 300-308; 6 (January 1915): 50-68.

Beresford, William. *A Voyage round the World; but more particularly to the North-west Coast of America; performed in 1785, 1786, and 1788, in the King George and Queen Charlotte, Captains Portlock and Dixon.* London, 1789.

British Columbia, Archives. *Report of the Provincial Archives Department of the Province of British Columbia for the Year ended December 31st, 1913* Victoria, B.C. [correspondence re: George Vancouver expedition].

Broughton, William Robert. *A Voyage of Discovery to the North Pacific Ocean.* 1804. Reprint. Amsterdam: N. Israel [1967].

Cleveland, R. J. *A Narrative of Voyages and Commercial Enterprises, 1792-1818.* London, 1842.

Colnett, Capt. James. *Journal of, aboard the "Argonaut" from April 26, 1789, to November 3, 1791.* Edited by F. W. Howay. Toronto: Champlain Society, 1940.

Cook, James, and James King. *A Voyage to the Pacific Ocean; Undertaken by Command of His Majesty, for Making Discoveries in the Northern Hemisphere; Performed Under the Direction of Captains Cook, Clerke, and Gore . . . .* 4 vols. London, 1784.

Corney, Peter. *Voyages in the North Pacific, Narrative of several trading voyages from 1813 to 1818, between the North West Coast of America, the Hawaiian Islands and China, with a Description of the Russian Establishments on the North-West Coast.* Honolulu, 1896 [reprinted from *London Literary Gazette* of 1821]. Reprint. Fairfield, Wash.: Ye Galleon Press, 1965.

Dalrymple, Alexander. *Plan for Promoting the Fur-Trade, and Securing it to this Country, by uniting the Operation of the East India and Hudson's Bay Company's.* London, 1789.

―――. *The Spanish memorial of 4th June Considered, by A. Dalrymple.* London 1790.

―――. *The Spanish Pretensions fairly discussed by A. Dalrymple . . . .* London 1790.

Dixon, George. *Remarks on the Voyages of John Meares, esp., in a letter to that gentleman.* London, 1790.

Elliott, T. C. "The Log of the H.M.S. 'Chatham'." *Oregon Historical Quarterly* 18 (December 1917): 231-43.

―――. "Oregon Coast as Seen by Vancouver in 1792." *Oregon Historical Quarterly* 30 (March 1929): 33-42; 384-94.

Greenhow, Robert. *Memoir . . . on the N.W. Coast of North America.* Washington, 1840.

Harlow, Vincent, and Frederick Madden, eds. *British Colonial Developments, 1774-1834: Select Documents.* Oxford: Clarendon Press, 1953.

Howay, F. W., ed. *The Dixon-Meares Controversy, containing Remarks on the Voyages by John Meares, by George Dixon, An Answer to Mr. George Dixon, by John Meares, and Further Remarks on the Voyages of John Meares, by George Dixon.* Toronto: Ryerson Press, [1929].

―――. "Four Letters from Richard Cadman Etches to Sir Joseph Banks, 1788-1792." *British Columbia Historical Quarterly* 6 (April 1942): 125-30.

―――. "The Last Letter of Captain James Cook." *Canadian Historical Review* 7 (September 1926): 222-32.

―――. "Letters Concerning Voyages of British Vessels to the Northwest Coast of America, 1787-1809." *Oregon Historical Quarterly* 39 (September 1938): 307-13.

―――. *Voyages of the "Columbia" to the Northwest Coast 1787-1790 and 1790-1793.* Boston: Massachusetts Historical Society, 1941.

Landsdowne, William Petty, 1st marquis of. *The substance of the Speech of the Marquis of Lansdowne in the House of Lords on the 14th December, 1790, on the subject of the Convention with Spain which was signed on the 28th of October 1790, by One Present.* London, 1790.

Ledyard, John. *Journal of Captain Cook's Last Voyage.* Edited by James Kenneth Munford. Corvallis: Oregon State University Press, 1963.

Lloyd, Christopher, and R. C. Anderson, eds. *A Memoir of James Trevenen.* London: Navy Records Society, 1959.

Mackenzie, Sir Alexander. *The Journals and Letters of Sir Alexander Mackenzie.* Edited by W. Kaye Lamb. Cambridge: Hakluyt Society, 1970.

———. *Voyages from Montreal, on the River St. Lawrence, through the Continent of North America to the Frozen and Pacific Oceans, in the Years 1789 and 1793.* 2 vols. London, 1802.

Meany, Edmond S. *A New Vancouver Journal of the Discovery of Puget Sound, by a member of the Chatham's Crew.* Seattle, 1915.

———, ed. *Vancouver's Discovery of Puget Sound: Portraits and Biographies of the Men honored in the naming of geographic features of Northwestern America.* 1907. Reprint. Portland: Binfords & Mort, 1957.

Meares, John. *Memorial of John Meares, Lieutenant in His Majesty's Navy, to the House of Commons.* London, 1790.

———. *Voyages made in the Years 1788 and 1789, from China to the North West Coast of America.* 1790. Reprint. Amsterdam: N. Israel, 1967.

Menzies, Archibald. *Menzies' Journal of Vancouver's Voyage, April to October 1792.* Edited with botanical and ethnological notes by C. F. Newcombe, and a biographical note by J. Forsyth. Victoria: Archives of British Columbia Memoir no. 5, 1923.

Moziño, José Mariana. *Noticias de Nutka: An Account of Nootka Sound in 1792.* Translated and edited by Iris Higbie Wilson. Toronto: McClelland and Stewart, 1970.

Pipes, Nellie B., ed. *The Memorial of John Meares to the House of Commons Respecting the Capture of Vessels in Nootka Sound.* Portland, Ore.: Metropolitan Press, 1933.

Portlock, Nathaniel. *A Voyage round the World: but more particularly to the North-West Coast of America.* 1789. Reprint. Amsterdam: N. Israel, 1968.

[Rickman, John]. *Journal of Captain Cook's Last Voyage to the Pacific Ocean on Discovery . . .* London, 1781.

Roe, Michael, ed. *The Journal and Letters of Captain Charles Bishop on the North-West Coast of America, in the Pacific and in New South Wales, 1794-1802.* London: Hakluyt Society, 1967.

Strange, James. *James Strange's Journal and Narrative of the Commercial Expedition from Bombay to the North-West Coast of America.* Introduction by A. V. Venkatarama Ayyar. Madras: Government Press, 1928.

Sturgis, William. *The Journal of William Sturgis.* Edited by S. W. Jackman. Victoria, B.C.: Sono Nis Press, 1978.

Suría, Tomás de. *Journal of Tomas de Suría of his Voyage with Malaspina to the Northwest Coast of America in 1791.* Translated and edited by Henry R. Wagner. Glendale, Calif: Arthur H. Clark, 1936.

Vancouver, George. "In Need of Financial Help." *Washington Historical Quarterly* 17 (April 1926): 125-28.

———. *A Voyage of Discovery to the North Pacific Ocean and round the World.* 3 vols. and atlas. 1798. Reprint. Amsterdam: N. Israel, [1968].

Wallace, W. S., ed. *Documents Relating to the North West Company.* Toronto: Champlain Society, 1934.

Zimmermann, Heinrich. *Zimmerman's Account of the Third Voyage of Captain Cook. 1776-1780.* Translated by U. Tewsley. Wellington, N.Z.: Alexander Turnbull Library, 1926.

3. Monographs: Books and Articles

Aker, Raymond. *Report of Findings Relating to Identification of Sir Francis Drake's Encampment at Point Reyes National Seashore: A Research Report of the Drake Navigators Guild.* Palo Alto, Calif.: Drake Navigators Guild, [c. 1976].

Akrigg, G. P. V., and Helen B. *British Columbia Chronicle, 1778-1846: Adventurers by Sea and Land*. Vancouver: Discovery Press, 1975.

Anderson, Bern. *The Life and Voyages of Captain George Vancouver, Surveyor of the Sea*. Seattle: University of Washington Press, 1960.

Andrews, Kenneth R. "The Aims of Drake's Expedition of 1577-1580." *American Historical Review* 73 (February 1968): 724-41.

———. *Drake's Voyages: A Re-assessment of their Place in Elizabethan Maritime Expansion*. New York: Scribner, 1967.

———. "The English in the Caribbean, 1560-1620." In K. R. Andrews et al., eds., *The Westward Enterprise: English Activities in Ireland, the Atlantic, and America, 1480-1650*. Liverpool: Liverpool University Press, 1978.

Archer, Christon I. "Retreat from the North: Spain's Withdrawal from Nootka Sound." *BC Studies* 37 (Spring 1978): 19-36.

———. "The Transient Presence: A Re-Appraisal of Spanish Attitudes towards the Northwest Coast in the Eighteenth Century." *BC Studies* 18 (Summer 1973): 3-32.

Bancroft, Hubert H. *British Columbia, 1792-1887*. San Francisco, 1887.

———. *History of Alaska, 1730-1885*. San Francisco, 1886.

———. *History of the Northwest Coast*. 2 vols. San Francisco 1884.

Bancroft Library. *Plate of Brass Re-examined: A Report Issued by the Bancroft Library, University of California, Berkeley, 1977*. Berkeley: Bancroft Library, 1977.

Beaglehole, John C. *The Life of Captain James Cook*. London: Hakluyt Society, 1974.

Begg, Alexander. *History of British Columbia*. Toronto, 1894.

Bishop, R. P. "Drake's Course in the North Pacific." *British Columbia Historical Review* 3 (1939): 151-82.

Boone, Lalla Rookh. "Vancouver on the Northwest Coast" *Oregon Historical Quarterly* 35 (September 1934): 193-227.

Boissonnault, Charles-Marie. "Mirabeau donne la Colombie espagnole à l'Angleterre." *Transactions of the Royal Society of Canada/Mémories de la Société royale du Canada*, ser. 4, vol. 10, sec. 2 (1972): 103-13.

Bowman, J. N. "Cook's Place in Northwest History." *Washington Historical Quarterly* 1 (April 1907): 113-21.

Buell, Robert Kingerly, and Charlotte Northcote Skladal. *Sea Otters and the China Trade*. New York: David McKay, 1968.

Chevigny, Hector. *Russian America: the Great Alaskan Venture, 1741-1867*. New York: Viking, 1965.

Cook, Warren L. *Floodtide of Empire: Spain and the Pacific Northwest, 1543-1819*. New Haven: Yale University Press, 1973.

Corbett, Sir Julian S. *Sir Francis Drake*. London, 1890.

Coxe, William. *Account of the Russian Discoveries between Asia and America*. London, 1780.

———. *A Comparative View of the Russian Discoveries with those made by Captains Cook and Clerke; and a Sketch of what remains to be ascertained by future Navigators*. London, 1787.

Craig, Hardin, Jr. "Peter Puget: An Active and Zealous Officer." *Mariner's Mirror* 38 (February 1952): 34-52.

Davidson, Gordon C. *The North West Company*. Berkeley: University of California Press, 1918.

Day, Vice-Admiral Sir Archibald. *The Admiralty Hydrographic Service, 1795-1919*. London: Her Majesty's Stationery Office, 1967.

de la Sierra, Benito. "The Hezeta Expedition to the Northwest Coast in 1775." *California Historical Society Quarterly* 9 (September 1930): 201-42.

Dermigny, Louis. *La Chine et L'Occident: La Commerce a Canton au XVIIIe Siècle, 1719-1833*. 3 vols. Paris: S.E.V.P.E.N., 1964.

Dillon, Richard H. "Convict Colonies for the Pacific Northwest." *British Columbia Historical Quarterly* 19 (January-April 1955): 93-102.

Duff, Wilson. *The Indian History of British Columbia; Volume I, the Impact of the White Man*. Victoria, B.C.: Provincial Museum, 1964.

Elliott, Barbara Coit. "Cape Disappointment in History." *Washington Historical Quarterly* 14 (October 1923): 262-68.

Elliott, T. C. "Captain Cook's Approach to Oregon." *Oregon Historical Quarterly* 29 (September 1928): 267-77.

————. "John Meares' Approach to Oregon." *Oregon Historical Quarterly* 29 (September 1928): 278-87.

Evans, Howard V. "The Nootka Sound Controversy in Anglo-French Diplomacy—1790." *Journal of Modern History* 46 (1974): 609-40.

Fisher, Raymond H. *Bering's Voyages: Whither and Why.* Seattle: University of Washington Press, 1978.

Fisher, Robin. *Contact and Conflict: Indian-European Relations in British Columbia, 1774-1890.* Vancouver: University of British Columbia Press, 1977.

Fry, Howard T. *Alexander Dalrymple (1737-1808) and the Expansion of British Trade.* Toronto: University of Toronto Press, 1970.

Gibson, James R. *Imperial Russia in Frontier America: The Changing Geography of Supply of Russian America, 1784-1867.* New York: Oxford University Press, 1976.

Godwin, George. *Vancouver: A Life, 1757-1798.* New York: D. Appleton and Company, 1931.

Golder, Frank A. *Russian Expansion in the Pacific, 1641-1850.* Cleveland: Arthur H. Clark, 1914.

Gough, Barry M. *The Royal Navy and the Northwest Coast of North America, 1810-1914: A Study of British Maritime Ascendancy.* Vancouver: University of British Columbia Press, 1971.

Greenhow, Robert. *History of Oregon and California and the Other Territories on the North-West Coast of North America.* London, 1844.

Gunther, Erna. *Indian Life of the Northwest Coast of North America as Seen by the Early Explorers and Fur Traders during the Last Decades of the Eighteenth Century.* Chicago: University of Chicago Press, 1972.

————. "Vancouver and the Indians of Puget Sound." *Pacific Northwest Quarterly* 51 (January 1960): 1-12.

Hallward, Norman L. *William Bolts, A Dutch Adventurer under John Company.* Cambridge: Cambridge University Press, 1920.

Harlow, Vincent T. *The Founding of the Second British Empire, 1763-1793.* 2 vols. London: Longmans, Green, 1952-1964.

Howay, F. W. "Authorship of the Anonymous Account of Captain Cook's Last Voyage." *Washington Historical Quarterly* 12 (January 1921): 51-58.

————. "Early Followers of Captain Gray." *Washington Historical Quarterly* 18 (January 1927): 11-20.

————. "Early Navigation of the Straits of Fuca." *Oregon Historical Quarterly* 12 (March 1911):

————. "Early Relations between the Hawaiian Islands and the Northwest Coast." *Publications of the Archives of Hawaii* 5 (1930): 11-38.

————. "The Fur Trade in Northwestern Development." In H. Morse Stevens and Herbert E. Bolton, *The Pacific Ocean in History* (New York, 1917): 276-86.

————. "A List of Trading Vessels in the Maritime Fur Trade, 1785-1825." Royal Society of Canada *Transactions,* ser. 3, sec. 2, 24 (1931): 111-34; 25 (1932): 117-49; 26 (1933): 43-86; 27 (1934): 119-47; and 28 (1935): 11-49. Reprinted in Richard A. Pierce, *A List of Trading Vessels in the Maritime Fur Trade, 1785-1825.* Kingston, Ont.: Limestone Press, 1973.

————. "An Outline Sketch of the Maritime Fur Trade." *Canadian Historical Association, Annual Report, 1932* (Toronto, 1932): 5-14.

————. "Some Notes on Cook's and Vancouver's Ships, 1776-80, 1791-94." *Washington Historical Quarterly* 21 (October 1930): 268-70.

————. "Some Remarks Upon the New Vancouver Journal." *Washington Historical Quarterly* 6 (April 1915): 83-89.

————, ed. "Vancouver's Brig Chatham in the Columbia." *Oregon Historical Quarterly* 43 (December 1942): 318-27.

————, ed. "The Voyage of the 'Captain Cook' and the 'Experiment,' 1785-86." *British Columbia Historical Quarterly* 4 (October 1941): 285-96.

———— and E.O.S. Scholefield *British Columbia.* 4 vols. Vancouver: Clarke, 1914.

Kenyon, Karl. W. *The Sea Otter in the Eastern Pacific Ocean.* Washington, D.C.: Government Printing Office, 1969.

Kuykendall, R. S. *The Hawaiian Kingdom, 1778-1854*. Honolulu: University of Hawaii Press, 1938.

Lower, J. Arthur. *Ocean of Destiny: A Concise History of the North Pacific, 1500-1978*. Vancouver: University of British Columbia Press, 1978.

MacKay, David. "British Interest in the Southern Oceans, 1782-1794." *New Zealand Journal of History* 3 (1969): 124-42.

Makarova, Raisa V. *Russians on the Pacific, 1743-1799*. Translated and edited by Richard A. Pierce and Atlon S. Donnelly. Kingston: Limestone Press, 1975.

Manning, William R. *The Nootka Sound Controversy*. Washington, D.C.: American Historical Association, 1905.

Mills, Lennox. "The Real Significance of the Nootka Sound Incident." *Canadian Historical Review* 6 (1925): 110-22.

Morison, Samuel Eliot. *The European Discovery of America: The Southern Voyages A.D. 1492-1616*. New York: Oxford University Press, 1974.

———. *The Maritime History of Massachussetts, 1783-1860*. Boston: Houghton Mifflin, 1921.

Morton, Harry. *The Wind Commands: Sailors and Sailing Ships in the Pacific*. Vancouver: University of British Columbia Press, 1975.

Nicholson, George. *Vancouver Island's West Coast, 1762-1962*. Victoria: privately printed, 1962.

Norris, John. "The Policy of the British Cabinet in the Nootka Crisis." *English Historical Review* 70 (1955): 562-80.

Ogden, Adele. *The California Sea Otter Trade, 1784-1848*. Berkeley: University of California Press, 1941.

O'Neill, Marion. "The Maritime Activities of the North West Company, 1813-1821." *Washington Historical Quarterly* 21 (October 1930): 243-67.

Ormsby, Margaret A. *British Columbia: A History*. Toronto: Macmillan, 1958.

Parizeau, Henri D. "The Development of Hydrography on the Coast of Canada since the Earliest Discoveries." *Proceedings of the Fifth Science Congress, Pacific Science Association*, 2 (1934).

Parry, John H. *Trade and Dominion: European Overseas Empires in the Eighteenth Century*. London: Cardinal, 1974.

Pethick, Derek. *First Approaches to the Northwest Coast*. Vancouver: J. J. Douglas, 1976.

Quinn, David B. "Some Spanish Reactions to Elizabethan Colonial Enterprises." *Transactions of the Royal Historical Society* 5th ser., 1 (1951): 1-23.

Rickard, T. A. "The Sea-Otter in History," *British Columbia Historical Quarterly* 9 (January 1947): 15-31.

———. "The Strait of Anian." *British Columbia Historical Quarterly* 5 (1941): 161-84.

Rose, J. Holland. "Sea Power and the Winning of British Columbia." *Mariner's Mirror* 7 (March 1921): 74-79.

Sandilands, R. W. "The History of Hydrographic Surveying in British Columbia." Association of Canadian Map Libraries, *Proceedings* 4 (1970): 22-40.

Stackpole, Edouard A. *Whales and Destiny: The Rivalry between America, France and Britain for Control of the Southern Whale Fishery, 1705-1825*. Amherst: University of Massachusetts Press, 1972.

Taylor, E. G. R. "Master John Dee, Drake and the Straits of Anian." *Mariner's Mirror* 15 (April 1929): 125-30.

———. "More Light on Drake: 1577-80." *Mariner's Mirror* 16 (April 1930): 134-51.

Thurman, Michael E. *The Naval Department of San Blas: New Spain's Bastion for Alta California and Nootka, 1767 to 1798*. Glendale, CA.: Arthur H. Clark, 1967.

Tracy, Nicholas. "The Falkland Islands Crisis of 1770: Use of Naval Force." *English Historical Review* 90 (1975): 40-75.

Twiss, Sir Travers. *The Oregon Question Examined in Respect to Facts and the Law of Nations*. London, 1846.

Von der Porten, Edward. "Drake's First Landfall." *Pacific Discovery* 28 (1975): 28-30.

Wagner, Henry R. "Apocryphal Voyages to the North-West Coast of America." *Proceedings of the American Antiquarian Society* 41 (April 1931): 179-234.

————. *The Cartography of the Northwest Coast of America to the Year 1800.* 1937. Reprint. Amsterdam: N. Israel, 1968.

————. *Sir Francis Drake's Voyage around the World: Its Aims and Achievements.* San Francisco: John Howell, 1926.

————. *Spanish Explorations in the Strait of Juan de Fuca.* Santa Ana, CA.: Fine Arts Press, 1933.

————. *Spanish Voyages to the Northwest Coast of America in the 16th Century.* San Francisco: California Historical Association, 1929.

Walbran, Capt. John T. *British Columbia Coast Names, 1592-1906.* Ottawa: Government Printing Bureau, 1909.

————. "The Cruise of the *Imperial Eagle.*" Victoria *Colonist,* 3 March 1901.

Wheeler, Mary E. "Empires in Conflict and Cooperation: The 'Bostonians' and the Russian-American Company." *Pacific Historical Review* 40 (November 1971): 419-41.

Williams, Glyndwr. *The British Search for the North West Passage in the Eighteenth Century.* London: Longmans, Green, 1962.

Whitebrook, Robert B. *Coastal Exploration of Washington.* Palo Alto, Calif.: Pacific Books, [1959].

————. "From Cape Flattery to Birch Bay: Vancouver's Anchorages on Puget Sound." *Pacific Northwest Quarterly* 44 (July 1953): 115-28.

4. Dissertations, Theses, and Unpublished Reports

Bartroli, Tomas. "The Spanish Establishment at Nootka Sound, (1789-1792)." M.A., University of British Columbia, 1960.

Boone, Lalla Rookh. "Captain George Vancouver on the Northwest Coast." Ph.D., University of California, Berkeley, 1939.

Brock, P. W. "H.M.S. *Resolution,*" "H.M.S. *Discovery,*" and "H.M.S. *Chatham.*" Dossiers in Maritime Museum of British Columbia, Victoria.

DeLongchamp, Mildred K. "Explorations to the Northwest Coast of America before 1800." M.A., Adams State College, Colorado, 1946.

Elliott, George Reid. "Empire and Enterprise in the North Pacific, 1785-1825: A Survey and Interpretation Emphasizing the Role and Character of Russian Enterprise." Ph.D., University of Toronto, 1957.

Hacking, Norman. "Early Marine History of British Columbia." B.A. (Hons.), University of British Columbia, 1934.

Jones, Oakah L., Jr. "The Spanish Occupation of Nootka Sound, 1790-1795." M.A., University of Oklahoma, 1960.

Little, Margaret E. "Early Days of the Maritime Fur Trade, 1785-1794." M.A., University of British Columbia, 1934.

Mills, John E. "The Ethnohistory of Nootka Sound, Vancouver Island." Ph.D., University of Washington, 1955.

Roper, William James. "The Achievements of Capt. George Vancouver on the British Columbia Coast." M.A., University of British Columbia, 1941.

Sandilands, R. W. "The History of Hydrographic Surveying in British Columbia." Typescript. [Victoria]: Canadian Hydrographic Service, 1965.

Stewart, Charles Lockwood. "Martínez and López de Haro on the Northwest Coast, 1788-1789." Ph.D., University of California, Berkeley, 1963.

Tate, Vernon Dale. "The Juan Pérez Expedition to the Northwest Coast, 1774." M.A., University of California, Berkeley, 1930.

Wike, Joyce Annabel. "The Effect of Maritime Fur Trade on Northwest Coast Indian Society." Ph.D., Columbia University, 1951.

Index